The Predatory Society

THE
PREDATORY SOCIETY

Deception in the American Marketplace

PAUL BLUMBERG

New York   Oxford
OXFORD UNIVERSITY PRESS
1989

Oxford University Press

Oxford New York Toronto
Delhi Bombay Calcutta Madras Karachi
Petaling Jaya Singapore Hong Kong Tokyo
Nairobi Dar es Salaam Cape Town
Melbourne Auckland

and associated companies in
Berlin Ibadan

Library of Congress Cataloging-in-Publication Data

Blumberg, Paul.
The predatory society : deception in the American marketplace /
Paul Blumberg.
p. cm.
Includes index.
ISBN 0-19-503762-6
1. Economics—Moral and ethical aspects. 2. Capitalism—United
States—Moral and ethical aspects. 3. Industry—Social aspects—
United States. I. Title.
HB72.B59 1989
381′.3′0973—dc 19 88-39858
CIP

2 4 6 8 9 7 5 3 1

Printed in the United States of America
on acid-free paper

For Diane

Acknowledgments

Every book is a collective enterprise, including those with only one name on the cover. Many people have given me their time and assistance, and I am indebted to them for it. Gilbert Geis, Conrad Miller, Diane Bjorklund, and Ray Franklin read parts or all of the manuscript and offered their suggestions, criticisms, and exhortations, many of which I heeded, some of which I did not, possibly at my peril.

I am particularly grateful to Gilbert Geis, who not only gave me the benefit of his well-known expertise in white-collar crime, but spent more time making substantive and editorial recommendations than anyone has a right to expect or even hope for.

As always, I have gained immensely from long walks and talks with my friend Conrad Miller who has often had the misfortune of being a sounding board for many of my notions. His insights have always helped clarify and modify my own ideas.

To my wife, Diane, who is both companion and fellow sociologist, I owe special thanks for her gentle encouragement, imaginative suggestions, careful proofreading, and uncanny ability to locate undiscovered gems at the library and to track down sources that seemed to have hopelessly disappeared.

To Ray Franklin I owe double thanks, for help both on this manuscript and the last one, which went accidentally unacknowledged.

Several Soviet scholars helped me unearth a small piece of Russian history discussed in Chapter 1: Professors Victoria Bonnell, Stephen F. Cohen, Sheila Fitzpatrick, Lynn Mally, William G. Rosenberg, and S. A. Smith.

Robert Heilbroner and Robert Lekachman suggested works I might read on the morality of capitalism. Robert K. Merton steered me to the first use of his valuable concept of pseudo-*Gemeinschaft*.

Susan Rabiner, my first editor at Oxford, offered early encouragement of the project, and her successor, Valerie Aubry, helped bring it to fruition. Catherine Clements skillfully guided the book through production, and Linda Grossman did a fine job of copy editing.

My son, Ira, and my brother, Bob, put me in touch with at least part of the late twentieth century by persuading me to replace my typewriter with a computer, which made the writing (and rewriting) of this manuscript so much easier than it otherwise would have been, and, in fact, almost enjoyable.

My major debt, as the reader will soon discover, is to hundreds of my students over the last fifteen years at the City University of New York, without whom this book literally could not have been written. They are genuine coauthors of this work. It is their experiences on the job, and their description of those experiences, that made this project possible.

The first advice usually given to an aspiring writer is to write on a subject he or she knows something about. While students slog through years of term papers and exams, generally writing poorly about material that is often abstract and unfamiliar to them, they are transformed and their prose miraculously improved when describing something outside the scholastic net that they have experienced directly—their own jobs. The essays contained in this book are a testimony to the repository of wisdom workers have about their jobs and their impressive ability to communicate it. Specifically, these essays seem to confirm the view that no one knows the shady practices of a business better than the people who work there. I am grateful to my students for permission to reprint excerpts of their writing and for their generous and, in many cases, enthusiastic cooperation in this project.

For information on the merchandising policies and practices of the Consumers Cooperative of Berkeley, California, I wish to thank Nancy Snow, who until recently was Community Relations Director of the Berkeley Co-op. An unhappy postcript is necessary, however. In Chapter 11 I discuss the Consumers Cooperative of Berkeley as an example of an economic alternative to the predatory marketplace. Although the Berkeley Co-op grew vigorously for most of its fifty-year history, in recent years it fell on hard times. The Co-op overexpanded in its halcyon days in the 1960s and 1970s and was then squeezed between the enormous market power of such huge supermarket chains as Safeway and the small specialty food boutiques and markets that have blossomed in Berkeley as that city gained a reputation as a restaurant and gourmet mecca. Shortly after this manuscript was completed, the Berkeley Co-op announced that it would be forced to close.

Nonetheless, the arguments made in Chapter 11 still stand. The Berkeley Co-op did not fail because of its principles of honest merchandising, but in spite of them. Moreover, the failure of one cooperative obviously does not mean the failure of the entire form. Consumer cooperatives have been around since 1844 when those twenty-eight hardy British weavers—the renowned Rochdale Pioneers—opened the doors of the first store. And since then, tens of thousands of consumer cooperatives have grown and flourished throughout the world. (Indeed, consumer cooperatives account for about one-third of all food sales in Sweden.)

Despite the recent fate of the Berkeley Co-op, I have decided for two reasons not to delete that discussion or even put the description of that cooperative in the past tense. First, the practices of consumer cooperatives elsewhere in the United States and abroad are roughly similar to those described at the Berkeley Co-op; what applies to one applies to most others. And second, the Co-op has been for so long such a central part of the special sociopolitical culture that is

Berkeley, California, its followers are so many and so loyal, its experience after half a century so great, that one cannot but hope that, to paraphrase Mark Twain, the reports of its death are greatly exaggerated, and that in one form or another it will spring forth again from the fertile soil of that community.

Finally, I wish to thank Michael Harrington, not for any specific assistance on this book, but for the general influence he has had on my views over the years. Though I don't know him personally, his life and work have been an inspiration since as a young undergraduate in the 1950s I first heard his spellbinding oratory. Although I have heard him dozens of times since then and read his countless articles and books, the effect is always the same: When he explains our world, the lights suddenly go on, everything becomes clear, the chaotic jumble of social and political events takes form and meaning, and one can see forever. Better than anyone in our generation, Harrington has explained with extraordinary intellectual clarity America as it is, and with extraordinary moral vision America as it might be. The twentieth century has been enriched by this great and good man.

Contents

The Predatory Society

Never fight fair with a stranger, boy.
You'll never get out of the jungle that way.

ARTHUR MILLER
Death of a Salesman

For what's the sound of the world out there?
Those crunching noises pervading the air?
It's man devouring man, my dear,
And who are we to deny it in here?

STEPHEN SONDHEIM
Sweeney Todd

INTRODUCTION

The Paradox of Capitalism

Every few years the news media in this country discover a business crime wave. And when they do, they usually connect it to the trends of the times. In the 1980s, for example, business crime was blamed on such things as the swing of the generational pendulum from the social concerns of the 1960s to the personal concerns of the 1980s, the greed-is-good mentality fostered by the free-wheeling individualism of the Reagan administration, the moral example of corruption in high places in Washington, the merger mania in the corporate world that produced a speculative fever and created a kind of casino society, the bacchanalia of a long bull market on Wall Street, the unprecedented inflation in housing prices that separated wealth from work, and so on. In the past, business crime has been blamed on other transient events. In the future, still other trends of the moment will make equally plausible explanations.

What I have tried to illustrate in this book, by contrast, are not just fleeting events that might account for occasional flare-ups of business deception, after which things get back to the norm of honesty. I have tried instead to identify the constant built-in features of capitalism that, day in and day out, create incentives for people to behave dishonestly. While political developments, economic conditions, and social trends may have their independent effects, and may sometimes aggravate the problem, they do not create it. The roots of the problem lie in the system itself.

These built-in pressures for deception arise out of one of the great paradoxes of capitalism. On the one hand, the material achievements of capitalism over the last two centuries have been extraordinary. In conjunction with the forces unleashed by the Industrial Revolution, the private market system has created greater wealth than the world has ever known. Capitalism has not only further enriched the rich, but, more important, has raised living standards for the middle class and large sections of the working class to heights unimagined by the system's most enthusiastic nineteenth-century proponents. Recall the exuberant praise even Marx and Engels lavished on capitalism in that familiar passage from the *Manifesto:*

> The bourgeoisie, during its rule of scarce one hundred years, has created more massive and more colossal productive forces than have all preceding generations together. Subjection of nature's forces to man, machinery, application of chemistry to industry and agriculture, steam navigation, railways, electric telegraphs, clearing of whole continents for cultivation, canalization of rivers, whole populations conjured out of the ground— what earlier century had even a presentiment that such productive forces slumbered in the lap of social labor?

And in our own day, the great dynamism of the market system has even attracted the attention of contemporary communists in China, the Soviet Union, and Eastern Europe.

The prime moving force in this system—the energy that drives the machine—is the profit motive harnessed to the powerful impulses of self-interest. The dream of wealth and personal success creates enormous incentives for businessmen to produce, invest, innovate, and expand. But while the profit motive may be capitalism's greatest economic strength, it is at the same time its greatest moral weakness. The argument is elementary: an economic system that is driven by the seller's desire to maximize profits generates great pressures on that seller to deceive his fellow citizens when it is advantageous to do so as a means of increasing those profits.

This argument is not, of course, original; it goes back most notably to medieval Catholic teachings on commerce. But these teachings have long been neglected. At least since the publication of Max Weber's *The Protestant Ethic and the Spirit of Capitalism,* it has been customary to regard early Catholic views on commerce as hopelessly backward notions that for centuries restricted economic growth, while Protestant attitudes on economic activity have been seen as a progressive force helping to liberate the nascent powers of capitalism.

What is usually overlooked when dismissing medieval Catholic economic doctrine as quaintly reactionary and historically obsolete is that the Church had legitimate ethical concerns—as relevant now as they were then—that the world of commerce was morally corrupting. By warning against the sin of avarice and insisting on a just price for goods, the Church recognized that in the marketplace, temptations for immorality lurked everywhere. Those who would buy cheap and sell dear, the Church argued, were often tempted to lie, cheat, and defraud others to increase their wealth. Once it takes hold, the desire for gain is insatiable, and those who pursue it may easily be overcome by greed and callousness. Pope Leo the Great's fifth-century pronouncement that "it is difficult for buyers and sellers not to fall into sin" became accepted Church opinion for the next six centuries.[1]

Thomas Aquinas argued in a fascinating thirteenth-century treatise on business fraud—which has a distinctly contemporary ring—that in the pursuit of profit traders often try to conceal defects in the goods they sell, as, for example, "in the case of a man who sells a lame horse as a fast one, a ramshackle house as sound, decayed or poisonous food as good."[2] Of course, such behavior is unjust. Aquinas argued, in fact, that most forms of trade conducted for profit were inherently morally suspect: ". . . he who in trading sells a thing for more than he paid for it must have paid less than it was worth or be selling for more. Therefore this cannot be done without sin."[3] Aquinas's contemporary, theologian Jacques de Vitry, put it more forcefully: "Cheating, fraud, lying, perjury, circumvention, and deception roam through all market places."[4] Medieval church discomfort with commerce is traceable to varied pronouncements in the New Testament itself and from there back to the Greek and Roman world. Plato and Aristotle had no great respect for profit-seeking in the marketplace, and the Roman orator Cicero, echoing the common opinion of his day, asserted that "Sordid . . . is the calling of those who buy wholesale in order to sell retail, since they would gain no profits without a great deal of lying."[5]

Of course there are countervailing forces in the contemporary marketplace that offset strong pressures to deceive. Every firm needs to protect its reputation if it wants to stay in business; this is manifestly a great restraining force against blatant and obvious deception. Yet, as the literature on business crime in this country is sufficient to fill a small library, and as the modest testimony on marketplace deception in this book suggests, these countervailing pressures against deception are not always adequate to keep business honest. There often seems to be a delicate balance between the effort to safeguard one's reputation, on the one hand, and doing all one can to maximize profits on the other, which sometimes means deceiving the public. How much stress is put on each of these varies enormously from firm to firm and from industry to industry, depending on many conditions, some of which are discussed later.

Adam Smith wrote of man's "propensity to truck, barter, and exchange." But in the market system he described there is also an equal propensity to deceive, or, to alter Smith's famous phrase slightly, a propensity to trick, barter, and exchange. Smith's invisible hand may provide economic benefits, but at considerable social cost, for one must weigh into the economic equation the social consequences of deception.

An economic system in which deception and cheating are widespread undermines social cohesion and subverts that sense of trust and fellowship which is the foundation of a civilized community. True, the consumer in America today has more rights and recourse than ever before. The genuine gains in consumer protection in the twentieth century should not be overlooked or minimized. Yet, while the propensity to deceive can be mitigated, I have serious doubts whether it can ever be eliminated entirely, for it seems to be intrinsic to the private market system itself.

After all the consumer legislation of the 1960s and early 1970s, after all the contemporary assurances of corporate and business responsibility, after all the pronouncements of "soulful corporations" and corporate consciences, after all the majestic theories telling us that the market system has been civilized by the welfare state, modernized by advanced technology, and transformed from the grim, satanic mills of an industrial society into a clean, well-lighted, and benevolent postindustrial society, we end up with a marketplace where the most appropriate motto is *still* caveat emptor. The more things change. . . .

One of the major struggles of the twenty-first century—in both East and West—will be, in my view, to build a system that combines some of the powerful economic incentives of capitalism with more socially responsible motives of cooperative and communal forms.

CHAPTER 1

A Bit of Bolshevik Sociology: Workers Write About Their Jobs

> White-collar criminality is found in every occupation, as can be discovered readily in casual conversation with a representative of an occupation by asking him, "What crooked practices are found in your occupation?"
>
> EDWIN H. SUTHERLAND, 1940

This is a book about the ingenious ways business cheats consumers in the marketplace. It is based on over 700 essays written by workers in dozens of different kinds of enterprises who reveal the deceptions and tricks of the trade carried out at their place of work.

The book was inspired in part by a footnote to twentieth-century history. In the years following the Russian Revolution, the Bolshevik government, seeking to discredit capitalism and the former Czarist regime, encouraged workers to write their memoirs of life in Czarist factories, describing how their employers had cheated the public and exploited the workers, and contrasting their dreary lives in pre-revolutionary factories with their presumably brighter lives since the revolution. By the late 1920s, these memoirs of factory life had been widely written, one such series begun under the general editorship of Maxim Gorky.*

---

* Decades later, after the Chinese communists came to power, they also urged

This early bit of tendentious Bolshevik sociology was firmly grounded in Marx's well-known aphorism that philosophers and other social thinkers had for too long *interpreted* the world; the point is to *change* it. This study of workers' essays differs from its Russian counterpart in at least one respect. Though my theoretical predilections are apparent here, I did not bias the study to elict only tales of swindle and evil from my informants; I designed it to encourage accounts of both business dishonesty *and* honesty, depending on workers' actual experiences.

Over a period of some fifteen years, from 1972 to 1987, I asked over 700 students enrolled in sociology courses at one campus of the City University of New York to write personal essays about their jobs. To avoid possible biases of self-selection, I asked them to write about their current job, or, if they were not presently working, to write about the most recent job they had. This also assured that the incidents they described were fresh in their memories. In these essays, the writers first discussed the nature of their jobs and their exact responsibilities, indicated how long they had worked for the company, and described the firm they worked for (disguising its name and identity if they wished).

The writers' major focus was on the question of the company's honesty. How honest or dishonest was the firm in its dealings with the public? Was there a contradiction between the image the company tried to project of honesty and fairness, which all firms seek to convey to the outside world (its frontstage performance), and what actually went on behind the scenes (its backstage behavior)? Were there various tricks of the trade, deceptions, secrets, and shortcuts that the company concealed from the public? If the writers saw no discrepancy between what the firm *said* it did and what it *actu-*

---

workers to tell of the bad days before the revolution. This was part of the so-called "speak-bitterness" campaigns. I am grateful for details of the Russian workers' memoirs to Professor S. A. Smith of the University of Essex, in a personal communication, January 30, 1986.

ally did (i.e., if the firm was honest with its customers), I instructed them to say so and elaborate. If they did see contradictions between the company's public image and what actually went on behind the scenes, I asked them to describe these practices and their evidence for it in detail.[1]

It might appear at first that students would make very poor informants. They are too young, too immature; they are untrained and their observations are likely to be unsystematic and haphazard. They are in most cases part-time or temporary workers, and thus perhaps less perceptive than permanent, full-time workers. Before the study began, I suspected that some of this criticism might be valid. Actually, however, the reverse turned out to be true, and these young people proved to be almost ideal informants for a number of solid reasons.

First, the fact that these writers are part-time or temporary workers proved not a drawback at all but a decided advantage. Because they are marginal to their workplace, they have all the insight and perception for which outsiders have long been known. These young people fit almost perfectly sociologist Georg Simmel's classic description of the *stranger*. Simmel observed that the stranger occupies a contradictory social position. He is inside and yet outside. He is both a member and a non-member. He is in but not of. He is near and yet remote. And it is this dual position that allows the stranger to see things that natives no longer notice. Local people of every region may think they speak without an accent; a stranger detects their accent instantly. Proximity gives the stranger knowledge and insight; distance gives him perspective and objectivity. As Simmel noted, because the stranger stands apart, he is free of the involvements "which could prejudice his perception, understanding, and evaluation of the given."[2]

In their jobs at the supermarket, department store, garment factory, or restaurant, these students *are* strangers just passing through, on their way up and out, using their mainly menial jobs to help them through college. Here they encounter a new world of work, inhabited by workers older and different from themselves. As temporary visitors to this workplace, students stand at a distance, and precisely because they stand at a distance, they are able to see the larger picture.

Students also proved to be excellent observers for another reason. Most are at an age where they still retain their youthful idealism.† They are not yet so old or cynical as to believe that fraud is an inevitable tool of human relations in the marketplace, and so do not, as do so many of their elders, dismiss it as business as usual. And while most are young enough to retain their youthful ideals and a capacity for moral outrage, they are at the same time old enough to know what is going on—to see it, remember it, and in this case, report it.

The sensitivity of these young people to their work experiences recalls one of Arthur Miller's fine plays, *A Memory of Two Mondays,* based on Miller's own work experience as a boy growing up in New York. In the play, a high school lad takes a temporary job in an auto parts warehouse to save money for college. He is different from the other workers in the shop, not only in age but in interests, aspirations, and ultimately in social-class destiny. He too is on his way up and out, but finds himself for a short time in this strange and incongruous environment. Because he is so different and so marginal, he sees it all clearly—the hopes, dreams, and disappointments of the younger workers, the pathos of the older workers who have spent their lives in this place, and the wondrous warehouse with its thousands of auto parts, a museum of the industrial age. Miller's play suggested to me that young people might have an important story to tell about work in America.

† A few students, attending college after years as workers or housewives, were considerably older than most undergraduates.

Indeed, this proved to be so. Not only do these young people have an important story to tell, they tell it extremely well. Freed from the academic constraints of term papers and examinations, some students displayed surprising literary gifts, and even students of average ability waxed eloquent when describing work situations familiar to them. While some showed righteous indignation recounting business fraud, others wrote straight journalistic accounts, making no moral judgments, and still others used touches of irony, humor, and sarcasm, employing a wry wit appropriate to the exposure of pious hypocrisy.

Finally, the fact that these students were drawn from the City University of New York (CUNY) enhanced their value as informants. A public university with minimal fees, CUNY has always drawn a student body from predominantly lower-middle- and working-class backgrounds. The vast majority of these students have to hold down a job—after classes, weekends, summers—in order to pay their college expenses or to help out at home. A recent study of CUNY graduates found that 89 percent of the students at the campus where this study was done worked either part-time or full-time while in school.[3] And in our study, well over 90 percent of the students were working currently or had worked at one time.

For most of these lower-middle and working-class students, a job is as much a fact of life as school. And by the time they graduate from college, many already have lengthy and diverse work experience. One student's description of his search for a summer job conveys the situation of most of his peers; a job is essential and is simply taken for granted. "This spring I was quite anxious about getting a job for the summer," he writes. "The rumors that it was going to be an exceptionally difficult year for college students to find summer jobs prompted me not to allow a repetition of last summer's disaster. Last spring I waited too long to begin searching for a summer job and ended up working in a car wash ten hours a day, six and a half days a week for the minimum wage. This year I began during Easter vacation the annual ordeal of looking for summer work."‡

As hundreds of workers wrote essays describing their work situation, and as the study was set in the New York metropolitan area with its huge population and enormous economic diversity, the range of occupational subcultures touched by these writers was extraordinary. These young people worked not only in supermarkets, department stores, and restaurants, but in factories, hospitals, nursing homes, bakeries, florist shops, summer camps, shoe stores, weight-reducing salons, gas stations, and stationery stores; for furriers, jewelers, pharmacists, physicians, and veterinarians; as semiskilled clerks, cashiers, salespeople, cab drivers, and postmen; and as skilled plumbers, carpenters, social workers, engravers, engineers, and so on.

At a time when ethnic, regional, and even national subcultures are being leveled by the homogenizing forces of modern technology, occupational and industrial subcultures continue to flourish. These cannot be homogenized by technology simply because a modern economy requires specialization and a vast division of labor. The *Dictionary of Occupational Titles,* for example, lists some 20,000 different occupations in America, most of which are totally unfamiliar to the ordinary citizen.

Each form of economic activity—whether a steel mill, garment factory, bank, or airline—must, by the very nature of the activities required to produce its product or service, create its own distinctive world, one generally unfamiliar to outsiders. Thus, each industry has in that sense a specialized subculture with its own organization, rules, customs, procedures, authority structure, and a peculiar jargon often strange or even incomprehensible to the general public. Beyond that, each *firm* within an industry has *its* own subculture based on its unique character. For example, all res-

‡ Some of the workers' essays quoted here were edited slightly for style, punctuation, and grammar, never for meaning or content.

taurants serve food and are thus alike, but each one is distinctive and has its own miniature subculture familiar only to the workers in that restaurant.[§]

An industrial subculture is thus fully known and understood only by the people who work in it. The public are outsiders and, as customers or clients, encounter only the very edge of these subcultures. Consumers may catch a glimpse of the inner workings of a bank or an auto dealership, but, for at least two reasons, their understanding remains superficial. First, their contact with the firm is not long or deep enough for a thorough understanding, and second, much of the inner workings of a business are intentionally closed off to outsiders. Like prisons, mental hospitals, and military installations, most enterprises are foreign and mysterious territory in our own land. Aside from their own place of employment, most persons have never been inside a factory, mine, mill, or behind the scenes of any enterprise; people are acquainted with these firms only through the products that emerge from them and appear on store shelves.

Just as most people are outsiders to the vast network of American business, so too are they outsiders to the crimes of business. Employees, however, are insiders. And in these essays, workers pull back the curtain and give us a glimpse of the unexplored industrial subcultures that flourish in America. Here, in essence, hundreds of sociological field-workers have given us diaries of the darker recesses of the American marketplace, revealing from within practices that have never been studied in quite this way.

In order to make some preliminary numerical generalizations about these essays, I classified each one according to the ex-

[§] It is true that corporate concentration and franchising have led to some standardization in occupational practices. Fast food outlets under one corporate umbrella, for example, standardize food preparation and work organization.

tent of business deception the writer reported. This involved several steps. First, I placed in the category of "No Deception" those testimonies in which the writer stated that insofar as he or she was able to judge, there was no contradiction between the image of fairness and honesty the firm presented to the public and what actually went on behind the scenes. I also placed in this category essays in which the deception the writer described was, in my judgment, simply too insignificant to matter. Even if the public discovered it, it would probably be regarded as inconsequential to the vast majority of people.

Second, in the "Unknown" category I placed all those essays that did not provide enough relevant information, where there was no coherent statement of whether the company did or did not engage in deceptive practices. These were cases where the writer did not really address the issue of business deception, but instead discussed such other matters as the boredom of the work, how the employees cheated the boss, how the employer took advantage of the workers, the personality traits—positive and negative—of employer, supervisor, manager, and the like.

Third, in considering these essays, I did not include as deception any of the numerous examples of company inefficiency, incompetence, or even negligence. I counted only those practices that involved conscious deception or fraud in its strict legal sense: "an intentional perversion of the truth for the purpose of inducing another . . . to part with some valuable thing belonging to him."[4] As distinguished from simple negligence, fraud is intentional deception, not carelessness, and in these accounts it took the form of attempts to induce the customer to part with something valuable—in most cases, money.

In weighing the evidence of business deception reported in these essays, I disregarded hearsay, rumor, and secondhand reports unless they were corroborated by direct firsthand observation. I also discounted unsubstantiated subjec-

tive judgments, such as "prices are too high," "the boss is
unfair to his customers," "repairs are not done well," and
so on. Finally, in a very few cases I dismissed evidence which
seemed, merely on the face of it or by the way it was presented, to be inaccurate, exaggerated, or otherwise suspicious.

Of the 728 essays written over a fifteen-year period, 638
(88 percent) were usable, that is, they addressed the issue of
whether these firms engaged in deceptive practices and provided evidence to support their case. And of these 638 writers, only 29 percent indicated that, to the best of their knowledge, the company for which they worked was honest. Most
writers, however—71 percent—reported that their firm did in
fact deceive the public and provided convincing evidence to
substantiate their claim.

Depending on the severity of these practices, I classified
each instance of deception as minor, moderate or serious (see
table below). This classification, though it has the advantage
of quantitative neatness, is nonetheless somewhat arbitrary.
In general, I counted as seriously deceptive those firms that
regularly swindled their customers and/or whose deceptions
cost customers substantial amounts of money. For example,
I considered seriously deceptive a gas station that consistently charged customers for repairs not done and sold mislabeled gasoline.

I considered moderately deceptive those firms that cheated

Extent of Business Deception	Number	Percent
None	183	29
Minor	284	45
Moderate	137	21
Serious	34	5
Subtotal	638	100
Unknown	90	—
Total	728	

the public less frequently and/or whose deception was neither a negligible nor major cost to consumers. Thus, a catering establishment that often substituted cheaper brands
of food and liquor and often surreptitiously overcharged
customers was considered a moderately deceptive firm.

The best examples of firms committing minor deceptions were those engaged in the kinds of false and misleading
advertising discussed in the following chapter.

These categories of minor, moderate, or serious deception provide only a rough indication of the precise degree
of business cheating found in these testimonies, for it was
difficult to establish a clear dividing line between, say, what
might reasonably be defined as serious deception and what
might be considered moderate deception. But while I cannot guarantee that other readers would make the same judgments in every instance, I believe that in most cases there
would be substantial agreement and whatever changes might
be made by others would not alter the general findings that:
(1) a large majority of all firms deceived their customers; (2)
while most of the deception was minor in nature, a significant amount (over one-quarter) must be considered, by conventional standards, moderate or serious.

Although students generally made excellent informants,
most do share a common defect: as marginal workers they
are not likely to know the full extent of the deception that
might go on in their firms. Even though students are perceptive about what goes on around them at work, and while
many of them have been directly involved in deceptive practices, if for no other reason than because employers must
draw their employees in to help perpetrate the swindle, few
students have access to the books or to top levels of company secrecy. Where it exists, business fraud may be con-
ceived as a series of concentric circles usually emanating from
the center, and while students may be aware of what occurs
toward the periphery, there may be many inner rings where
information is concealed, not only from the public, but from

the bulk of the employees as well. The practices reported here are those that students—usually on the perimeter of the enterprise—have observed; by using students as informants, therefore, we can be sure that there is *at least* as much business deception as is reported here and perhaps much more.

Naturally, however, even the most serious cases of business deception reported in this study do not match in severity major white-collar crimes of national significance—price-fixing, collusion, bribery—that may cost the public billions of dollars. Yet ultimately what is of concern here is not merely business crime itself but the impact of that crime on the social fabric. We know that "less important" events that happen at home often have greater personal impact than "more important" events that happen far away. A small storm close to home causes more local concern than a hurricane far away. If people are repeatedly, or even occasionally, deceived in their everyday dealings in the marketplace, this direct personal experience may do as much damage to the social fabric and to the climate of trust in a community as larger scandals farther away. True, these local deceptions are often small. Yet, deception, however minor, is the rust of society; it may work slowly, but ultimately its consequences can be devastating.

From this brief quantitative summary, it is apparent that in these workers' accounts business deception is widespread. But a quantitative picture alone is inadequate, for it cannot convey the actual substance of these deceptions. Throughout the book, therefore, I have cited many excerpts from these essays, for they bring us far closer to the social reality of the marketplace. And yet, reading just one or two of these essays alone, regardless of how flagrant the deception, doesn't reveal the larger picture, because singly each seems unique and without pattern. The whole here really is greater than the sum of its parts. A single deception has little meaning. A great number, taken together, convey a sense of the entire system at work, and from them one gets an overview of the imaginative perversity and elaborate deviousness of it all.

And yet, business deception, though widespread, is neither universal nor evenly distributed. Some firms are scrupulously honest, others are highly deceptive, and still others are moderately or marginally so. What explains these variations? Are there characteristics of the customers, the product, the environment, the industrial subculture, or the market situation that help account for these variations? After a general discussion of deceptive sales practices in Chapter 2, I turn in subsequent chapters to some of the principles that seem to explain this "propensity to deceive," and conclude with a general discussion of morality and the marketplace in American society.

CHAPTER 2

Selling It: The Seamy Side of the Marketplace[1]

ADULTERATION

Things are seldom what they seem,
Skim milk masquerades as cream;
Highlows pass as patent leathers;
Jackdaws strut in peacock's feathers.
                    W. S. GILBERT, *H.M.S. Pinafore*

Adulteration of products is one of the most common deceptions practiced on the public. And for good reason. If the cardinal rule of capitalism is to buy cheap and sell dear, then it's understandable why adulteration is so widespread; it allows the seller to alter one side of that equation in his favor and indeed buy cheaper than would otherwise be possible.

Unlike the snake-oil salesman of old who proudly announced to his gullible audience that his product was "100 percent adulterated," today's sellers don't boast about it. Yet adulteration continues, albeit surreptitiously, and innumerable products are diluted by means of a wide variety of imaginative techniques. The informants reported numerous examples of human ingenuity employed in the ceaseless quest to cheat one's neighbor.

Water, Water Everywhere (and Other Liquid Adulterations)

Water is naturally a favorite adulterating substance—so common, in fact, that one meaning of the word itself, used as a verb, is to adulterate. Its adulterating properties are so useful that sometimes water is even used to adulterate *water*. A cook at a sandwich shop explains: "A salesman for a spring water company talked my boss into featuring their spring water as a soft drink. My boss was reluctant at first but decided to give the drink a try. Surprisingly, the spring water was popular even at 55 cents for 10 ounces." But as the worker goes on to explain, this gave his boss an idea for an even more lucrative way to market the product. "My boss made a deal with the spring water distributor and now he orders just the empty bottles. It was hard to believe that he was going to fill the empty bottles with tap water, but that's what he did. Through a plastic tube he would fill each bottle with tap water, ever so careful not to get the label wet."*

A counter clerk at a local delicatessen told a similar tale about the secret of the store's "imported" water. "In the store," he writes, "we sold 'imported' water. Except this 'imported' water was water 'exported' from our sink in the rear. I had the misfortune to have to fill the bottles and display them in the window. Thus our customers, even one as consumer-conscious as Bess Meyerson [former New York City Consumer Affairs Commissioner] couldn't tell the difference between the two types of water."

A supermarket worker also observed how tap water was put to similar use, not regularly but when necessary. She

---

* To protect the anonymity of these workers' accounts, I have changed or deleted the names of all persons and firms, altered the location of all companies or described them in such a general way as to make identification impossible, and changed the names of many products. Also, because these essays were written over a fifteen-year period, I have tried as much as possible to standardize the prices for goods and services mentioned by workers to levels prevailing in the late 1980s.

writes that when spring water is delivered to the store with some of the bottles leaking, "regular tap water is added to fill them up. This is then sold at the normal price rather than take a loss on the item." When necessary, other products are also watered—mouthwash, for example: "Some bottles come in which have not been completely filled. They are then filled with water and placed on the shelf. A customer would never know what happened unless he had seen it."

Water makes an appearance in innumerable other products as well. A waiter who worked in a prestigious New York catering hall reveals that the caterer found many uses and disguises for water aside from its appearance in drinking glasses. For example, the waiter writes, "if the chefs made a mistake on the amount of soup that was needed to cover the affair, they would just take our magic ingredient and place it in the pots and there you have enough soup for everyone in the party. This would also be done with sauces and dressings as well. And it's simply amazing how far a bottle of ketchup can go these days." A worker in a small supermarket, well known for its quality meats, notes that water is particularly useful in the meat department. He writes that "a most important tool in the meat department is the water pump. It is with this pump that tongues, corned beef, pastramis, etc., are instantly made to weigh more."

A local drugstore in Queens faced a problem similar to that of the partly filled mouthwash bottles, but involving cologne. A cashier who worked in the store for eight months stated that sometimes the colognes would partially evaporate and the store was left with half-filled bottles. This posed no particular problem; clerks were instructed to mix two bottles to get one full bottle. In this situation, customers were not cheated for they got a full bottle of cologne. Another situation, however, called for a more imaginative solution. She writes, "At times we found ourselves with half-filled cologne bottles but of two different makes. We combined them anyway and sold the concoction as the brand with the higher price. To illustrate, one day we took a half-filled bottle of Night in Tunisia cologne and mixed it with the remains of the more expensive Paradise fragrance. We sold our mixture in the latter bottle and at the higher price."

Alcoholic beverages of all kinds are prime candidates for adulteration because they are expensive and easy to adulterate without being detected. Workers report widespread adulteration or substitution of cheaper alcohol in catering establishments, bars, and restaurants. A very common practice, and one widely suspected by the public, is selling cheap liquor as a more expensive brand. The technique is time-tested and easy to carry off. A waiter for a New York caterer spells it out simply: "My manager purchases cheap liquor and then pours it into empty bottles of premium liquor."

Many bars do the same, of course, regardless of how fashionable the clientele or neighborhood. A waiter at an expensive East Side Manhattan pub writes that "when you ask for a 'scotch on the rocks,' you are going to get cheap bar liquor. When you ask for 'Chivas on the rocks,' chances are you are still going to get the cheaper scotch, but you will be paying extra."

Many restaurants play the same game. A worker at a restaurant at an airport in the northeast observed a similar switch. He writes that a customer ordering an expensive whiskey, scotch, or brandy will probably be served a cheaper brand. If the customer complains, the bartender would "feign innocence" and claim that it was a "misunderstanding."

Something's Fishy

Seafood is easily adulterated, and cheaper fish is readily substituted for more costly because many types of seafood look and even taste enough alike to deceive most consumers. A young woman who worked the counter at a local fish store itemized in a most matter-of-fact fashion the routine substitutions typical of this market:

1. Our prepared crabmeat salad is usually made from shredded, frozen halibut that is boiled first. It tastes just like crabmeat;
2. Ingredients other than the traditional whitefish, pike, and carp are ground up and used for gefilte fish;
3. Lobster tails from other locations are sold as South African tails;
4. Flounder filleted are sold as fillet of sole;
5. Danish frozen brook trout thawed out is sold as fresh Idaho rainbow trout;
6. Frozen steaks (halibut, salmon, cod, etc.) can be thawed out, displayed, and sold as fresh.

She concludes with her employer's rationale for these practices. "These are just a few of the devices that are used which the public is unaware of. But they are really not considered to be that bad (by the owner of the store) since [he claims] all fish stores do this and in competing with other stores one must do this."

Restaurants have their own tactics for adulterating seafood. A waitress in an Italian restaurant describes the strategy of stretching the baked clams. She writes, "Appetizers in our restaurant are often deceptive. Baked clams, for instance, should be called 'baked breading.' The fresh clams are first chopped up very small and then mixed with bread crumbs and placed back in their shells. The proportion of clams to breading is astounding. About one whole clam is used to make about six baked clams. Naturally, since you use so little clam and so much breading, you lack shells. Thus after people eat the baked clams the busboys are told to clear the table, taking the empty shells back into the kitchen to be used again and again. They are filled by more breading and then served to another customer." A waiter in another restaurant described the same practice of reusing clam shells. Fortunately, he said, clam shells are "dishwasher safe."

Fillets of ouija board. A waiter who worked at a small neighborhood seafood restaurant for a year and a half describes what happens when customers order fillet of sole, a maneuver that might instead be called fillet of ouija board.

"A popular choice at our place are broiled dinners, especially broiled flounder fillet or sole fillet, the difference being that sole is a bit more expensive than flounder. When I have two people, one of whom orders flounder and the other sole, what happens is that they will both receive flounder since they look and taste very similar, and we usually only have flounder fillet to begin with. When the order is ready, I will go back to pick it up, whereby I will ask the cook which order is which. He will then turn to me, walk over to the two dinners, close his eyes, and with a circling motion of his fingers bring it down on the counter, where he will say with a smile, 'I guess this is flounder and that's sole,' and continue on with his other orders." In this restaurant, there are a few other substitutions and adulterations, but the waiter claims that here "the public does not get taken for a long ride, but only for a brief scenic tour."

One Man's Meat

Restaurant menus are often an imaginative mix of fact and fiction. The head chef at one location of a large restaurant chain "translated" some items on his restaurant's menu. The "fresh-squeezed orange juice" is actually frozen concentrate. The "fresh-cut french fries" are frozen. The "butter" is margarine. And the "All-Beef Steer Burger" is stretched with soybean meal with an admixture of blood to "give it that fresh look." Restaurant inspectors for the New York City Health Department are supposed to monitor for "truth-in-menu" violations, but even Health Department officials concede that this is a low priority item considering their more important health concerns.[2]

Although it is generally easier to disguise fish than meat,

the latter is not impossible, as our informants reveal. The adulteration of hamburger was very commonly reported by workers. And a busboy who worked in an Italian restaurant for over four years wrote that, among other adulterations and substitutions, "I have seen lean cuts of beef sold as veal at veal prices because someone forgot to order the veal."

A cashier at a neighborhood self-service butcher shop disclosed that occasionally cheaper meat was disguised and sold as a more expensive cut. "For example," she writes, "if we had an excess amount of chuck steak, the butcher would cut the chuck steak into the shape of a porterhouse. After this was done, one couldn't tell the difference between the two." Naturally the chuck steak turned porterhouse was sold at porterhouse prices.

Seconds and Irregulars

Department stores don't ordinarily sell products that can be adulterated, but surreptitious substitution of inferior—and cheaper—goods for their more expensive counterparts was quite common. A young woman who worked for three years in the receiving department of a large New York department store reported that the store often passes off irregulars and seconds as first-quality merchandise. She adds that "many times damaged and soiled goods are sold rather than repairing or cleaning them or sending them back to the manufacturer." The lesson she learned? "Every time I buy an item in the store I always check for damages." A worker at an expensive and well-known department store "which is practically worshipped by middle-class suburban housewives" alleged that the store also sold seconds without informing customers. She writes, "Many sales at the store offer irregular merchandise which the manufacturer is glad to sell to [the store] for a fraction of the usual cost, and of course the public is not told of the imperfections."

I Can Adulterate It for You Wholesale,
or Trickle-Down Larceny

Most of the examples given above involve adulteration at the retail level. But there is no reason to assume that adulteration begins there. In fact, it often begins earlier, at the manufacturing or wholesale level, and ultimately trickles down to the consumer.

A young man worked in a chemical plant outside New York State that sells aromatic chemicals to leading cosmetic houses, which in turn produce well-known perfumes. The writer reports that the company occasionally deceived a client by adulterating one of its most exotic oils, one that is extremely difficult to produce naturally and which sold for hundreds of dollars a pound in the late 1970s. "On one occasion," he writes, "we had an order for fifteen pounds of X. One of the chemists in the plant told me that he mixed the pure liquid with an artificial substance, so the fifteen-pound order was filled without fifteen pounds of the genuine natural product."

Government regulations in this area are flexible enough so that the company can also make money adulterating other products. "An example of this is Y, where the government issues certain specifications for the liquid. As it is a natural substance, there has to be a range in the specifications. Therefore, the company buys the substance at the upper range and dilutes it down with chemicals to the lower part of the range, thereby making the product one-third to one-half cheaper. They then sell this product at the market price and reap a very nice profit."

All That Glitters: I

The esoterica of precious gems and jewelry provide a lucrative opportunity for adulterating the product. One informant with an unusual skill worked as a florentine engraver for a jewelry contracting firm. The company manufactures jewelry from gems and unfinished gold pieces furnished to them by their customers—large casting firms. The company carried out major deceptions against unwitting customers, which centered on the process of florentine engraving. The worker explains. "In order to understand this trick of the trade, one must know how a florentine finish is applied. A small hand tool is scraped across the side of a ring to create a 'criss-cross' design. In the process of doing this, bits of gold are removed from the ring. The scraps from a week of florentine engraving are worth a considerable amount of money. The customers expected these filings, which they would melt and reuse, to be returned to them with the finished work. Actually, what they were getting returned was 10 percent gold and 90 percent brass. My boss urged me to scrape as hard as I could in order to maximize the gold scraps. This would result in extra profits for my boss and cramped hands for me. Instead of going to its owners, the filings would go to a refinery which paid the boss cash for them."

The owner played an even more lucrative game with diamond rings. In setting several diamonds into a ring, workers were often instructed to substitute smaller diamonds than the customer had ordered. The worker writes, "My boss would inspect all work before assigning it to his workers. If a ring took many diamonds, he might choose to have all but one of them set. The empty spot would be filled with a smaller, less expensive diamond. For example, I once saw the boss approach a setter with an unset cocktail ring which took thirty two-point diamonds which were supplied by the customer. The setter was given, with the ring, only twenty-nine two-point diamonds and one one-point diamond. The smaller diamond was set in an inconspicuous area of this massive cluster ring. After it was polished it was almost impossible to detect that one of the stones was only half the size of the others. The two-point diamond would be used in place of a larger diamond at a later time. This process, if continued, can be very lucrative."

The engraver notes that sometimes his company's swindles amounted to more than returning brass filings instead of gold or setting smaller diamonds in place of large. Occasionally, whole rings were stolen from customers. He writes that "if the ring count on a delivery bag was less than the actual number of rings inside, the difference was kept. Once, for example, after counting a pile of rings, I told the boss that there were 145 rings in the bag but that the bag said there were only 143. He simply put two rings in his pocket and said, 'Now there are 143.' "

This firm's practices are not unique, for a salesman in another large jewelry firm revealed similar sleight of hand. "We used to receive these very small stones on consignment from sellers, and we would take half of them out and mix the other half with cheaper goods and return them to the seller and say we couldn't sell them."

SHORT-WEIGHTING

You shall not have in your bag two kinds of weights, a large and a small. You shall not have in your house two kinds of measures, a large and a small. . . . For all who do such things, all who act dishonestly, are an abomination to the Lord your God.

DEUTERONOMY 25:13–16

Short-weighting may be seen as a kind of adulteration, and workers reported an array of interesting techniques for doing this that they observed on the job. One young man who worked for two and a half years in a delicatessen observes that "the process of short-weighting is accomplished in many ways. One way is conveniently having the scale placed off in a corner, behind the counter where the customers cannot view the actual weight of the product they were about to buy. This was useful to my employer because he or some of the other employees could easily slip a thumb on the scale to make the cold cuts weigh more. My boss weighed various salads (chicken, tuna, fruit, etc.) in a container to make them weigh more. Another trick was using spring weights, and tipping the scale to make the produce weigh more in order for my employer to make a greater profit."

Another informant worked for five years as a billing clerk at a meat supplier in New York which sells large quantities of meat to restaurants, camps, hotels, and other large meat purchasers. She reports that the smaller firms receiving meat deliveries from her company "do not have their own scales readily available to them and therefore must take the word of the meat packer who sometimes does not include 16 ounces to the pound."

Short-weighting of meat is common because the product is so expensive that even a small short weight can be profitable. A worker with four years' experience in a local supermarket noted frequent short-weighting of meat. He writes, "Very often the scales in the meat department were tilted in favor of the boss's profit. The law requires that in fixing prices of meat or any other packaged goods, the weight of the container and packaging must be allowed for. Not in our supermarket, however. Every sale made on packaged meat meant a few cents in the boss's pocket. A few cents doesn't sound like a lot, but if you multiply it by all the customers that are ripped off, it adds up."

Larger, systematic studies by New York's Department of Consumer Affairs have confirmed these workers' observations of short-weighting of meat in city markets. In a surprise sweep of city meat warehouses, where consumers buy meat in large quantities at a discount, the Consumer Affairs Department found short-weighting and mislabeling in *all* twenty-eight locations they surveyed.[3]

Short-weighting is a serious problem, not just in the sale

of meat, but for many goods sold retail. For example, in 1982 inspectors for New York City's Department of Consumer Affairs purchased over 465,000 packages of meat, vegetables, fruit, cheese, and so on in retail markets throughout the city. Approximately 122,000 of these packages, or 26 percent, were short-weighted.[4] Thus, consumers were routinely overcharged for more than one out of every four weighed packages they purchased. The cost to the public of this enormous rip-off is impossible to estimate, but it must run into tens of millions of dollars annually. The Department found that consumers were being cheated in many different ways: store scales were improperly set; customers were illegally charged for food wrapping; prepackaged goods arriving from suppliers were short-weighted (for which retail stores are legally responsible).

Why is short-weighting so common? Because it so often pays. The pecuniary rewards are many; the penalties are usually slight. The Department of Consumer Affairs, like so many agencies charged with protecting the public interest, is no match for the industries it is supposed to regulate. It inspects food stores infrequently, averaging only once a year at best. Fines for violators are usually nominal (from $50 to $400) and can normally be considered just part of the cost of doing business. Moreover, the department's enforcement powers are meager and cumbersome, and it often has difficulty collecting the fines it imposes. By the late 1980s, for example, 1,100 supermarkets in the city had accumulated a backlog of more than 40,000 unpaid fines dating back as long as five years.[5]

Besides all this, in the past bribery has undercut proper enforcement. A number of workers in this study wrote that they had indirect evidence that stores they worked for made payoffs to inspectors. In 1980, after a two-year undercover investigation by the city, nine of the eighty inspectors for the Department of Consumer Affairs were arrested and indicted for taking bribes from supermarkets to overlook short-weighting and false advertising.[6] Several pleaded guilty and many were imprisoned or placed on probation. Besides these inspectors, thirteen food stores and supermarket chains, including such well-known New York area chains as A&P, Key Food, and Waldbaum's, were also charged, along with fifty-seven store employees who were indicted for bribery. The district attorney in Brooklyn, where the investigation was centered, noted that bribery reached high into supermarket management, including district supervisors, district managers, and store managers. During the undercover investigation, supermarket managers allegedly bribed inspectors so promiscuously that the city's Consumer Affairs commissioner commented, "Almost every store the undercover inspector walked into, an offer was made."

PHONY SALES

The biggest liar has the edge.
CHICAGO RETAILER

Nothing in American culture is so contradictory as public attitudes toward social class and inequality. On the one hand, Thorstein Veblen *was* referring to America, at least in part, when he coined the phrase "conspicuous consumption"— demonstrating one's social position by a lavish display of expensive and often useless objects. On the other hand, the classless and egalitarian tradition in American life has shaped the national penchant for the practical rather than the showy, the functional rather than the pretentious. America has long been the wealthiest nation on earth, and one might expect that the products that symbolize America to the world would be costly, extravagant, and ostentatious. Yet that is not so. The artifacts that best express American culture and values are inexpensive, practical, and accessible. The garment that best symbolizes America to the world is not a Brooks Brothers suit but blue jeans; the food that best expresses American taste is not caviar but hamburgers; the beverage that says

America internationally is not champagne but Coke—all commodities of a common-man tradition.

And aside from a small upper class, what is valued among most Americans is not how expensively one can buy but how inexpensively, how cheaply, how economically. Americans love to boast, not about how much they paid for something but about how little. Veblen notwithstanding, Americans have a genuine bargain psychology, and surely one of the public's favorite four-letter words in the marketplace is "Sale!"

The weakness of American consumers for the word "sale" has not been lost on advertisers. Accordingly, one of the most widespread deceptions practiced on consumers in retail trade is the outright manipulation and falsification of so-called sales. The conventional wisdom defines a sale as a temporary markdown from the regular price. But what advertisers pass off as a sale is often very different from this. Capitalizing on the pervasive bargain mentality of American consumers, retail firms often engage in what might be called "Markup/Markdown" sales. Shortly before a "sale," the store will mark its prices up, then mark them down, creating the illusion of substantial savings.

Such practices violate long-standing Federal Trade Commission (FTC) guidelines on deceptive pricing, as well as New York City's Consumer Protection Law of 1969. The FTC guidelines state, for example, that in advertisements where sale prices are compared with previous regular prices, the regular price must be "one at which the product was openly and actively offered for sale, for a reasonably substantial period of time, in the recent, regular course of . . . business, honestly and in good faith—and, of course, not for the purpose of establishing a fictitious higher price on which a deceptive comparison might be based."[7] But since the FTC rarely prosecutes deceptive pricing cases at all, and state and local agencies look into only the most egregious cases, the practice is widespread and largely unchecked.

According to the informants, deceptive Markup/Markdown sales are not just employed by an occasional neighborhood shop, but are a common practice of many large department stores in New York. The practice is so common, in fact, that accounts of it appear time after time in the workers' essays. As the following cases illustrate, the similarity of the stories is striking; only the store and the product vary.

A salesman in a local clothing store writes: "A good deal of the sale merchandise in our store is first marked up to a higher price, then sold for the sale price. Right before the merchandise is to be put on sale, I usually destroy the old price tags on the clothing and replace them with new ones. On each new price tag I write on it a higher price, then put under this price the sale price, showing the consumer how expensive the garment is and what a large discount he is getting."

A clerk at a well-known New York discount department store reports a similar practice. "It is not unusual for merchandise to be recalled for reticketing a week or two before it is to go on sale at a slight reduction," she writes. "In the reticketing area, the items are then marked up to a higher price and then replaced on the floor. When the sale date finally rolls around, [the store] can then print ads telling what the item had previously sold for in our stock, thus dramatizing and exaggerating the true extent of the reduction."

In these cases, while the savings to consumers were exaggerated by boosting the "regular" price, the sale price was in fact slightly lower than the usual price, so consumers could save some money, though not a great deal. In the case of some "sales," however, this is not true; the sale price is identical to the usual selling price. A woman who worked for a year at a small clothing store in the Bronx reveals, "We often had the common 'half-price sale.' Naturally, all the prices were first marked up as much as 100 percent and then reduced.

For example, a dress usually selling for $48 would be marked on the ticket $96 and crossed out and marked down to the original $48. By doing this, the store could claim that the item was on sale. However, if an item is on sale in our store, the customer can neither return nor exchange it. We did this to sell the merchandise that had been sitting on the shelves for a long time, or if the item was damaged."

A salesman who worked in the bath shop of a large New York department store reported a similar practice. He writes, "The manager of our department had me remove stickers from a product. He then made up new price stickers with higher prices and had me place them on the merchandise. I was then told to use this special red marker and cross out the price on the sticker and reduce the price. The price was originally $7.95, the new price sticker read $9.95, which was crossed out and marked back down to $7.95." Thus the sale price was the same as the regular price.

A stock boy at the warehouse of a large New York department-store chain notes that during the company's so-called warehouse sales, "items such as lamps and luggage are supposedly marked down about $10 to $15 to a sale price when actually they aren't. What seems to be done is that a price higher than the regular prices is written on the sale tag. This higher price is then crossed out and the regular price, not a sale price, is placed under it." This particular case was unusual because the worker himself didn't realize that the sale price was the same as the regular price until some of his customers noticed it and mentioned it to him. He writes, "I first became aware of this when a few customers came to me and said that the supposed sale price was the same as the regular price in the store. Since I couldn't tell them what was going on because I didn't know, I told them to see someone who was in charge. . . . A few days later I happened to be in one of the many branch stores and I saw that the customers were right about that item; it wasn't on sale. Also I saw a few other things in the store that were the same price as at the warehouse sale. Ever since then I've noticed that all the sales at the warehouse have this discrepancy."

What is extraordinary about the Markup/Markdown gambit is that sometimes the sale price is actually *higher* than the regular price. A young woman who worked for two years in the ladies' dress and coat department of a New York department store related the following incident. "We were about to have a sale on certain gowns, and the store advertised that these gowns would be marked down 15 percent from the regular price. Not mentioned in the ad was that we had just marked the gowns *up* 33⅓ percent."

Another writer with three years' experience in a large department store worked in the receiving department, where new merchandise is checked in, counted, and ticketed. Her job was to price merchandise. She describes the kinds of sales the store occasionally ran. "Sometimes the prices of items are actually raised for a sale. As incredible as this may sound, I can vividly remember re-marking merchandise which originally sold for $3.99 to $4.99 for a sale. Another time I re-marked bracelets that were selling for $5.99 to $8.99 for a special advertising supplement."

A cashier for a well-known department store on Long Island reports similar tactics in several departments of the store. In the men's department, for example, a sweater that regularly sold for $36.99 was marked up to $46.50. The sweater appeared in the store's advertising circular with copy reading: "Save 18%. Men's fisherman knit sweaters, $37.99. Regularly $46.50." The sale price was thus $1.00 higher than the regular price. The cashier checked the cash register tapes and found that during the "sale," the sweater sold better than ever.

And indeed, given the bargain psychology of American consumers plus the genuine need of many families to keep spending down, it isn't surprising that consumers respond to advertised sales. Unfortunately, advertisers readily exploit the public's naïve bargain psychology. The device of sales is cleverly used by merchants against those who respond to it.

During a Christmas shopping season in Chicago some years ago, business was particularly slow. To increase sales, retailers waged a price war, fought in part by genuine price-cutting and in part by phony sales, or as the president of a well-known Chicago retail chain called it, "spurious comparative pricing." What all these phony sales at Christmas meant, he said, was that "the biggest liar has the edge."[8] A more fundamental issue, however, is whether the biggest liar has the edge only at Christmas or all year round.

A final example of the Markup/Markdown gimmick adds an element that spells more bad news for consumers. A young man who worked for two and a half years in the receiving department of a large department store reveals that sales run by his company can be very inflationary. He explains, "One of the most popular devices used by this department store is employed when there is going to be a sale. During a sale the price of an item is supposed to be lower than the regular selling price. This department store might do this except for one thing: a week or two before the sale they raise the retail price. This means that the sale price is now the old selling price. Then when the sale is over, the price is raised again to the new retail price. This gives the store an opportunity to raise their prices without the consumer being aware of it. In this way they have cheated the consumer in two different ways but with only one method."

Besides the Markup/Markdown technique, workers reported several other patterns of deceptive advertising or general misrepresentation. First, the "As Advertised" sleight of hand is a variation of the phony sale. It works as follows. Goods are advertised, but at their regular price. In the store near the advertised merchandise is the sign reading, "As Advertised," which, of course, is literally true; the goods have been advertised. But most people assume that goods that are advertised are on sale and thus assume that "as advertised" means "on sale." Although the stores are technically telling the truth, the intention is obviously to mislead.

A saleswoman in the dress department of a popular New York department store describes this deception. "Most of the discrepancies between the public image and the actual store policy stem from misleading advertising. There are many times when a dress is advertised in the newspaper and a sign is put up saying 'As Advertised.' This leads customers to believe that these items are reduced in price while in reality they are being sold at their regular price and the store is merely publicizing the merchandise."

A saleslady in a woman's shoe concession of a department store reports a similarly deceptive practice. "When I see something advertised in the newspaper, like most people I think 'Sale,' especially when the ad says 'Only $15.99.' This is one of the tricks of the trade, for the ad never stated 'Sale.' But many times a customer has seen an advertisement and asked me, 'How much were they originally?' When I tell them that they were always that price, they are astonished. This to me is one of the biggest tricks of the trade."

Besides the "As Advertised" gimmick, another semantic device used by one New York department store is the term "Sale Price." An employee explains, "In this department store 'Sale Price' means that the price ends in .99 or .88. When they advertise something like this, specially ticketed merchandise is sent to the store marked $19.99 or $15.88. These items never sold at a higher price. If they had been marked regularly they would have been $20 or $16."

In another form of phony sale, merchandise that a store does not normally carry—usually cheap, shoddy, old, or damaged—is specially purchased, unknown to the customers, and offered at "sale" prices. One woman writes of the junior sportswear section of the department store in which she worked. "The largest and most involved deceptions which I saw concerned their so-called 'sale' merchandise. The sale clothes were not really sale clothes at all. The buyers for the specific departments would prepare for sales weeks in advance. They would buy the cheapest possible clothes when they went to the market. This made the store look like they were giving genuine bargains. These sale clothes are most often merchandise which the manufacturer couldn't sell to any other store because of its poor quality. I saw this happening over and over again. During the period that I worked there the store had giant pre-Thanksgiving Day sales. Two weeks in advance the buyer for my department went to the market looking only for things that were the least expensive so they could fill the newspapers with ads of big savings."

Finally, many workers reported that their employers used one of several variations of the familiar bait-and-switch technique: (a) The store has the advertised goods but tries to switch the customer to something more expensive; (b) The store has only a limited quantity of the advertised merchandise, insufficient for the demand created by the advertising; (c) The store never had any of the advertised merchandise at all.

A writer who worked in the shoe department of a local department store describes how she sees the store advertise shoes that she knows are carried in only limited quantities. She writes, "On Sunday mornings I usually read the newspaper, not only to keep up with what is happening, but also to see what is on sale, as most women do, I guess. As I scan the newspaper, I usually see an advertisement from my department. In the last six months, at least five times I have seen a shoe or slipper advertised in my department of which I know we don't have enough stock. When I get it on Monday night we usually have just a few pairs left, since we only had a little to begin with and what we had went during the day. Meanwhile, the ad stated that we have all sizes and colors in all stores. My manager instructs us to tell the customers that there was such a demand for them, all our stock went; or to tell them that they are coming in (which may or may not be true)." Such practices clearly violate New York

City's Consumer Protection Law, which requires sellers to have "sufficient quantities" of advertised merchandise on hand to satisfy "reasonably anticipated public demand."[9]

Of course, an extremely well-informed consumer could probably navigate his way around most of these Markup/ Markdown and bait-and-switch deceptions. But one would have to be virtually a full-time shopper to do so. Most people simply don't have the time, energy, or patience to check accurate prices of the hundreds of products they might have to buy at one time or another. But the only alternative to being an omniscient consumer and avoiding the swindle is to be constantly suspicious and on guard. In the contemporary American city, one must be watchful everywhere—physically watchful in the streets, mentally watchful in the market.

DEATH OF A SALESMAN: THE CORRUPTION OF AN OCCUPATION

Killers are those who merely take orders, but Hunter-Killers are those who are not just content with getting the sale, but selling what is most profitable.

Salesman in a consumer electronics store

Imagine for a moment a completely rational economic system in which goods are advertised honestly to appeal to rational needs, and people are not deafened by a cacophony of voices urging them to spend beyond their means on an endless array of consumer trivia. In such an economic system, what would be the function of a salesman? In this hypothetically rational economic system, a salesman would simply match the customer with the most suitable product. Because salesmen generally know more about the products they sell than do their customers, in this rational system a salesman would display his goods, explain their features, and guide the customer to the one most appropriate. If he didn't have a suitable product, the salesman would discourage the customer from buying or refer him elsewhere.

If that description of how a salesman ought to function sounds naïve or even utopian, it is a measure of how accustomed we have become to living in a world where we routinely expect a salesman not to perform his "natural" function of selling us what we need, but to sell us all he can. We have come to expect the worst simply because we know that most salesmen are under vast pressures to maximize their sales regardless of their customers' needs. These pressures obviously derive from the commission system, from management's orders, and from the constant threat of competition from other salespeople and other firms. Whatever the source of these pressures, the system of rewards is so arranged as to corrupt the most natural, rational, and useful functions of a salesman. Hence, one normally finds in a salesman not a valued adviser but a suspected adversary. In fact, the behavior of salesmen in a market system can, without too much exaggeration, be compared to a physician who correctly diagnoses his patient's illness and then intentionally prescribes the wrong medicine.

Why are we both surprised and grateful when we encounter a salesman who tells us *not* to buy or to buy a less expensive product? Because we realize that in doing so the salesman has resisted the temptations of the system and is working against his own self-interest in order to serve the customer. Ironically, however, in a predatory society, even honesty can become a tool for deception.

Many astute salesmen have noted that the best way to gain a suspicious customer's trust is to create the illusion of honesty. One way to do that is to steer the customer away from one product by confiding supposedly inside information about that product's deficiencies. Customers are often so grateful for the salesman's candor that he can easily convince them to buy a product he actually preferred to sell all along.

A seasoned car salesman, who chronicled the tricks of

the auto trade in a recent book, cites an example of how he used "honesty" to deceive his customers. An ancient Lincoln had been sitting on the dealer's lot for months, apparently unsalable. The dealer offered a $200 bonus to any salesman who could unload it. A young couple drove onto the lot and began looking seriously at a late-model Nissan. The salesman approached them. " 'Hi, folks, I'm [Bob DeMarco]. Boy, I'm glad I saw you! The guys have been trying to sell that car [the Nissan] to someone for a month. It's just not a car you would want to own.' The people stop walking and look at him. Here is an honest man, just what they've been looking for." Of course, the salesman "knows just the car to fit their budget: the Lincoln with the $200 bonus."[10]

The conflict of interest between customers and salespeople is a recurrent theme in the testimonies of many of our informants who worked in sales. In these accounts we see in microcosm how young people are socialized into this occupation: honest people are transformed into deceivers and the potentially useful occupation of salesman is thereby corrupted.

The owner of a shoe store taught a young saleswoman the rules of the selling game. The worker writes, "While I was being trained as a salesgirl, I was informed by my boss that I was to sell shoes no matter what." She was to use her knowledge of stock not only to help her customers but also, when necessary, to deceive them. She mentions one technique noted by many shoe store employees. "If we were out of a lady's size in a particular shoe, I was to give the customer a half size bigger or a half size smaller and withhold the information from her. Then, after slipping the shoe on and letting the customer get the feel of it, I was to inform her that the shoe 'runs large' so I gave her a smaller size, or the shoe 'runs small' so I gave her a half size larger." She concludes, "It was obvious that many of the shoes should not have been worn by some of the women, but this was no concern of mine. My job was to be a decent con artist, and this made me a good salesgirl."

Another saleswoman was trained in a similar manner. She had been working for about a year for a woman who operated a small clothing boutique, and confessed that she was trained to sell clothes to the customer regardless of whether they fit the customer's needs or figure. She writes, "Now, I know that the ultimate goal of business is to make money. Yet for Carol, my boss, this is the only goal. I am embarrassed to admit that Carol has me trained fairly well. I flatter women on how they look even if a dress looks only fair. Luckily, I'm nowhere near as bad as Carol. She will tell everyone how wonderful they look even if they look terrible in a particular dress. Once a lady came in and was debating whether she should take a blue skirt or a red one. She asked me which I liked better and I answered honestly, 'the blue one, you look better in it.' Immediately after the customer left the shop, Carol said to me, 'Next time someone asks, tell them the red skirt, it's more expensive.' According to Carol, everyone looks good in everything they try on. Nothing is ever too tight or too loose—all you ever have to do is move a button. Now that is absolutely ridiculous."

As noted, there are many whips that drive a salesperson to deceive. In a shoe store described by one writer, the whip was management's order to "make the day"—to meet or beat the total sales of last year on the same day. Under this pressure, one salesman used a device similar to that mentioned above: "If a customer asks for a size 6 and you legitimately do not have a size 6, bring out a 6½ and don't say anything. Usually they won't know the difference."

In a well-known women's clothing store, the pressure to make the day often backfired, according to one saleswoman. The order from top management to make the day thundered down to every department head, merchandiser, and floor manager, each of whom was judged by this one criterion. Under this constant pressure, therefore, sometimes departments arranged to make the day in ways that were actually detrimental to the store. Often, for example, when store traffic was slow, the only things that would make the day would be the volume of mail orders sent out. The saleswoman continues: "Following the instructions of my merchandiser, the salesgirls would be sure to fill all the mail orders even when it meant sending out the wrong colors or sizes. The inconvenience to the customer didn't matter, contrary to the company's policy of satisfying the customer. There was one instance where we had sold our total stock of an advertised robe, leaving many mail and phone orders unfilled. In order to make the day, this same merchandiser marked down and had us send the customers a moderately similar robe that had not been selling. I have no way of knowing the customers' reactions to this, or the excuses and apologies made to them by the store. I just know I will never order anything by mail or phone from any store."

The commission system obviously creates incentives for salespeople to sell whatever they can regardless of their customers' needs. Some firms, in fact, offer an extra commission for selling undesirable items. One saleswoman who worked for a popular New York women's clothing store explains the system used there. "Besides my base salary, I work on commission, receiving 1 percent of what I sell, and P.M.'s, which vary with each department. P.M. stands for push money, that is, a bonus besides the commission for pushing what otherwise doesn't sell. For example, last year after Christmas, we had practically the entire stock of silver and pink lounging pajamas reduced from $32 to $4.99. For every one sold the salesgirl would make $1.50 in P.M.'s. Oddly enough, these hideous creations were gone within two weeks."

In another Manhattan clothing store, a salesman revealed that the commission system had an especially pernicious effect on the customer's pocketbook. In this store, the prices of some items were intentionally left unmarked; salesmen sold the goods for whatever they could get. Besides the straight commission system on priced goods, salesmen were paid an extra bonus on the unpriced goods—25 percent of anything an item sold for in excess of its regular price.

In the conflict between customers and salesmen, customers are especially disadvantaged—and salesmen correspondingly advantaged—when the product in question is inherently complex.†

Few products are as confusing to the public as life insurance. One writer, who worked for three years as a salesman for one of the nation's largest insurance companies, described how the public's relative ignorance about life insurance left them vulnerable to ambitious salesmen. From every level of the organization, salesmen felt pressure to sell new policies. Besides the commissions and the usual rewards for sales, the company offered prizes of all kinds to top salesmen. Perhaps the most coveted was the trip to the company's annual winter convention in Hawaii. The company kept turning the screws tighter, so that each year salesmen had to sell more in order to qualify for the trip. These incentives drove many to mislead their customers in order to get new business.

From his own experience at the company, the salesman writes, "People sign form after form not knowing what they are doing. They don't know, for instance, that they are borrowing the cash value from one policy to pay the big premium on the new contract. They know nothing about the interest charges with respect to such loan values. They don't know that they surrender all the accumulated dividends on one policy to pay the first annual premium on the other."

When the public's comparative ignorance is combined with the salesman's need to write new policies, patterns of deception are inevitable. According to the salesman, "many agents were guilty of what is known in the industry as 'twisting.' Twisting may be defined as 'delivering any incomplete

† Chapters 3 and 4 examine the relationship between consumer ignorance and business deception.

comparison of policies for the purpose of inducing or tend-
ing to induce a person to lapse, forfeit, or surrender any policy and replace it with another.' "

Twisting is to an insurance agent what "churning" is to
a stockbroker—generating excessive commissions from transactions not in the customer's interest. Our salesman notes
that "naturally, twisting is prohibited by the state [insur-
ance] code, whether the policy to be discontinued was written by a different company or by the same company as that
which the agent represented. In most instances it is in the
best interests of the insured not to replace the existing insurance with that of another policy. Yet in my office it was a
common practice."

When a salesperson is an employee of a firm, the pressure to maximize sales normally comes, in one way or another, from the employer. Nonetheless, self-employed salespeople, though not driven by an employer, play the same
game with the same rules, and the incentive to maximize
sales produces the same conflict of interest with customers.
The experience of one young man illustrates how the impulse to be honest is often subverted by the constraints of the
market system. For six months he was a sweater vendor at
one campus of the City University of New York, selling che-
nille sweaters to students. He bought them from the whole-
saler for $6 and sold them for $12.

He describes his metamorphosis. "When I started selling
the sweaters it was going great. I was making a huge profit
because people were buying more than one. Then after a
few weeks business started slowing down and I began losing
money. One of the questions that most people asked was
whether the sweaters had to be dry-cleaned. The answer that
I gave was yes, because machine washing would cause the
sweaters to fall apart.

"Well, people didn't really like spending money dry-
cleaning such an inexpensive item, so quite a few people
didn't buy sweaters for that reason. So when business really

got bad, I had to begin telling people that the sweaters were machine-washable so that they would buy them. I sold very well after that and quickly closed up. I found out later from another vendor that a lot of people returned to get their money back because their sweaters fell apart. The business was honest until sales began to fall. Things like this happen all the time in merchandising because the retailers have to move their merchandise."

Thus the education of a salesman.

Of course, instead of deceiving his customers he might have tried to buy sweaters that were genuinely machine-washable and then sold them honestly. Yet, there are always strong pressures to sell what one has. And it is the great misfortune of the salesman in a private market system that so often he cannot be what he rationally ought to be—a genuine adviser in the marketplace. He is too often not someone who aids our judgment, but someone who clouds it. He is thus alienated from his own sensible purpose and ultimately from his own integrity. The marketplace takes a skilled human resource, squanders it, and turns it against those who might be helped by it. Everybody loses.

CHAPTER 3

Ignorance: Dumb Customers and Distracted Customers

A fool and his money . . .

Some firms are honest, some are not. Of those that are not, some are more dishonest than others. What explains the wide variations in deceptive behavior in the marketplace? The most obvious generalization one can make about the propensity to deceive is that, broadly speaking, the more ignorant the customer, the more likely he is to be cheated, just as in the wild, the weaker and more vulnerable the prey, the more likely it is to be set upon. In a sense, ignorance is a precondition of every successful swindle, for if the victim were not ignorant, the ruse could not be carried off. Ignorance, however, as Caesar said of Gaul, can be divided into three parts. I will discuss the first two in this chapter and the third in the following chapter.

DUMB CUSTOMERS

By "dumb customers," I mean people who know less about the situation in which they find themselves than do ordinary people in the community. Who are dumb customers? Foreigners and tourists, confused and unfamiliar with their environment, are proverbial easy prey. Persons who are less alert or less intelligent than most are also more easily deceived than others. Occasional shoppers for unfamiliar prod-

ucts or in an unfamiliar milieu are often spotted as out of
their element and accordingly cheated—women in auto repair
shops, men in butcher shops, and so on.[1]

Cab drivers are notorious for taking advantage of tourists who obviously know less about the city than natives. Horror stories abound, and the worst incidents often make the
newspapers. In a recent case, two confused travelers from
China took a cab from Kennedy Airport to the Chinese mis-
sion to the United Nations, a ride of about seventeen miles.
The fare? Eighty-five dollars plus a mandatory fifteen-dollar
tip. Unfamiliar with American currency and prices, they
paid it.[2]

In an even more egregious swindle, three young Mexi-
cans who spoke no English arrived in New York for a visit. A
cab driver spotted them at Kennedy Airport and offered to
drive them to their destination on the Upper West Side of
Manhattan. The fare? $167.[3] This story made the newspaper,
but for every one that does, there must be hundreds of others that don't.

Cabbies who work the airports have similar tales to tell.
One cab driver in our study tells how the game is played and
how the victims are selected. "An experienced cab driver can
quickly recognize a good opportunity to take advantage of a
naïve foreign visitor. They're easy to spot with somewhat be-
wildered looks on their faces and holding pieces of paper
with addresses scribbled on them. Besides, if they're not going where the cab driver wants to go, he can always look
them straight in the eye and tell them apologetically, for instance, that he never even heard of Flatbush. One cab driver
described to me how he drove a Spanish-speaking couple from
the airport to the south Bronx by way of the Brooklyn Battery Tunnel, a detour that doubled the regular fare."

Such practices are common. In fact, it might be stated as
an axiom that the longest distance between two points is
taken by a cab driver with tourists as passengers. Another
cab driver confirms the practice; he reports that "regular

cab drivers who happen to be at the airport are hungry for a few extra dollars and often pride themselves on taking a longer and hence more expensive route to the passengers' destination. The fastest and cheapest route to midtown Manhattan [from Kennedy Airport] is the Long Island Expressway through the Midtown Tunnel or over the 59th Street Bridge. Many drivers, however, take their fare over the Triborough Bridge (25 percent more) or around the Belt Parkway (60 percent more)."

Cab drivers who work the airports are also fond of an illegal practice known in the trade as doubling, tripling, or quadrupling up. By doubling up, for example, a driver will take two separate fares (two people unknown to one another) in the same cab to a common destination (such as Manhattan) charging each one the full fare. This practice is especially common when the airport is "stripped" (that is, many passengers, few cabs).

A part-time cab driver with a definite flair for narrative offers these amusing accounts of the many ways strangers are welcomed to the city. " *'Air is extra, lady.'* Many cab drivers have a nasty habit of charging extra fees for everything. Everything. A gentleman arriving on a plane from Rio de Janeiro who doesn't know a word of English (except 'Americana Hotel, please') has a very good chance of being charged a dollar for every suitcase he brings in the cab. Plus the surcharge for going over the 59th Street Bridge, plus the extra charge for the use of Queens Blvd., plus. . . . Another favorite of many drivers is to charge an extra dollar to any person who sits in the front, either because there are already three in the back, or if he has crutches, or if, well, anything. If you can get away with it, take it."

The cabbie then goes on to discuss the special procedure for taking passengers outside the New York City limits. *"Bartlett's Famous Quotations.* The meter is not the only means for determining the amount one pays to be taken to a destination. If you are traveling to a point outside New York

City, you may bargain with a cab driver for a flat rate in this situation. Cab drivers love the rate scale for out-of-town jobs, as they earn about two and a half times what they would have earned if they let the meter run. Is this enough for the cab driver? No. The standard rule is add at least $5 to the stated rate, and when you've just gotten off a plane from Acapulco with five suitcases, you will pay $75 to get to Montclair, N.J. (a 45-minute ride). Sometimes you'll be asked by some unknowing soul to quote a rate from Kennedy Airport to the Bronx. This trip should be run on the meter [because it is within the New York City limits], but if the cab driver seizes the advantage of this ignorance, he may quote $55. I personally saw this done at the airport, except the prospective passenger was a plainclothes hack inspector. They took the driver away in handcuffs."

Out-of-towners are not the only ones duped by ambitious cab drivers. Drunks may also be considered dumb customers, for their faculties are dulled, their judgment impaired, and, if not belligerent, they make perfect victims. The cab driver quoted above relates a humorous episode which, though he supplies no evidence for its veracity and it sounds as if it may be part of the folklore of New York cab culture, nevertheless bears repeating.

He writes, "Drunks of a passive nature are preferred customers of cab drivers in that they don't disturb the driver and are quite vulnerable to being rooked. One evening at La Guardia Airport a drunk asked a cab driver to take him to Newark Airport. The passenger and driver agreed on a $55 flat rate. The drunk promptly fell asleep as the cab left the curb. The driver capitalized on this fact by merely driving from the upper level of the airport to the lower level and awakened his passenger with news of their arrival at 'Newark.' The drunk paid the fare and departed."

Tourists and other unknowing citizens are not only being taken for a ride in New York City taxis, but apparently in hansom cabs as well. These picturesque horse-drawn carriages, so appealing to tourists and other romantics, add local color to Central Park and midtown Manhattan. The price of these carriage rides is fixed by law at $17 for half an hour, but when inspectors for the Department of Consumer Affairs posed as customers, drivers quoted prices ranging from $20 to $60 for rides lasting only ten or fifteen minutes. Although rates are supposed to be posted in the carriages, investigators found them often obscured by lanterns, blankets, and miscellaneous decorations. When the rate signs were visible in the carriage, drivers told the undercover inspectors that those rates only applied during daytime hours or on weekdays.[4]

In many instances the ghetto poor may also be considered dumb customers. Two workers, unknown to one another, wrote similar essays detailing their experiences working for a company that sold $500 vacuum cleaners door-to-door in poor and ghetto neighborhoods in Brooklyn and the Bronx. Poorly educated and unsophisticated, many of these people were understandably dumb customers and were accordingly exploited. The sales tactics were those often used in poor neighborhoods: salesmen concealed the purpose of their visit, concealed the total cost of the equipment they were selling, concealed the interest and late-payment charges, and concealed the customers' legal right to terminate or cancel the contract.

A gas station attendant who worked in a poor Hispanic neighborhood in Brooklyn told how his boss cheated unsophisticated customers during the turmoil of the energy crisis. In the late 1970s when the price of gasoline rose above $1 a gallon for the first time, many gas pumps that were manufactured with only a two-digit price for gasoline could not record the correct gallon price. To compensate, many dealers adjusted the meter for half a gallon of gasoline and doubled the final reading. Thus, for example, gas selling for $1.10 a gallon was set on the meter at 55¢ and the final total simply doubled. Nonetheless, the service station attendant reports that after the oil companies had replaced the pumps or adjusted the old pumps to register the actual price of gas, "the practice of doubling the final charge continued in our gas station."

A number of photo-electronic stores in Manhattan are renowned for cheating tourists, foreigners, and naïve New Yorkers who maintain less than the requisite level of paranoia when dealing with them.[5] With their display windows jammed with a dazzling array of cameras, lenses, tape recorders, record players, radios, televisions, video recorders, calculators, binoculars, watches, and other wonders, the stores' high-tech glitter often proves irresistible to passing shoppers.

A salesman for more than two years at one of these emporia reveals some of the company's favorite swindles. First, he says, the store regularly sells reconditioned or rebuilt products as new. For example, "Manufacturers of electronics goods sometimes turn out defective items which are then reconditioned and put back on the market. These reconditioned items have to be clearly marked with a sticker or stamped 'reconditioned' on the item itself. Our store purchases several models of name-brand calculators that are rebuilt or reconditioned. When the units reach the store, my boss immediately orders me to take the 'reconditioned' stickers off the backs of the calculators and dispose of them. Though the store buys these calculators at a reduced price, they sell them as new and the public is not aware of the subterfuge."

Selling used electronic equipment as new is not a practice limited to midtown Manhattan. In a study of 121 appliance and electronics stores throughout New York City, the Department of Consumer Affairs made the extraordinary discovery that over one-third were selling used T.V. sets as new. Many of these sets were eight or more years old, and the department suspected that many were reconditioned sets that had been used in hotels, motels, and hospitals. Deception on such a large scale suggests there may be a formal network of unethical suppliers.[6]

The camera and consumer electronics market in New

York City is fiercely competitive, and to meet the competition merchants must often set prices just a few dollars above cost. To compensate, sellers often try to boost profits in surreptitious ways. Dumb customers are perfect victims.

A merchant may enhance his profits by removing accessories that are supposed to be included with a product and selling them separately (a practice known in the trade as stock-splitting), or by substituting cheaper accessories for the ones included. The electronics salesman writes, for example, that when selling personal walkaround stereos, "a common trick is to take the original headphones out of the box and replace them with inexpensive headphones. For instance, original Sony headphones in an expensive Walkman wholesale for about $30. Our store would buy cheap headphones for $8, place them in the Sony box, and then sell the Sony headphones for as much as $80."

Similar tricks abound in the highly competitive retail camera market. The list price on cameras is greatly inflated to make the apparent discount price seem much larger. Equipment originally included with the camera—batteries, straps, and so forth—is often removed from the box and sold separately. The prices of camera cases, filters, and accessories usually purchased with cameras are inflated or sold at the high list price. And so on.

These tactics are certainly not unique to this informant's store; they are widespread and often reported in the press. According to the salesman, however, this firm's greatest profit-generating device is its adding machine. The adding machine ploy is used almost exclusively on foreigners and tourists who are either unfamiliar with American currency or with New York State's sales tax. It works as follows: "When tourists buy several items, the boss adds them up and decides how much extra he wants to make on the sale. On all sales to tourists above $300, a $40 or $50 charge is affixed to the total sale depending on how much the boss thinks he can get away with. This he accomplishes by punching, say, $40 into the machine and then ripping off the piece of calculator tape that has the imprint of $40. Therefore, the customer will never see the $40 physically on the tape, but the total will be $40 over the prices printed on the tape."

The merchant also has a novel method of calculating the sales tax for tourists. The salesman reports that "usually, when tourists purchase several items, the boss just takes a number off the top of his head and charges it as sales tax. The number is usually twice or three times the actual sales tax that should be charged. Both added charges boost profits tremendously on tourist sales." The salesman claims the system is fairly foolproof, for if the tourist discovers the extra charges, "the boss apologizes and tells them there must be something wrong with the adding machine and then retotals the items correctly to maintain the sale."

DISTRACTED CUSTOMERS

In certain businesses the customer's purchase takes place in an atmosphere that is inherently distracting and renders the customer less discerning a judge of whether the product or service he is buying is satisfactory. Thus, although the customer is ignorant, he is more distracted than dumb.

On festive occasions, such as weddings, birthdays, bar mitzvahs, anniversaries, or other "affairs" (as they are called in New York), the host is likely to be so inundated with details and preparations, besides the usual social anxieties surrounding these events, that he will often simply be too busy or nervous to judge the quality of all the things he has purchased, especially if they are marginal to the occasion.

Many workers told of how distracted customers were deceived. A saleswoman in a large florist shop on Long Island writes: "The motto in the basement [of the store] is, 'If you don't have it, fake it,' and that's exactly what we do. Oh, you might have asked for irises or daisies for your wedding centerpiece, but you may get gladiolus instead. And, if mum are too expensive this week, you'll probably find last week's mums in this week's arrangement. . . . If you are wondering why people accept these arrangements, I will remind you that the greatest advantage is taken of weddings and bar mitzvah parties. During a joyous occasion, how many people are concerned with the quality of flower arrangements, or even remember what they ordered? Place a parasol on top of wilting flowers and you still have an usual centerpiece. Add balloons for an 'around-the-world' theme and customers will call to compliment you."

Restaurant-caterers often capitalize on distracted customers hosting large catered parties by delivering less food than the customer ordered. One worker employed at a delicatessen that catered parties and engagements notes, for example, that "when we receive orders for, say, 100 sandwiches, my boss usually gives about 95 sandwiches and charges for 100. He would usually joke that the people who were short-changed on the sandwiches would never notice the difference. The same short-changing practice was used for large orders of beer, soda, etc."

Having delivered many orders to catered parties, another worker observed, "It seems that people are so wrapped up in the excitement of the event they are ordering food for that they only sign the bill and never really look at it."

An employee in the central accounting office of a large New York caterer observed frequent overcharging of customers for catered affairs. On one occasion, for example, the manager made a simple arithmetic error and overcharged the customer nearly $200, which the customer paid. The employee describes what happened next. "I assumed that the manager made an unintentional error and I put a note on the vice-president's desk explaining the situation. The next day the note was returned to me with the comment: 'Michael, don't worry about the overpayment unless the person calls us.' Of course I needn't say what his reaction would have been if some customer underpaid the company."

In the last chapter it was noted that adulterating food and drink is common. Accordingly, many catering employees wrote that their managers often substituted cheaper food and drink at catered events, a sleight of hand easily accomplished because the customer is too distracted by the social whirlwind to take note. A waiter at a catering establishment writes, for example, that "shrewd management buys less expensive brands of alcohol and carefully transfers the cheaper liquor into expensive bottles; after a certain number of drinks the guests don't care what they're drinking anyway. And after serving the guests a couple of nice stiff drinks, the bartender begins adding more mixer and less liquor. This is a very good way to keep costs down."

A woman who worked for several years as chief hostess for a New York caterer describes a similar procedure: bartenders pour cheap liquor into expensive-brand bottles. There is even a kind of perverse honesty about it. As she explains, "People paying for their affair are promised top-brand labels, and that's exactly what they get—top-brand labels on every bottle of cheap liquor."

A waiter for four years at a catering house reveals systematic deception of distracted hosts and their celebrants at weddings, receptions, dinner-dances, baptismal parties, and retirement testimonials. The caterer's frontstage image "is one of graciousness and do anything to please the customer—promise them anything," but their backstage policy is "cut corners, skimp, and save." The worker writes that the company's basic assumption is that "anything can be put over on the naïve public—as long as it is done with a smile. . . . I know for a fact that the customers are told that all the meats that are used are fresh and prepared on the premises; however, all meats are precooked and prepared elsewhere. . . . I've seen canned fruit being mixed with fresh fruit. . . . They use all the leftover food at other times for other parties, whether those parties are on the same weekend or the following weekend. We as waiters are told to give the best food to people who are paying for the affair and to give the other food to their guests. . . . They rip off the public by giving them off-brands of liquor, or by refilling name-brand bottles with cheaper, inferior liquor. . . . At least one quart of water is added to every gallon of premixed drinks. . . . At especially large functions, when the main course is rib steak or filet, the chefs just happen to run out of meat so that the last few people are served roast beef or less expensive prime rib. The customer pays full price for the band's meal, although they are always served a less expensive meal."

Festive occasions provide good opportunities for defrauding distracted customers, but somber ones open up profitable avenues also. Years ago in *The American Way of Death,* Jessica Mitford exposed the ways the funeral industry takes advantage of distracted customers. This study gives a glimpse of something similar. A delivery boy for a local florist claims that funerals provide an ideal opportunity to cheat the bereaved. He writes that "the biggest rip-off in the florist industry is the funeral basket. People are not concerned with price when they come in to buy one. They typically say, 'I don't care about price. I just want something nice.' They would pay (as much as $75 to $100) and leave. At this point my boss would go down to his basement and bring up a basket which is made out of cardboard and costs him twenty cents. He would fill it with greens which cost next to nothing. Then he would very sparingly add flowers. With all the greens it looked like a lot, but for the price it wasn't much at all. On top of this he would use his oldest flowers because they only had to last one day."

CHAPTER 4

Ignorance in the "Knowledge" Society: The Technically Uninformed Customer

> . . . to determine the quality of a thing great skill is needed, which most buyers lack.
>
> THOMAS AQUINAS, 1271

> Oh, I know I'll probably get taken. I just hope it isn't for too much.
>
> Customer in an auto repair shop waiting room, 1987

THE CENTRALITY OF THEORETICAL IGNORANCE

According to almost unanimous contemporary opinion, America has become a postindustrial society. Writers differ on details, but the one theme upon which all agree is that the postindustrial society is one in which education is fundamental. Ours is an age of information, a knowledge society. As sociologist Daniel Bell argued in his influential book, *The Coming of Post-Industrial Society,* one of the major features of a postindustrial society is what he called the "centrality of theoretical knowledge."

But there is a fundamental confusion in the argument of these fashionable postindustrialists. It is obvious that our economy and society, today as never before, depend on technical knowledge and the flow of information. But for that very reason individual citizens in this society find themselves increasingly ignorant about the knowledge-based world they inhabit. While Bell claims that we now live in a society based on the centrality of theoretical knowledge, one can just as easily stand Bell on his head and argue that the prime feature of our age is actually the "centrality of theoretical ignorance." In advanced societies, technical specialists learn more and more about less and less and have, as Thorstein Veblen once observed, a trained incapacity to understand anything outside their own narrow beam of expertise. The jeweler can fix watches but knows nothing about his car. The auto mechanic can repair cars but is baffled by his broken television set. The electronics repairman can fix televisions but is helpless when he gets a toothache. The dentist can ease the toothache but can't fix his watch. And so on.

Meanwhile, the typical citizen knows less and less about more and more as technology soars beyond his capacity to understand. The ordinary person is hopelessly ignorant of the workings of the everyday material environment on which he depends—electricity, the automobile, T.V., computers, medicines. Even such elemental activities of life as growing food and constructing shelter, which were second nature to earlier generations, are beyond the technical skill of today's typical urban dweller. In that sense, contemporary postindustrial people living in today's "knowledge" society are far more ignorant of their workaday world than the most ignorant "primitive" living in preindustrial society ever was.[1]

George Bernard Shaw made this precise observation decades ago in a comment on Adam Smith's classic discourse on a pin factory. Before the elaborate division of labor that we associate with the modern factory, one craftsman made an entire product—in this case, pins—from scratch, slowly but skillfully. Later the craft was subdivided into innumerable semiskilled factory operations, so that, as Smith notes, instead of one skilled worker making an entire pin, the task was now accomplished by ten workers, each doing a small and repetitive piece of the whole. This division of labor produces enormous gains in efficiency, but at the cost of diminishing each worker's skill. The consequence, Shaw wrote, "is that with the exception of a few people who design the machines, nobody knows how to make a pin or how a pin is made: that is to say, the modern worker in pin manufacture need not be one-tenth so intelligent and skillful and accomplished as the old pin maker; and the only compensation we have for this deterioration is that pins are so cheap that a single pin has no expressible value at all."[2]

"It is a funny place," Shaw adds, "this world of Capitalism, with its astonishing spread of ignorance and helplessness, boasting all the time of its spread of education and enlightenment."[3] And, says Shaw, on his travels contemporary man is "surprised to find that savages and Esquimaux [sic] and villagers who have to make everything for themselves are more intelligent and resourceful!"[4]

In his classic treatise, *The Division of Labor in Society,* the early French sociologist Émile Durkheim examined the sources of social solidarity—those forces that bind people together in society. Durkheim linked solidarity to the division of labor. Preindustrial societies have only a rudimentary division of labor, and most persons of similar age and gender perform similar tasks (hunting, gathering, fishing). Durkheim argued that the similar occupations pursued by most people in simple societies forge social bonds based on likeness, or what he called "mechanical solidarity."

In industrial societies, with their complex division of labor and thousands of specialized occupations, mechanical solidarity based on likeness breaks down. But Durkheim believed it is replaced by a new form of social solidarity resting on a foundation of human interdependence. In a society with an elaborate division of labor, each person comes to be dependent on others. Society becomes an organic whole, and the interdependence of its component parts creates what Durkheim called "organic solidarity," which he believed was at least as effective in knitting the social fabric together as the mechanical solidarity of simpler and more uniform societies.

While Durkheim's thesis has been gospel for generations of sociologists—his book was first published nearly a century ago—it is in at least one respect naïve. What Durkheim overlooked when he argued that social solidarity arises naturally out of the interdependence of a complex division of labor is that in the context of a predatory marketplace, a complex division of labor produces not so much social solidarity as mutual exploitation.[5] Interdependence in a predatory society means that each person is enormously vulnerable to the specialized skill and knowledge of others. Thus, as in the examples just given, the auto mechanic may very well be cheated when he takes his television set to the repairman, the T.V. repairman may be deceived by the jeweler, and the jeweler may be ripped off by the auto mechanic. Our modern interdependence means that everyone is able to exploit the ignorance of his neighbor, and at the same time everyone finds himself at the mercy of others who sell the complex products and services on which his dependence is as great as his ignorance. If, amid the simple technology of the thirteenth century, Thomas Aquinas observed that most people lacked the skill to determine the quality of a product, then we may readily understand how much more accurate that observation is today.

The kind of ignorance I wish to discuss in this chapter is based on the paradox that in the so-called "knowledge" society, many people are inevitably and grossly ignorant about much of the man-made technical environment around them. The technically uninformed customer, like the distracted customer discussed in the last chapter, has about as much knowledge as the typical citizen and thus differs from the so-called dumb customer. But he may nonetheless be cheated in the marketplace because he is purchasing a product or service that is technically so complex that he cannot be expected to possess an adequate understanding of it.

LOOKING FOR MR. BADWRENCH

The mechanic's best tool was his paint can.

Service station attendant

The automobile is unquestionably the quintessential twentieth-century American product. In this century it has reshaped not only the American city and countryside, but American culture itself. How significant, then, that the automobile is not only a central symbol of American life but also a central symbol of deception and fraud in the marketplace. As the typical consumer cautiously steers his car through its life cycle, from new car showroom to repair shop to body shop to used car lot, at every turn he confronts cheats, hustlers, and wheeler-dealers.

Americans approach a new car dealer with only slightly less trepidation than they do a used car dealer. It was not until 1958 that Congress passed the Automotive Information Disclosure Act, which required manufacturers to post their suggested retail price on the window of each new car.[6] Congress was urged to act because before this law was passed, car buyers were often totally in the dark about the price of a new car; the price was frequently anything the salesman felt like saying it was. After 1958 car buyers at least knew where to begin to bargain.

Undaunted, however, dealers have figured a way to get around the sticker price. Many now print up their own official-looking supplementary stickers, with such expensive dealer add-ons as underseal, rustproofing, paint and fabric protection, and so on, most of which, according to Consumers Union engineers, are of little or no value, but which add hundreds or even thousands of dollars to the price. Sometimes dealers selling scarce foreign cars don't even bother to masquerade their additional markup by giving customers underseal or fabric protection. They just brazenly print on their supplementary sticker: "ADDITIONAL DEALER PROFIT:

$2,000." Customers either accept this inflated price or have a long way to go bargaining down to the actual manufacturer's suggested retail price.

Besides the supplementary sticker, car dealers have an additional bagful of tricks.[7] And the public is generally aware of them and appropriately suspicious. A 1986 Louis Harris survey, for example, asked Americans whether they thought automobile salespeople are "thoroughly reliable to deal with, the same as most other salespeople, or types you have to watch like a hawk." Only 22 percent described auto salespeople as thoroughly reliable, one-quarter said they were the same as most other salespeople, but 48 percent said they had to be watched like a hawk.[8] And used car salesmen have for so long held the dubious honor of being among the least trusted people in the land that the occupation itself has passed into the language as synonymous with sleaze.

The way automobiles have been sold in this country for decades suggests that a tenacious subculture of deception may be rooted into the general traditions of an industry. Ironically, consumers themselves become part of that subculture when they begin to expect and even grudgingly accept deception as the norm. They become that industry's willing, or at least passive, victims and tolerate practices in it they would never put up with elsewhere. Customers in a department store, for example, would not abide for a moment the kind of hustle they willingly endure in an automobile showroom. If a clothing salesman employed the same tactics that car salesmen routinely use, most customers would simply leave the store in disgust. Yet they accept it in the auto showroom as part of the unpleasant but inevitable process of buying a car.

The automobile repair industry shares a similar subculture of deception. Despite the reassuring commercials of oil companies and auto manufacturers about kindly, patient, and honest mechanics, evoking images of small-town trust and goodwill, in real life, as opposed to Madison Avenue fantasy, finding an honest and competent mechanic is regarded by most people as a rare and unexpected piece of good fortune. In a 1978 Roper Poll, for example, over 70 percent of respondents suspected that they were either "quite often" or "almost always" misled or overcharged by auto repairmen.[9] Auto-repair fraud investigations conducted over nearly half a century more than confirm public suspicions. In 1941 *Reader's Digest* magazine hired two researchers, who conducted the most ambitious study of auto repair rip-offs ever done in the United States.[10] The investigators drove a Lincoln Zephyr from coast to coast and back again in a route that took them through all forty-eight states. They traveled some 20,000 miles and en route visited 347 repair shops. They kept the car in perfect mechanical condition throughout the trip, but before visiting each shop they simply disconnected the wire from one of the car's two coils. Then they brought the car in for diagnosis and repair. Although the problem was minor and obvious, only 37 percent of the mechanics in these garages reattached the coil wire for nothing or for a nominal charge. The majority—63 percent—"overcharged, lied, invented unnecessary work, or charged for work not done, for parts not needed, for parts not installed."[11] In all, mechanics gave the investigators seventy-four different—and incorrect—explanations for what was wrong with the car.

Has a generation of consumer activism in America reduced auto repair fraud? In 1987, forty-six years after their first investigation, *Reader's Digest* repeated the study. They got the same results.[12] The magazine hired an automotive writer who drove a perfectly maintained three-year-old car on a 10,000-mile triangle from Boston to Los Angeles to Orlando, Florida, and back to Boston. He passed through thirty-three states and en route visited 225 garages, including gas stations, dealerships, independent repair shops, and chain automotive outlets. Before entering each garage, he disconnected one spark plug wire from the engine, a problem that is as simple and obvious in a repair shop as an unplugged appliance is at home. Yet in only 28 percent of the garages did the mechanic quickly make the right diagnosis and reattach the wire. Nearly three-quarters of the time the investigator was either denied immediate service and made to wait hours or days, or sold unnecessary repairs. When a mechanic did work on the car, he made the correct repair only 44 percent of the time. In the other 56 percent of the cases, the investigator wrote, using almost the same words as the authors of the 1941 study, "mechanics performed unnecessary work, sold unnecessary parts or charged for repairs not done." Among other diagnoses, mechanics told him he needed tune-ups, valve adjustments, carburetor repairs, and even a rebuilt transmission. Mechanics recommended about a hundred unnecessary parts, ranging in price from $2 to $500, including catalytic converters, air pumps, engine control modules, distributor caps and rotors, and valve lifters.

In the late 1980s Americans were spending about $65 billion annually on auto repairs. Current government estimates are that approximately 32 percent of that, or almost $21 billion, is wasted on unnecessary or fraudulent repairs.[13] By simple arithmetic this means—however incredible it may seem—that every day of the year auto repair shops cheat Americans out of $57 million.

The New York picture duplicates the national situation. Undercover investigations of auto repair shops in New York City over the years have shown the same high levels of fraud as elsewhere: deception is the rule, honesty the exception.[14] In our study, workers employed in gas stations or auto repair shops described similar situations. These garages exemplify the technological complexity of modern society and illustrate the manner in which the technically ignorant customer is deceived and his ignorance turned to someone else's profit.

A young man who worked pumping gas and fixing flat tires in a gas station for three years described in graphic detail how the station swindled its customers. One illustration: "On cold winter mornings many people would phone the station because their automobiles would not start. Usually the problem was a weak battery, which could be fixed by a simple charging. But the mechanic would often tell the customer that he needed a new starter motor. The customer, ignorant of the workings of an engine, would permit the mechanic to install a new starter. The mechanic would then tell one of the attendants to run down to the hardware store and buy a can of black paint. He would then take out the old starter and paint it. As soon as the paint dried he would put it back in. The customer was charged $90 for a rebuilt starter but in reality just had his old one painted."

The mechanic painted not only starters but other parts as well. The worker continues: "Customers used to come in with generators that weren't charging. Many times the trouble was just a loose or broken fan belt, but the mechanic would say that it was the generator. He would take the old generator out and paint it with his can of black spray paint. The bill came to $85 and again the only thing that was done was a paint job. The painting of parts and selling them as new got to be so widespread that the attendants used to say that the mechanic's best tool was his paint can. Almost everything that could be painted or cleaned was sold as new. Radiators, water pumps, starters, generators, and carburetors—few were ever replaced, just painted."

Consumers do have some protection from the paint-can ploy. New York State law provides that customers can request a mechanic to return all the parts he claims he's replaced.[15] But the customer must put that request in writing before the mechanic works on the car. Moreover, the law is not well publicized and most customers are probably unaware of their rights. Besides, how is a technically uneducated customer to know whether the water pump the mechanic returned to him came from his car or from someone else's?

A second service station attendant revealed similar deceptive practices. He noted at the outset that his boss had fully mastered the appropriate demeanor to put the customer's concerns to rest—"his smiling, almost innocent face and his reassuring manner quieted any anxieties of the customer that either the car was beyond repair or in incompetent hands."

Yet despite the boss's reassuring carside manner, he cheated his customers as brazenly as the owner of the gas station discussed above. The worker writes, for example, that during oil changes, "It was common practice to put low-grade oil in the car and charge for the highest grade. An employee would watch to see if the customer was coming while the other employee would be putting in the oil and he would quickly stop if the other whistled a few bars of 'Dixie.' "

This station regularly abused the state law requiring automobiles to be inspected annually for safety and emissions. Only the most superficial examination was given to vehicles belonging to occasional customers. Mechanics here also used the lucrative paint-can gimmick. The worker cites a typical case of a woman whose car had broken down. "Mrs. H. comes into the station upset because her car won't start. Being a true gentleman, my boss will send someone to bring it into the station. The mechanic finds that an ignition wire is loose, but tells Mrs. H. she needs a new starter. The mechanic, being an expert painter, takes the old starter out, paints it, replaces it, and charges Mrs. H. $85. As a crowning joy for the mechanic, Mrs. H. tips him for his kindness and good work. This story may sound inflated, but actually it is worse than that. The mechanic where I work said to me as he was throwing out a paint can, 'That can was worth $400.' A $400 profit on a $3.98 can of paint is nothing to laugh at; that is a 10,000 percent profit."

The first gas station attendant quoted above also revealed that his employer not only cheated customers when they brought their cars in for repairs, but even when they came in just to get gas. He writes, "In order to make a higher profit, the owner used to mix the high test tank half with regular. Since regular gas costs the owner much less, his profit was increased by selling regular gas as high test. Usually, when the owner ordered high test, he would need about 1,800 gallons. But when he called up the company for delivery, he would order 900 gallons high test and 900 gallons regular and mix them in the high test tank."

This worker's essay was written years before government officials at federal, state, and local levels realized that gasoline contamination was a problem. In 1980 complaints began coming in to the Federal Trade Commission from all parts of the country that some gas stations were selling low-octane gas in high-octane pumps and charging high-octane prices.[16] In 1986 alone the New York City Department of Consumer Affairs fined 135 gas stations for selling mislabeled gasoline. Apparently many station owners did not regard these fines as much of a deterrent, for twenty-four of them were cited two or more times during the year for the same offense.[17] In the same year a New York congressman called on the General Accounting Office to investigate the problem of gasoline mislabeling nationwide, and New York State officials recommended creation of a state testing and enforcement unit to control fraudulent gasoline retailing.[18]

In its own studies, the U.S. Environmental Protection Agency (EPA) has discovered even more serious problems of gasoline mislabeling and adulteration. Selling regular fuel as premium is illegal and costly to consumers. But the problem goes beyond that. Some gas stations have been mislabeling leaded fuel and selling it as unleaded. Why? One easy and inexpensive way to raise gasoline octane ratings is to add tetraethyl lead. But using leaded fuel in new cars designed exclusively for unleaded gasoline can rapidly destroy a car's expensive catalytic converter and cause other damage. In 1985 the EPA did a sweep of gasoline stations in the New York City area and found that about 3 percent of the stations it sampled were selling leaded fuel as unleaded.[19] The EPA suspected, however, that their study underestimated the actual contamination rate; word of an EPA investigation spreads rapidly among station operators and they can quickly correct violations before they're discovered. An earlier study of automobiles rather than gas stations found higher rates of lead contamination. In 1984 the EPA randomly surveyed cars in the New York City area and found that 11 percent of cars requiring unleaded gasoline had leaded fuel in their tanks.[20]

As leaded gas is gradually phased out of the U.S. gasoline supply, other illegal contaminants and octane enhancers are finding their way into gas station pumps (e.g., alcohol, which, when used without proper additives, causes engine damage).

Workers in other kinds of auto repair facilities also disclosed how customers were deceived and manipulated. A mechanic for a franchised muffler replacement firm described the psychology of selling parts to technically uninformed customers. In most repair establishments, the actual work of restoring the customer's product is done when the customer is absent. This serves a number of functions. It allows the repairman to conceal the actual amount of work done (or not done); it allows him to conceal the difficulty (or simplicity) of the job; and it maintains the requisite mystification of the occupation. In this muffler shop, however, the owner encouraged each customer to remain and watch his car being repaired. According to the informant, this is part of the technique of gaining the customer's confidence, so that the mechanic can sell him additional hardware. He writes, "The shop I work for is set up in such a way that the customer is actually in the work area viewing the repairs being done to his or her car. My boss says this creates a more 'friendly atmosphere,' where the customer is watching the mechanic install all of the parts and not feeling 'ripped off.' . . . As with any sales job, my objective is to sell as much as I can to the customer. While under the car I tell the customer that he needs the 'whole line' (the entire exhaust system), even though I know that one or two of the parts may still be good. Selling the whole line makes the job easier and faster for the mechanic and obviously puts more money in the boss's pocket."

The mechanic knows how to meet the customer's objections. "Sometimes a customer will tell me that he thinks a part is still good and does not want it replaced. I then tell him that it is 'too old, rusty or weak to save' and that 'if you don't replace the old pipe it might break due to stress and you would lose your whole investment.' "

In order to sell additional parts, the mechanic sizes up not only the car but the owner. "My boss instructs me, 'While under the car try to sell the customer shocks or springs, depending on how much money you feel he is ready to spend.' If I had no trouble selling him the whole exhaust system I can then tell him that his shocks are leaking or that his springs are collapsed or sagging, and that they should be replaced. Once he looks interested and has taken the bait I can close the sale by saying that 'if you don't replace them it could be unsafe.' A line like that usually works better with women."

CONSUMER ELECTRONICS: MAGIC, SCIENCE, AND RELIGION

Even paranoids have enemies.

DELMORE SCHWARTZ

A long history of undercover investigations of other kinds of repair services reveals a level of fraud comparable to that in auto repair. When the ambitious research team drove the Lincoln Zephyr through forty-eight states in 1941, testing the honesty of auto mechanics, they carried with them a number of other items for "repair." On their well-running wristwatches the researchers simply loosened the central screw on the crown wheel, something any competent jeweler would notice immediately. Yet, of the 462 jewelers the researchers visited, 226, or 49 percent, made or suggested unnecessary and expensive repairs.[21] With typewriters, the researchers introduced a malfunction correctable in a few seconds by a simple adjustment. Yet, of the 150 repair shops they visited around the country, 98 (65 percent) deceived them and claimed that much more elaborate and expensive repairs were needed.[22]

On portable radios, the researchers either loosened a tube or disconnected a conspicuous wire. When they took the radios to 304 repairmen in shops from coast to coast, 195—64 percent—lied, gave phony diagnoses, or charged for unnecessary work.[23]

There are few areas of public ignorance more profound, in fact, than that surrounding modern consumer electronics products. An automobile may be a mystery to the most mechanically inept white-collar workers, but the visibility of moving parts provides a minimal level of comprehension even among the most untrained. But probably not more than one person in a hundred can describe in even the most general way how the image of a person, sitting in a studio 3,000 miles away, can suddenly appear on a screen in their living room. Paradoxically, this scientific achievement is for most people a matter of almost religious faith. Only slightly less incomprehensible than television are radios, phonographs, and tape recorders. And just when we think we might be catching on, new developments in consumer electronics—the compact disk and digital tape recorders—create anew hopelessly broad chasms of consumer ignorance.

This ignorance does not often surface, however, for one doesn't need to understand these products to use them. If only those people who fully understood the technical principles of television were allowed to watch, A. C. Nielsen's task would be far simpler. In fact, if people were permitted to use only those machines they fully understood, modern life itself would be far simpler—and more primitive. Fortunately for most of us, understanding is not a prerequisite for use, and even people who have never even heard of an integrated circuit are perfectly able to switch on a television set and turn the dial to their favorite show.

User-friendly products protect us from our own ignorance. But not forever. We inevitably come face-to-face with our own ignorance when these products break down and suddenly become inert pieces of metal, unresponsive to our customary commands. And in a predatory marketplace, when this occurs, our ignorance leaves us particularly vulnerable to those who have the technical expertise to repair these products and get the magic working again.

Recent undercover investigations of T.V. and electronics repairmen reveal a level of fraud on the same order of magnitude as that discovered nearly a half century ago in the *Reader's Digest* study. Despite decades of consumer activism and legislation, deception is still the norm. In the mid-1970s, New York City's Department of Consumer Affairs conducted a study of television repairmen. Three staff members visited twenty-one randomly selected T.V. repair shops in the city. They brought with them T.V. sets that had been certified by technicians as in perfect condition except for a minor, easily visible problem (such as a loose speaker wire or an unplugged cable). Of the twenty-one shops they visited, fifteen (more than 70 percent) gave estimates of up to $73 for unnecessary repairs.[24]

Some consumers cannot suppress the paranoid suspicion that when they have something repaired the mechanic surreptitiously breaks something else—on some mysterious time-delay basis—to ensure another visit to the repair shop within a short time. Paranoia should not be automatically dismissed. In a predatory society, paranoia is not a symptom of mental illness but a sign of a good mental health and a perceptive mind—there really *is* a plot. In the case of these twenty-one T.V. repair shops, four of them in fact returned the sets to the investigators with more damage than when they had been brought in. New York's Commissioner of Consumer Affairs concluded from this study that a high proportion of T.V. repairmen in New York City are "either highly dishonest or extraordinarily incompetent."

Consumers are apparently no better off in the suburbs than in the city. In Suffolk County, a Long Island suburb of New York, the local department of consumer affairs conducted a similar investigation of electronics repair shops.[25] Technicians took a perfectly operating videocassette recorder and replaced its fuse with one that was blown out. An investigator posing as a customer then took the recorder to seven shops in the county, reporting in each case that the machine was "dead" and requesting repair estimates. In the case of a completely dead machine, the most obvious place to begin is to check the fuse. Yet none of the repairmen reported that the problem was a blown fuse. Instead, they "discovered" a variety of defective parts, including the power supply, transformer, regulator, diodes, idler, and chip. While a 25¢ fuse would have fixed the machine, the seven shops gave repair estimates ranging from $85 to $147. Again, paranoia is vindicated—two of the repairmen sabotaged the machine after the customer refused the recommended repair.

In our study, a young man who had worked for three years in a reputable electronics repair shop illustrates how the public's technical ignorance in this area is exploited. The shop repaired the full range of high-fidelity equipment, including amplifiers, tuners, receivers, record players, and tape recorders. Besides doing minor repairs, the young man took in equipment from customers and wrote up work orders for the technician. He relates the following incident and claims it is not uncommon. "A customer came in with an expensive, professional-quality tape recorder. He said that the recorder was running slow and he requested a complete overhaul to bring it up to factory specifications. We told him with a smile that there would be no problem with the repairs and he would hear from us within a week. He appeared to be quite pleased and left believing that his recorder was in good hands. This is where our frontstage behavior stopped.

"Once the machine was on the technician's bench, our backstage policy took over. The technician simply oiled the motor. That completed the necessary repairs. But on the back of the work sheet which we return to the customer, he listed the following: 'repaired take-up assembly, rewind assembly, fast forward assembly. Replaced belts, adjusted record and playback levels.' The technician took an old belt from another tape recorder and placed it in a small bag along with the machine to show the customer that the belt had been replaced. Actually, that particular tape recorder does not even have any belts in it. The total repair charge was $75.

"One week later the customer picked up his unit and was greeted with the same courteous smile he received when he brought the tape recorder in. He tried it and was totally satisfied. Naturally he was completely ignorant of the actual work done."

In a democratic society with egalitarian ideals, one might expect that those with technical knowledge would try to share it with the public, that those who know would try to narrow the knowledge gap with those who do not. There is something egalitarian and anti-elitist about doctors who educate patients about their own bodies or mechanics who educate customers about their automobiles.

In a predatory society, however, public ignorance is useful to the expert. The more ignorant the public, the more dependent and powerless that public is at the hands of the expert and thus the more economically vulnerable. The more uninformed the public, the less that public is able to challenge the word of the expert. Hence public ignorance gives the expert leverage to maintain and enhance his earnings, power, and status.

Note, for example, the electronics worker's account of a

customer who brought in a tape recorder with a simple problem. The customer reported that one channel of the recorder was distorting. The worker writes, "In most cases like this I can usually determine what the problem is. The manager, however, discourages me from telling the customer anything, claiming the less a customer knows the better it is for us.

"At this particular time we were not very busy, and I was able to spend a little more time with the customer. I knew that if one channel was distorting it would be one of two things: either the heads on the machine needed replacement or they needed a simple cleaning. I tried the latter, hoping that was all it was. I cleaned the heads with a felt applicator and some alcohol. This did the job, for both channels sounded perfect again. I didn't even charge the customer, for the entire operation took only a few seconds.

"When my manager found out he became very angry. He told me I would make a very poor businessman. He would have taken the tape recorder in and charged the customer $45 for the repair."

DRUGSTORE DECEPTIONS

For most people the world of medicine is fraught with mystery, faith, and anxiety. Nowhere is the average citizen's dependence on the technical expertise of others greater than in the healing of his or her own body, and nowhere is deference to the experts more complete than in modern medicine. Public ignorance about health, illness, and medication means that blind faith in health professionals replaces accurate knowledge. This is most apparent in patients' attitudes toward physicians, but it operates more or less down through the medical hierarchy. One pharmacy employee in our study observed, for example, that the "public looks at a pharmacist the way a child looks at his father."

Most health professionals benefit from this mystification of their trade, which shields them behind a wall of technical knowledge and social distance. In the case of the pharmacist, this mystification is physically symbolized by the high barrier behind the prescription counter, which hides the area where the mysterious healing elixirs are mixed.

Self-employed pharmacists have an ambiguous status; they are both professionals and businessmen. As professionals they are obliged to make service to the public their first priority; as businessmen they are tempted to maximize their income. These two roles occasionally conflict. Many pharmacy employees in our study wrote of this potential role conflict and how the pecuniary ambitions of the businessman sometimes took precedence over the obligations of the professional.[26]

One perceptive observer worked for eight years in a pharmacy in a working-class area of New York. In the same neighborhood for twenty years, the store had a regular clientele, and the owner managed over the years to establish a reputation for trust and reliability. The trust was occasionally abused. The pharmacy offered a 10 percent discount on drugs to senior citizens, a discount calculated, our informant notes, after a surreptitious 10 percent price increase.

The pharmacists at this drugstore also abused the generic drug laws in ways that increased their earnings. In New York State, when a physician writes out a prescription, she either designates that it be dispensed as written or that a less expensive generic substitute be used instead. If the doctor allows the generic option, the pharmacist must give the patient a state-approved generic equivalent if one exists. If the doctor designates that the brand-name prescription be dispensed as written, the pharmacist must give the patient that drug and no other. Our pharmacy worker writes, however, that his pharmacists were able to make extra money illicitly when the doctor directed that the prescription be dispensed as written. He explains: "If the doctor signs the prescription 'Dispense-as-written,' the pharmacist can illegally substitute a cheaper brand of the same medicine and still charge the price of a brand name. Thus the customer is paying for an expensive brand-name drug but getting a generic. This is especially hard to detect in liquids because the two types of drugs look the same."

This same pharmacy also increased cash flow by the razzle-dazzle of taxing nontaxable items and charging higher than the prescribed sales tax on taxable goods. Most people are uncertain which items in a drugstore are taxable and which are not. Accordingly, our informant writes, "Among the more blatant rip-offs used by the pharmacists include taxing items that are not supposed to be taxed. Most people cannot compute the tax as quickly as it can be rung up on the cash register, and the pharmacist used his quickness of hand to register taxes on items such as vitamins or aspirin and other nontaxable items. Also, if the customer buys some shampoo, aspirin, toothpaste, Pepto Bismal, and Christmas cards, it is very easy to get away with taxing everything, even though aspirin and Pepto Bismal should not be taxed. Most of the customers do not know this and thus are unaware they are paying a few cents extra. Furthermore, many people cannot figure out that a subtotal of $16.29 should be taxed $1.34, and it is quite easy to ring up $1.74 at tax time. This may seem like an insignificant amount, but it adds up."

In still another lucrative practice in this pharmacy, the druggists sold free samples of drugs that doctors had given them. According to the worker, the scheme operates as follows. "Doctors often receive sample drugs from companies that manufacture them. Since the number of sample drugs the doctor receives always exceeds the number he will give his patients, he often has a rather large quantity of various drugs piling up in his office. Come cleaning day, the doctor wants to rid himself of this messy pile of pills and liquids. He does this by giving them to the pharmacists, often in huge plastic bags and cardboard boxes. For the doctor, this is no great loss. For the pharmacist, this messy heap is a pile of gold. He will use the sample drugs and sell them to his customers. This is not supposed to be done, and the message on the box or bottle clearly states so: 'Professional Sample: Not To Be Sold.' The pharmacist ignores this message like a smoker ignores the warning on a pack of cigarettes, and he goes right ahead and sells these samples. Unfortunately for me, some of the medicines have the word 'sample' engraved on the tablet, and since the pharmacist cannot let his customers know they are getting sample drugs, my job is to take a razor blade or emery board and scrape the 'sample' away. One can imagine how painful this is by holding his thumb and forefinger about ¼ inch apart, flexed tightly, for about forty-five minutes."

This practice may actually be fairly common. A clerk in a Queens pharmacy describes the same operation with goods derived from a slightly different source. He calls this dealing in "contraband."

"My boss makes a deal with a drug salesman to buy the samples which are supposed to be given to doctors. My boss pays the salesman about 10 percent of the cost price, giving the salesman a few extra dollars and giving my boss a savings of 90 percent of what the drug should cost him. The doctor gets hurt by not getting the correct amount of samples, and indirectly this hurts the public because they aren't getting the free samples from the doctor. A few of the doctors know about this 'trick of the pharmacy trade' and don't care or even get some of the action by selling my boss samples themselves. . . . Often my employer and I are back behind the counter with an emery board, razor, alcohol, Q-tips, or knife— all implements of contraband—trying to erase the word 'sample' from the drug."

Another writer, who worked for four years in a New York drugstore, describes how the pharmacists took advantage of customers who naïvely presented a doctor's indecipherable scribbles written on a prescription form. When prescribing several different medications, some physicians will write out prescriptions for both over-the-counter (nonprescription) as well as prescription drugs. This gives the pharmacist an opportunity to charge a prescription price for an over-the-counter remedy. The worker writes, "Many items which could be sold over the counter are prescribed by doctors. When the pharmacist receives a prescription from a customer which is for, say, Vitamin 'X,' Donnagel, or Emetrol, he sees it as a chance to get more money out of the customer. In my time working in the pharmacy, many liquids, tablets, and capsules have been transferred from their original bottle to a dispenser used only for prescriptions. This way the pharmacist earns that extra profit and the customer is none the wiser. I'm surprised that customers don't look at the prescriptions before they hand them to the pharmacist."*

They don't because the technical complexity of modern life has made ignorance endemic, and hence many people simply abdicate their own judgment and passively put their lives in the hands of experts.

The abuses workers reported here are undoubtedly not unique or anecdotal. In 1985 the New York City Department of Consumer Affairs conducted a citywide study of pharmacy pricing and practices, especially as they affected the city's elderly population.[27] Among their major findings:

1. In one-third of the pharmacies surveyed, prescription drug prices were not posted, as the law requires, or were illegible or partially or completely hidden;
2. In 40 percent of the pharmacies where drug prices were posted, the actual drug prices differed from and in most cases were higher than the posted prices;
3. The old pay more. While over 90 percent of the pharmacies surveyed advertised discounts for seniors, actual discounts were usually much less than advertised. And offsetting whatever slight discounts seniors received, in neighborhoods with many elderly residents pharmacists charged as much as twice the price for the same drugs as in other neighborhoods.

* It must be said here, though, that in this pharmacy, patients suffering from heart disease, diabetes, and epilepsy who needed medicine on a continuous basis to survive were sold their drugs at cost.

OTHER ENCOUNTERS OF THE TECHNICALLY UNINFORMED

All That Glitters: II

The essays contain many other examples of customers, otherwise individuals of normal intelligence, who were deceived simply because their knowledge could not possibly match the expertise and the carefully rehearsed staging of the mechanic, the T.V. repairman, the building contractor, the veterinarian, the jeweler. For example, a worker employed for two years as a saleswoman in a jewelry store relates this scenario of a young man and woman buying a ring.

"When a couple comes in to purchase a diamond ring, they usually don't know too much about diamonds in general. For this reason they get a mouthful of double-talk from the salesman and sometimes get talked into buying a ring that is completely different from what they anticipated. When they inquire about the quality of the ring, the salesman usually lets them look through the eye loop. Only if you know how to use the loop will you be able to see the flaws or the quality of the stone. Since few know what to look for, they see nothing. When the salesman looks through it he can see if a stone is cracked, its color, how well it's cut, and how well it's set into the setting."

If the couple decides they want the ring, they may say they would like to have it appraised. But according to the writer, having an appraisal was not a foolproof method of getting one's money's worth in this jewelry store. She gives an example. "In one case I witnessed, my manager told a couple where to go to have a ring appraised. He even told them he would pay for the appraisal. After they left he phoned his friend the appraiser and said, 'Joe, a couple is coming down with an emerald stone with diamonds around. They paid $400; make it $500 and don't tell them one of the stones is cracked.'

"The next day Joe called my manager to tell him that he had told the story to someone else working there. When the customer came in, Joe appraised it for $500, but the other employee came over and said it was worth at least $650. (The ring cost the store $175.) The couple came back to our store and apologized for not trusting the salesman, and left very much satisfied with the ring."

And so it goes in the knowledge society. The typical consumer is not knowledgeable at all, but technically ignorant, dependent upon the expert who can turn his specialty to profit at the expense of the uninformed customer. Thus our writers describe other experts: the doctor who performs "abortions" on women who aren't pregnant but believe they are; the contractor who uses subgrade building material; the oil delivery men who tamper with the meter to pad their customers' bills; and exercise and weight-reducing salons that use the mumbo jumbo of high tech to bilk their clients.

The Mysterious Bust Machine

One young woman worked for over a year at a well-known weight-reducing salon. She was an instructor at the Eliza Doolittle Figure Salon, "the only qualifications being a fairly thin physique and the ability to do all the exercises."

With figure rearrangement, it is difficult to judge in a short time whether the services provided are honest, adequate, and effective, or simply fraudulent. Positive results are often slow in coming, and failure can always be attributed to the customer, for disciplinary lapses and the like.

In the early 1970s, when the young woman worked for this company, some figure salons had come under investigation for a variety of deceptive practices.[28] Many allegedly sponsored misleading advertising, hired untrained instructors, and made fraudulent claims. Some figure salons implied, for example, that, without dieting, members could lose weight effortlessly and reshape their figures simply by such "passive exercise" as reclining on vibrating lounge chairs. According to our worker, the most blatant deception at the Eliza Doolittle Salon involved this kind of exercise equipment, or rather, what the company claimed this exercise equipment would do. She writes, "The district managers came around every few months and told us what we needed to know about the machines and their use. For the first few months I was there, we were to tell the members that the vibrators are used to 'break down the fatty tissues.' No one knew exactly what that meant, how it actually happened, or what it ultimately had to do with losing weight, but it sounded legitimate and as long as no one questioned it, everything was O.K. Usually it wasn't questioned, but occasionally we would be forced to reveal that we really didn't know what we were talking about. Anyway, after a few months we were told not to say that the vibrators break down the fatty tissues, but that they relax the muscles for exercising."

The most inflated claim, apparently, involved the bust machine, which, for several weeks after it was introduced, "no one knew whether it was supposed to build up or reduce the bust. Finally we were told that it could do either, depending on whether you used it at a slow or rapid pace. Of course, there was always some disagreement about which did what, but it hardly mattered, since the only thing the machine really did was build up the arm muscles. If there was any machine we knew for a fact didn't work, believe me, it was the bust machine. So ultimately we had a lot of very strong flat-chested or buxom women."

"FROM EACH ACCORDING TO HIS ABILITY . . ."

On the periphery of capitalist business practice lies a curious parody of the fundamental communist principle, "From each according to his ability, to each according to his need." There seems to be an unwritten rule in some firms that customers should be charged according to their ability to pay. For believers in distributive justice, this does involve a kind of puny redistribution of wealth. An implicit principle in some repair establishments, for example, is that the wealthier the customer (as indicated by the cost of the item to be repaired), the more he shall be charged. While in communist parlance this may be "From each according to his ability," in capitalist practice it works out to be "Charge all the market will bear."

In the electronics repair shop discussed earlier, for example, the writer offers the following observation. "One common practice in the shop is that we charge more for repairs on expensive stereo systems than we do for the more inexpensive ones, regardless of the repairs done. A customer who brings in two stereo receivers, one more expensive than the other, can expect to be charged more for the more costly unit. The idea behind this practice is that the more money a customer pays for a stereo system, the less likely will he be to quibble over the price of repairs, even though the same amount of time and labor has gone into both units. Our explanation to the customer who doesn't know the first thing about the unit is, 'The technician had to spend more time with it because it is more complicated.' "

Another worker employed in an auto repair shop reported the same operating principle there. "Usually when someone brought their car in to have the radiator flushed the charge was $25. But one time a man came in with a BMW and he was charged $75, not because the job required more labor, but because he was regarded as someone who could afford to pay more."

While it is true, as has often been reported, that the poor pay more, they can take some small solace in the knowledge that the affluent are also cheated.

CHAPTER 5

Helpless Customers
and Potemkin Villages

CHILDREN AND OLD MEN NOT CHEATED
Sign in a Canton market in
prerevolutionary China

INMATES

In the marketplace, the strong subdue the weak. As we've
seen, one form of weakness is ignorance. Another form of
weakness is . . . weakness itself. Especially victimized are
those persons who are not so much ignorant of their exploitation as helpless to do anything about it. Inmates of mental
hospitals, prisons, nursing homes, and schools for retarded
and handicapped children all have two things in common:
their essential helplessness vis-à-vis the institution, and their
susceptibility to abuse by the personnel because of it. Helpless
inmates are especially vulnerable to the worst excesses of the
profit motive; such persons are unable to oppose the kinds
of relentless cost-cutting that endangers their welfare and
sometimes their lives. Then, too, the utter dependence and
often pathetic weakness of helpless inmates occasionally pro-
voke anger and cruelty among those employees charged with
their care. Shocking revelations of inmate mistreatment in
these institutions appear regularly in the press, and despite

momentary public furor only confirm that helplessness goes ignorance one better in provoking victimization.

In a New York sanitarium for elderly, ill, and senile patients, an employee described a not unfamiliar horror story. She writes that "since many of the patients were senile, the staff did what they wanted with them. They made fun of patients right to their faces, cursed them, and often told them to shut up. Once I walked into a room and saw a nurse proceeding to 'doll up' a ninety-year-old woman. The nurse teased her hair up in a beehive and put little pink bows in it. Then she wheeled her up and down the corridors, laughing hysterically, while all the other nurses and some of the patients made fun of the poor old woman who could do nothing but mumble a few nonsense words."

The writer of that account was a kitchen worker in the sanitarium. She delivered meals to patients and thus had a regular overview of the patients' condition and the behavior of the nursing staff. The nurses' indifference and neglect was apparent. She writes, "If the patients wouldn't sit up immediately and eat their dinner when it came, the nurses would tell them to go to hell, because they weren't going to feed them, and they would tell me to take their trays back to the kitchen.

"By each of the nurse's stations there was a board with lights and the corresponding room numbers. I could walk by that board and look at which numbers were lit up, and on my way back to the kitchen, about twenty minutes later, the same numbers would be lit up. Their response to the board was typically, 'Oh, her again, why the hell doesn't she leave me alone.' As for the very quiet patients, the ones who were near death, they got even less attention. The staff would close the doors to their rooms and let them moan away. When I would come in to deliver their food I would often find them half naked, sometimes totally naked, oblivious to everything, their bedpans full and smelling up the room. Often I would ask the nurse to look in on a patient like that. She'd shrug her shoulders and say O.K., just to put me off, I imagine, because a half hour later when I came back to pick up the tray everything would be exactly the same as when I left it. His tray wouldn't even be touched. They wouldn't even try to feed him."

A woman with twenty-two years of experience in an East Coast chronic-care hospital, which houses the severely disabled and the elderly, tells a strikingly similar story. While in one ward chronically ill patients received excellent care, in the other wards one is "caught up in a different world—the hospital world that is hidden from the public eye. It is a world that is very different from the public's image of what a hospital is like."

In this part of the hospital, she writes, "there is no such thing as efficient nursing care. Patients are often left in bed because it is easier for the staff (which is usually a skeleton crew). When patients call for bedpans they are not answered because they are either not heard or deliberately ignored. Patients will ultimately soil themselves and their beds and will lie in their excrement until a nurse or aide tires of the odor and changes the linen. As a result many patients suffer from bedsores that do not heal. . . . Meal trays are placed on the patients' stands and the patients who cannot feed themselves are either fed very quickly or not at all."

Despite such abuses, institutions that house these helpless customers are not entirely beyond the ken of public scrutiny. First, there are the friends and relatives of the inmates who are obviously concerned with their treatment (though such inmates may be at times an unpleasant and unwanted burden). In any case, attention must be paid by the institution to the children of the elderly in the nursing homes; attention must be paid to the parents of the children in schools for the retarded or handicapped; attention must be paid to the relatives of inmates of mental institutions, and, to a lesser extent, prisons. Second, there are also "the authorities," or the public or the financial benefactors to which these institutions are accountable and for which some kind of positive image must be maintained.

Consequently, whenever outside interested parties come to call, whether friends, relatives, or bureaucrats, they must be kept ignorant of the institution's dirty little secrets, and Potemkin villages must be hastily constructed.[1] Whatever sleaziness, neglect, or abuse usually goes on must be quickly, if temporarily, disguised and an acceptable facade presented. Why don't the inmates simply tell the outsiders what's going on? They may, but for two reasons their stories usually carry little weight: (1) the visitors are likely to be more impressed with the attractive Potemkin village which they observe with their own eyes than with secondhand stories; and (2) the testimony of inmates is suspect anyway, for, depending on the institution, the very fact of their incarceration calls their judgment and veracity into question.

Our workers noted several instances of Potemkin villages, where makeshift facades covered a more somber reality. An older woman worked as a nurse's aide for two years in a New York nursing home owned and managed by a married couple who spent most of their time on the premises. They had worked out an elaborate strategy for constructing a Potemkin village at a moment's notice. The worker writes that the owners' office was strategically located so they could "view and intercept any visitors on their way in. No one could enter without the owners seeing them. As a matter of fact, they had it arranged so that one of them could detain the visitors in the office while the other would check out the condition of the patient. If the patient was in a neglected condition, two or three aides were hastened to prepare the patient for his visitor. This practice was also used when the owner expected the health inspectors to visit. . . . Although some of the patients complained to their relatives about their neglected condition, the relatives were always impressed with what they saw more than with the ravings of neglect by their senile elders."

The ruse continues, according to the worker, and other actors are brought on stage. "After the relatives were greeted by the owners, they were greeted by a smiling nurse who assured them that certain patients were improving, which was often not true. She would even go so far as to tell the relatives that the doctors were called in frequently to check some patients. But the truth of the matter was that when the doctors did appear, they spoke to a few selected patients, picked up their black bags and took off for parts unknown."

Creating a Potemkin village involves, first, presenting good news, and second, withholding bad news. The worker notes, "To add insult to injury, when serious accidents occurred, the owners told us in no uncertain terms to keep quiet even though the relatives should have been informed. Many patients had fallen from their beds or through misjudgment had fallen and injured themselves. These incidents were easily covered up because the relatives' visits were very infrequent."

Another writer worked for two years as a teacher in a Midwestern school for deaf and multihandicapped children. When the Guild for the Deaf or other philanthropic organization was scheduled to visit, the teachers were notified a day in advance, and the school was transformed: "The filthy floors were mopped and cleaned. The bottom windows, which were usually left open and easy for a child to fall out, were kept closed. The teachers took off their dirty dungarees and the women actually put on dresses and the men their suits. No one smoked and all the ashtrays were put away. The well-behaved children were put in the most visible rooms, and the noisy and aggressive children were taken upstairs so as not to be seen. Some lunch tables were brought in and set up nicely. Each child was sure to get his medication a few minutes before the visitors were to come in so they would be calmed down and give a good impression. All in all, it was another school on these 'special' days. It was a make-believe school, not the real school."

SUMMER CAMP: "HELLO MUDDAH, HELLO FADDUH"*

In a much lighter vein, Potemkin villages flourish at summer camp when the "inmates" are visited by their parents. Many of our writers had worked as camp counselors, and while most of the deceptions practiced in the camp setting were not serious, many ex-counselors stressed that the camp situation did not quite measure up to the healthy, wholesome summer paradise suggested by the ads in *The New York Times Magazine* or the colorful promotional brochures. Sometimes the actual facilities are old and inadequate, the food tasteless and monotonous, and the counselors neglectful or borderline sadistic. But all this changed on parents' visiting day. "The biggest fake of the whole camping season was visiting day," writes one ex-counselor, who then describes how, for the entire preceding week, the camp was cleaned up for the "momentous occasion," the counselors told exactly how to behave, the campers dressed up, a bus hired for the day to take the parents around the extensive grounds, and the most dilapidated facilities carefully screened from parents' inquisitive eyes.

Another counselor writes in a similar vein about visiting day at a particularly anarchic summer camp. After the children had been in camp for one month of their two-month stay, "parents come up to visit, meet the camp staff, and see the campus. The camp on visiting day does not resemble the camp during the rest of the summer season. Instead of the camp being a shock to the parents, it is a shock to the campers. The campus is spotless, bathrooms are working properly, and the food is great. A typical remark a parent makes to his child is, 'I don't understand what you're complaining about. This camp is beautiful!' "

---

* The trials of summer camp have been immortalized in Allan Sherman's song, "Hello Muddah, Hello Fadduh," a comic letter home from a traumatized camper.

Another ex-counselor at a summer camp in Maine described how the camp informed the parents of the welfare of their loved ones. She writes, "Camp Wunderbar boasts of the great progress each and every camper makes in various fields of endeavor. After the third week of camp, each counselor is instructed to write a letter to the parents of each camper describing the 'tremendous leaps forward' their child has made in the first few weeks of camp. It was quite a challenge, but we exaggerated our way through. We were learning from the boss."

According to this counselor, parents also took pleasure in reading in the camp yearbook the following account of their children's personal growth: " 'Camp Wunderbar takes pride in the progress made by its campers in the many and varied activities offered at the camp. The following list indicates some of the fields in which campers have taken great forward strides.' Each camper's name was followed by two activities in which he had taken 'great forward strides.' Actually the selection of these two activities was quite arbitrary. Indeed, most campers did not exhibit even small forward strides in any activity. The activities placed next to a camper's name were often those in which he hadn't even participated. Kids who had never stepped on the softball field were credited with exhibiting 'great forward strides' in softball. Once again, deception was employed to salve the conscience of the parents who had paid $1,250 to get rid of their kids for the summer."

TAKE ME OUT TO THE BALL GAME

Not all helpless customers are institutionalized. They also exist outside institutional settings. One might consider patrons at a sporting event as midway between the institutionalized helpless and the non-institutionalized helpless. Such spectators are obviously not institutionalized, but they are confined—for several hours, anyway—and are in a sense trapped in the stadium. Accordingly, such "helpless" patrons are likely to be cheated.

Captive customers at a ballpark are in no position to shop around for the best price for beverages, mainly because the sellers have a monopoly, which is made airtight by the rule that canned or bottled beverages cannot be brought in from the outside. It comes as no surprise, then, that several young men who had worked as vendors at ballparks and football stadiums noted that customers did not get all they paid for. One vendor who worked at a ballpark in the Midwest wrote that both the beer and soda he sold were watered. A vendor at another sports stadium reported the same practices, with a couple of added twists. He writes, "A soda which sells for 90¢ consists of half a cup of ice and is filled with watered-down soda. The beer is also watered down, and air is injected into it to give you half foam and half beer." Moreover, the company employs an ingenious device that might be described as "Better cheating through chemistry," a variation on DuPont's old advertising slogan. The vendor writes, "Occasionally the beer becomes completely flat, and this is corrected by dropping a few grains of salt into the beer, causing it to fizz."

THE UNEMPLOYED AS HELPLESS CUSTOMERS

Few people in contemporary society are more helpless than the unemployed. Nothing confers power and status as much as a high-paying job; nothing creates powerlessness and dependency as much as joblessness. No wonder that one of the most consistent findings among all the studies of unemployment since the Great Depression is that men who are out of work for long periods lose status and authority not only in the community and larger society, but often at home with wife and children. No image of helplessness is more poignant than able-bodied yet idle men on street corners or lined up at the employment office.

Among the essays was one by a counselor at an employment agency who described the kinds of games her office played with unemployed workers seeking jobs. An employment counselor's immediate interest, of course, is to place the client in a job because most clients who accept a position pay several weeks' salary to the agency, of which the counselor may get a substantial share. These commissions are the counselor's chief source of income. Thus, the interests of counselor and client seem to coincide because the counselor is trying to place the client in a job and the client is seeking a job. But this is not necessarily so. The unemployed—helpless customers—are often misled and manipulated by the employment agency, as frequent investigations of these firms have shown.

Our informant noted that her agency's initial deception are the newspaper ads that the agency places. She reveals that "Practically none of these ads are for real positions. They are only come-ons. When a person calls us to find out where one of these jobs is located, the counselor tries to find out where the person lives and then states that this nonexistent job is fifteen minutes from his or her home. When a client comes in specifically for one of these imaginary positions, he or she is advised that they are too young, too old, not a good enough typist, needs steno, or that the position is already filled. However, they are advised that there are many other good positions at the counselor's fingertips."

The aim of the phony ads, of course, is to bring the client into the office. Once the client is there, the counselor tries to sell the person on whatever job is available, almost regardless of whether the client is suited for the job. The writer cites a not unusual example. "I remember clearly one girl who had applied for a receptionist's position. She was about eighteen years old, just out of high school, could type about twenty words a minute, and she was naïve enough to fall for my line which went something like this: 'What you need is six months to a year of stable job experience. You have to show companies that you'll come in every day. Through this job you can increase your typing skill and pick up any new skills that are available to you in the office. But what I know you're really going to like about this job is that you'll be working with all young girls, you'll meet a lot of people, and, because of this, you won't mind having to work from 9:00 to 1:00 on Saturday.' "

The position the counselor was describing to this young woman was that of a clerk, answering telephones in a T.V. repair shop. The counselor continues: "Who was deceived in this particular interaction? First, the company that may hire this girl was told that this girl is ambitious, excited about the position, and will really be worth her salary. Second, of course, the client herself has been a victim of deception by the very same tactics—namely by a gross exaggeration about the job and by actual lies concerning what the job offers."

But the ruse doesn't end here. Because the counselor's primary concern is the commission, she is not so much interested in placing *this* particular woman in the job as in placing *any* woman who passes through her office. The next step is predictable:

"No sooner has the counselor assured the client that this particular job is just what she wants, then, upon interviewing the next client, the counselor goes through the same line— for the same position. Ten persons are sent out for the same position on the same day at half hour intervals. The counselor's concern doesn't lie with the individual client—but rather having a person—any person—fill the position. We don't care what person gets the job, only that the job is filled, thereby assuring our fee."

This counselor's testimony was based on her experience at an employment agency in the mid-1970s. An unanticipated consequence of this—and probably other—agency's policies may have been to channel educated women into low-status, low-paid clerical jobs at the heart of the female occupational ghetto. The employment counselor describes how and why this was done: "When a female client has a college degree, the counselor *strongly* advises her not to divulge her college background. There is no attempt to place her in a position that would call for a college degree. Secretarial skills are the only asset a woman can really have in the eyes of the counselor. The reason for this is it is easier to find a position for a female with clerical skills, for this ensures that the counselor will collect her fee without too much difficulty."

Hence, from the agency's point of view, it is better to steer women into dead-end clerical jobs that can be filled quickly, thus assuring the agency its fee, than try to place women in nontraditional higher-status, higher-paid positions. These might take longer to find, and consequently the agency risks losing a fee. Given this modus operandi, employment agencies have probably been—and probably still are—an institutional force helping to perpetuate the segregation of women into traditional jobs.

CHAPTER 6

Scarcity

Even the most casual observer of social behavior knows that when the good and necessary things of life are scarce, people rarely behave in a commendable manner. When things are abundant, people can afford to be generous; when things are scarce, watch out. True, scarcity may occasionally bring out the best and most unselfish in people, especially during a temporary crisis as they share and help others, but over the long haul it usually brings out the worst. When there is not enough to go around, when people are pushed to the wall, when many people want the same scarce and desirable things—food, money, space, property, power—social conflict almost always ensues, as everyone grabs what he can for his own survival and comfort.

Given the sorry effect of scarcity on social relations, it is not surprising that many social philosophers have placed scarcity at the foundation of their dreary view of society.[1] For English philosopher Thomas Hobbes, competition for scarce goods, for property and the good life—the "convenient Seat," as he called it—caused most of man's quarrels, both in society and in the earlier state of nature. Cunning, envy, greed, and egotism spring from this struggle, for those who have the convenient Seat try to keep it and those who do not try to seize it.[2]

For Thomas Malthus, as we know, scarcity was the eternal sword of Damocles hanging over civilization. Mankind's unlimited desires threatened to overwhelm nature's scarce resources, and unless population growth was controlled, scarcity would wreak its revenge, bequeathing a world of famine, pestilence, and war.

Marx believed that economic scarcity was such a divisive force that a harmonious communist society could never be built on its foundation. By socializing scarcity one would only generalize *want*. In such a situation, Marx argued, with unsatisfied economic needs all around creating inevitable competition, "the struggle for necessities and all the old filthy business would necessarily be reproduced."[3]

Just as harmonious communism cannot be built on scarcity, neither apparently can harmonious capitalism, for business fraud flourishes in a framework of scarcity. The phrase "Business is business," often reluctantly expressed, captures the constraints that economic necessity and scarcity impose on sentiment and morality, and the unfortunate fact that the latter qualities must bow before the former.

One reason corruption pervades the marketplace is that scarcity is the essence of trade. Society has never achieved—not even in our affluent society—such a level of abundance that all things are plentiful, affordable, and available to everyone. Thus, in the context of scarcity, there is the inevitable scramble for personal advantage. In fact, one might argue that scarcity produces *all* the fraud we have described previously. "Profit scarcity," or the scarcity of money, which is eternal, induces businessmen to deceive—to put a thumb on a scale, sell tap water as imported water, fill a crankcase with low-grade motor oil and charge for high, and so on. This is in general true.

But by the principle of scarcity here, I mean something more specific. Goods themselves are frequently scarce, not only because society has not achieved universal abundance, but also because of problems of misallocation. Products are not always at the right place at the right time. Some firms are particularly susceptible to periodic scarcities or shortages, and these impair the firm's ability to do business. Hence, when shortages occur, many firms are inclined to employ deceptive means to conceal them from customers. They may secretly substitute a product that is available in place of the product the customer wanted. Because of shortages, they may give the customer less than what he ordered. They may pretend before the sale that there is no shortage, which the customer discovers only after he has paid his money.

A few examples may illustrate the point. A young woman worked for a sportswear manufacturer in New York's garment district where she did assorted clerical work. In the garment industry, manufacturers occasionally receive orders for goods they do not have. How this particular manufacturer responded illustrates the principle that scarcity of product often leads to business deception so the firm can conclude a sale that could otherwise not be made. The worker writes, "It seems that when my boss runs out of certain sizes, he will compensate by just putting a new label on the wrong size dress. For example, if the order calls for fifteen dozen size 10 dresses and he only has fourteen, he might put size 10 tickets on size 12 dresses."

Another writer with a similar story worked for a large ladies' garment manufacturer whose clothing was distributed nationwide through department store catalogs. At this firm the informant worked as a "picker." Her job was to take invoices for orders to be filled and pick the appropriate clothing from the large central racks. As a picker, she was well situated to observe how orders were filled and misfilled. She writes, "In manufacturing garments for department store catalogs, a lot of garments are needed because these orders are very big and are shipped all over the country. The operators just continue to sew garments by the thousands until they think they have approximately enough to fill the order. When the order gets close to being completely picked and filled and they run out of a size, they fill in with what they have. For instance, if they run out of size 12 and have too many size 14's left, we simply get out our little scissors and clip out the size tags. Then we are given a tag gun that has cardboard 'size 12' tags and put them on the garment and finish filling the order so it goes out on time."

Because of this practice, the worker hastens to reassure the reader, "If you have ever walked into a store thinking that you were a perfect size 8 and came out totally depressed because you just bought a garment that is a size 12, don't fret yet and swear you are going to join Weight Watchers immediately. There is a good chance that the size tag has been tampered with."

The same writer relates another mislabeling adventure in her firm. "One day the supervisor handed me a pair of cuticle scissors and seated me in front of a large carton filled with sweaters. She then instructed me to cut out the size labels inside the sweaters. After I did this, she gave me these little cardboard tags which had the letter 'M' printed on them which stood for Medium. She then told me to staple these tags to the bottom of the sweaters in the front. The size tags that I had clipped out said 'L.' "

Another writer who worked in the shipping department of a factory that produced expensive, high-fashion women's clothes, mainly pants, tops, and blazers, reported similar sleights of hand with the size tags. She writes, "If a company orders fifty-four size 5's and fifty-four size 7's, and we have all the 5's but only thirty size 7's, we will take twenty-four size 9's, change the size tag on the garment to read 'size 7,' and pass them off to our customers as 7's. This is done simply to fill a quota on an order and is a very common trick in the industry."

The same manufacturer sometimes also sends out substitute styles and colors without the customer's permission when those that were ordered are not available. Although the customer can return merchandise not ordered, the manufacturer has made it a *fait accompli;* shipping out the wrong merchandise in the first place makes returns inconvenient, and often the customer will simply keep the merchandise rather than take the trouble to send it back. Naturally, the manufacturer counts on this.

Several other workers reported similar practices. One who worked for an expensive handbag manufacturer said that if they were short of certain colors the company sent handbags to stores in colors that weren't ordered. And a man who worked for two years in the shipping department of a leading publisher of classical sheet music reported a dissonant practice: "If a person orders a piece of music that we don't have, but we do have a similar piece, we will give it to them without any notification." Of course, one might wonder what is a "similar" piece.

While scarcities impel manufacturers, wholesalers, and mail-order companies to deceive their customers, retailers turn around and do the same to their customers. A saleswoman working in a small boutique, for example, writes that "When a woman comes in and says, 'I'd like to see that dress in a size 8,' and there is only a size 6 or 10, my boss will pull the size tag off one of the dresses and say, 'Here is an 8.' She is constantly changing around size tags." A salesman at a neighborhood Army-Navy store describes a fairly common occurrence; a customer asks for two pairs of slacks, in this case tan, size 40 waist, 31 inseam. The salesman is able to find only one pair in the right size. So: "My boss went down to the basement and made his own check for the second pair of pants. When he determined that the pair wasn't available in the desired color, he grabbed a pair of the right color and inseam from the size 42 waist pile and ripped off its size label. He then took a label with the correct waist and inseam sizes and stapled it to the size 42 pants. He took the two pairs of pants upstairs and sold them, telling the customer they were both the same size. The boss said he kept a stapler in the basement to be used in situations where labels must be changed. He laughed because, according to him, the customer doesn't know the difference."

Scarcity is no stranger to the shoe business, for no store can possibly stock the vast combinations of styles and sizes that customers demand. Therefore, as we have seen in Chapter 2, deceptive accommodations must be made. If you don't have what the customer wants, sell him what you've got. The salesman in the Army-Navy store quoted above describes the situation in the store's shoe department. "If the customer asks for a particular size and we don't have it, we either try to give him the next nearest size or try to convince him to take a different style shoe. When the size of the shoe we show the customer is different from the size the customer asks for, the boss urges us not to tell the customer that there is a discrepancy, because if we do tell him, even if the different size shoe fits, the customer won't take it."

A problem of scarcity peculiar to shoe stores is the problem of mismates—one pair of shoes of two different sizes. The matched mates have disappeared or run off with someone they have little in common with, and the store must dispose of what remains. A worker employed for four years in a shoe store which is part of national chain describes how the store handled the problem of mismates. "Since the customers help themselves to shoes, and since some of the cashiers did not always check the shoes being sold for mates, it was not unusual to have pairs of mismates left at the end of the day when the stock was straightened. For example, there would be a left shoe size 7 and a right shoe size $7\frac{1}{2}$. These shoes should have been taken off the sales rack and kept in the back until inventory, when they would be recorded as mismates. Since mismates do not reflect well on the manager's store control, however, one of the managers was known to change the size inside the shoe. In the above example, he would change the size 7 to a size $7\frac{1}{2}$ by either inserting a $7\frac{1}{2}$ label or by writing a $\frac{1}{2}$ next to the 7. The shoes would then be placed back out on the rack and sold as a pair of $7\frac{1}{2}$'s."

This is apparently a common practice. A woman who

worked for five years in the shoe department of a well-known New York department store describes the disposition of mismates in the same fashion. "When one of the salespeople happens to stumble on a mismate—same shoes of two different sizes—do we return the shoes? Discard them? No. We sell them. Who would buy shoes of two different sizes? No one, if they knew. We have a size 6 and a 6½; we just erase the ½ and now you have two shoes that read size 6. The customer won't know; the fact is one foot is always a little larger than the other."

As we have seen, scarcity often leads to the surreptitious substitution of products. In one case described by a worker it led to the substitution of *persons*. A nurse's aide at a proprietary hospital in New York reported that, because of a serious shortage of registered nurses in the hospital, a cosmetic remedy was devised. "The hospital had only one registered nurse on each floor. The rest of us were either nurse's aides or practical nurses. For this reason they dressed the nurse's aides in nurse's uniforms. This was done to give the impression that the hospital was well-staffed with nurses. Many patients mistook me for a nurse—and thus, this little trick was quite effective."

Scarcity may tempt a firm not only to substitute sizes, colors, styles, products, or persons, but to give a customer less merchandise than he ordered and charge him for the full amount. The clerical worker for a New York sportswear manufacturer, quoted earlier, who reported that her employer occasionally substituted sizes, also reported that when her firm didn't have sufficient quantities to fill an order, it often simply shipped less and tried to camouflage it. She explains how this is done. "The garments are usually packed in dozens. If an order calls for fifty dozen garments and we have only forty-nine dozen available, the garments are packed in such a way as to give the impression of a dozen garments in each package. Here is how the little trick works: the first thirty-eight boxes are packaged correctly, but the last twelve boxes will contain, instead of a dozen in a box, eleven in each box. This is exactly how the order will be shipped. Sometimes this goes unnoticed by the department stores and at other times the 'mistake' is caught. When the 'mistake' is noticed it usually is passed off as a careless error of one of the shipping clerks. The error is then corrected and all is well. The department store gets the full order and the manufacturer still has his spotless reputation."

A similar numbers game is played in an entirely different industry. One writer worked for seven years in the shipping department of a machine shop that produces a variety of washers and gaskets. Sometimes the firm doesn't have enough of a particular product to fill the order. They solve the problem by shipping less than the full order. The worker writes, "Sometimes the shop runs out of material but will ship as if the order is complete. How much of a shortage they will ship depends on the amount ordered. If the order is for 1,000 pieces, the shortage can be up to 50 pieces. For an order of 100,000 pieces, the shortage can be up to 5,000 pieces. For an order of one million, the shortage can be up to 50,000. Once they shipped an order for one million pieces with a shortage of 100,000 pieces and the customer never complained. If the customer does complain of the shortage, they will make the washers and ship them out. The owners usually give the excuse that the counting machine probably wasn't working properly."

Under the press of scarcity this firm manipulates the quality as well as the quantity of the products it ships. According to the worker, "Sometimes they get a rush job and they don't have the right material. If the order says to use 304 stainless steel, they may use 302 stainless steel instead. Most of the time they get away with it. If the parts are rejected then they will have to buy the right material and make the washers again. At other times they will use material that is thinner than what the order says; that way they use less material."

ALL MY SONS

In Arthur Miller's early play, *All My Sons*, an aircraft manufacturer, an otherwise moral man, knowingly ships defective
cylinder heads to the army air force during World War II.
The fighter planes in which these heads are installed ultimately crash, killing many American pilots. How could a
businessman do such a thing? What conceivably could be his
defense? He claimed there was no time to correct the defect.
The army was "screaming for cylinder heads." If he didn't
ship them out he would have lost his contract with the army.
That would have jeopardized the business he had built up
over decades for his wife and sons. He had to do it for the
sake of his family.

The theme of Miller's play is a central moral issue of
our age. What is a man's moral responsibility, not just to his
immediate family, but to the entire human family?[4] In a
civilized society, can one simply throw strangers overboard to
make the voyage more pleasant for himself and his family? In
a society based on self-interest, does self-interest have any
moral limits? This is not merely an issue contrived by a play-
wright for an evening's entertainment, for the situation
Miller depicts arises again and again in our time.

It is a perplexing moral paradox. How is it that people
who are otherwise good citizens, generous neighbors, and
kind parents, who would never think of harming others face
to face, can, while at work, do things that cause injury or
even death to innocent strangers? How could otherwise moral
men—in real life and not on stage—knowingly manufacture
defective brake systems for a U.S. air force jet fighter?[5] How
could moral men sell to the army defective machine gun
parts that cause the guns to jam in battle?[6] How could moral
men knowingly manufacture defective fire-fighting equipment for navy ships?[7]

How could moral men design and market automobiles
they know are dangerous and that will inevitably cause accidents and death?[8] How could moral men in the asbestos in-

dustry intentionally conceal for so long the terrible hazards of their product?[9] How can moral men export to third world countries dangerous drugs and chemicals that have been banned in this country?[10] How could moral men promote and market infant food formula in developing countries where its use almost inevitably causes malnutrition and illness?[11] How could moral men at one of the nation's leading baby-food companies market a product for infants labeled "100% Apple Juice" that was a "fraudulent chemical cocktail" containing no apple juice at all?[12] How could moral men attempt to export from Europe powdered milk they knew had been dangerously contaminated with radioactive cesium 137 from the Chernobyl nuclear disaster?[13] And on and on.

In its most fundamental sense this behavior is a moral problem, a problem of human choice and responsibility. Looked at in a slightly different way, this behavior is merely a consequence of the quest for gain amid continuing scarcity. Because safe products are scarce or expensive or unavailable or hard to produce, defective or dangerous goods are sold in their place.

In our study we had a few such cases. One woman worked in the early 1970s as a salesperson for a large New York department store. Her rotating assignments took her to many different sections of the store. She reports: "I once worked in the boys' department. They had a whole showcase full of boy's pajamas. It was Christmas and people were buying in such a rush that often they didn't take the time to inspect their purchases. The pajamas were on sale for one-third their regular price. The reason was that they were flammable. The store buyer in this department had us put the "FLAMMABLE" warning tags inside the pajamas so that they weren't visible."*

There is no question that the profit system is the central

---

* This incident occurred during a transitional stage in the flammable fabrics law, when flammable pajamas were being phased out and flame-retardant pajamas were being phased in.

villain in all these instances of workplace immorality. In each case, calculations of gain simply superseded every other value. In an economic system based exclusively on motives of self-interest and profit, such behavior is inevitable. In such a system some persons will simply use the principle of profit, not just as the most important criterion, but as the *only* criterion of every transaction, regardless of how little they may benefit and how much others may be harmed. Carried to its logical conclusion, this leads to the tacit formula that if it is necessary to risk other people's lives in order to increase my income, then so be it. But it is often more complicated than this. There are additional social and psychological dynamics through which the profit motive works that help explain why otherwise moral people are capable of extraordinary immorality at work.

1. The injury done to others is often impersonal. Company employees don't know their victims personally. The people who suffer are anonymous, invisible customers far away, and as such don't exist except as abstractions; their humanity can be easily discounted or forgotten, which helps those responsible for their injury sleep with a clear conscience. People die in automobiles far from those who have designed them. Smokers die quietly far from those who manufacture and advertise cigarettes. Third world people suffer far from the plants that produced the chemicals that poison them.

In Stanley Milgram's classic experiment on obedience to authority, designed to test whether subjects were willing to follow orders to administer strong electric shocks to innocent victims, the further away the victim was from the subject (in another room, out of sight or hearing range), the more willing the subject was to administer high levels of shock. Conversely, the closer the victim was to the subject (in the same room, for example), the more reluctant the subject was to shock the victim.[14] An unfortunate consequence of twentieth-century technology and the political, economic, and military bureaucracies that employ it is that injury and death are now delivered by remote control, in many cases, very remote.

2. The division of labor in the modern enterprise is so elaborate that each worker performs but a small part of the whole operation. No matter how much harm the company does to its customers, responsibility is so widely diffused throughout the firm that no one need feel responsible for anything. Cigarettes cause cancer. Yet who is responsible for spreading the disease—the farmer who grows the plant; the factory worker who wraps the cartons; the secretary in the office of the tobacco company; the model who poses for a cigarette ad; the newspaper executive who accepts tobacco advertising? All would deny responsibility for spreading disease, and they are essentially correct. Certainly none of them is wholly responsible.

In terms of the diffusion of responsibility, some large companies are actually organized something like a firing squad. In a firing squad, a number of men shoot at the victim simultaneously, allowing each man on the squad to feel that his bullet may not have been the one to kill the victim. Furthermore, one rifle is normally loaded with blanks, permitting each man the moral luxury of thinking that he may not even have injured the victim. Thus, the condemned man lies dead, yet "no one" was responsible.

3. Employees can almost always avoid personal responsibility because someone else gave the order to do what was to be done. Almost everyone has a boss, a supervisor, or a manager, and then one is only following orders. As the twentieth century has unhappily demonstrated, people tend to obey orders—no matter how grotesque—if they are perceived as coming from a legitimate source.

4. Conformity is often both contagious and compulsory. Employees observe other workers going about what seems to be normal business, however antisocial it may be, and take their cues from them and join in. It is a kind of

emperor's-new-clothes situation, where each person's behavior validates and reinforces the behavior of everyone else. In the corporate world, as William H. Whyte observed long ago in *The Organization Man,* one is expected to be a team player. And as the well-known social psychology experiments conducted by Solomon Asch and others have demonstrated, group pressure exerts enormous power over otherwise rational and independent persons to conform.

5. The machinery is running, the wheels are turning. Employees enter an organization that existed before they came to work there and will continue to exist after they leave. The apparatus seems both immortal and too powerful to control or change. Milgram suggests in this context a psychological process he calls "counteranthropomorphism."[15] Behavioral scientists have long recognized the human propensity for anthropomorphism—the attribution of human qualities to animals and inanimate objects. In contrast, counteranthropomorphism is the tendency for people to assign nonhuman or superhuman properties to products of human society. Thus, in a large bureaucratic organization, the rules, although man-made, seem to take on an existence of their own; they are often seen as immutable truths, as if they had descended ready-made from heaven and were not of human design or subject to human modification. So, in the large organization, "the rules" are beyond question and must be obeyed. Just as in religion, people create gods and then worship them.

6. Most people are not, and cannot be expected to be, heroes and whistle-blowers. A recent study found that the vast majority of whistle-blowers in private industry end up being fired, not praised or rewarded for their courage.[16] Most people need to keep their jobs, need to pay their bills, need to get by and be accepted by others. They cannot afford to sacrifice their comfort and security for an abstract principle. So they go along.

7. Finally, in a large bureaucratic organization people

abandon their role as full moral human beings. At work they simply become functionaries with a specific and narrow job description, with no moral demands and no expectations about larger moral responsibilities made on them.[17]

And how did the saleswoman in our study feel about selling flammable pajamas to the public? She confessed that while she deplored selling these dangerous garments and wanted to stop, she sold them anyway. Why? She was only a functionary, she was simply obeying orders, she needed the job, and couldn't risk losing it by defying authority. She writes, "I was powerless to warn customers about the flammable pajamas, and I felt sick every time I sold one of them. I wish I had been in a higher position so I could have ordered the merchandise thrown out. But unfortunately, salespeople are a dime a dozen. I was a new employee and scared at the time and there were a lot of people waiting in line for my job. So I stuck it out passively."

CHAPTER 7

Perishability

Certain businesses trade in perishable commodities. I am not referring here simply to such obviously perishable goods as food. Photographic film ages and is thus perishable. Clothing styles are not eternally fashionable. In establishments that sell perishable products, there is always the danger that goods will spoil, rot, go sour, go stale, go out of date or out of style, or become obsolete. In such firms, depending on how perishable the goods are, there is a constant undercurrent of urgency to sell the product, for if the goods cannot be passed off on the customer quickly enough, they will perish, and large economic losses will ensue.

The perishability principle is obviously related to the scarcity principle, and may even be considered a subtype of it, for the fact of perishability means that some goods are scarce, in part because they may so easily become worthless if they are not sold rapidly. In any case, enterprises dealing in perishable commodities are highly likely to employ deceptive practices, for if goods cannot be sold before they perish, there are almost irresistible pressures to get rid of the goods *as* they are perishing or even *after* they have perished. This can usually be accomplished only by concealing from the buyer the actual condition of the merchandise. The following examples illustrate the general rule.

Meats, Fish, and Fowl

"Sell it or smell it" is an old adage in the meat business, and Benjamin Franklin once observed that "fish and visitors smell after three days," though with modern refrigeration the former can sometimes be kept fresh a bit longer. Because meats and fish are highly perishable, those who sell these products are under considerable pressure to sell them quickly. Failing this, merchants employ techniques involving cosmetics or concealment to move the spoiling or spoiled product along.

A man who worked in the meat department of a supermarket for five years described how his manager dealt with problems of perishable meat and fowl. After Thanksgiving, for example, the store is sometimes left with unsold turkeys with rapidly approaching expiration dates. The problem is easily remedied in the following manner. "We just bring the turkeys in and wipe the old ticket off so it is not visible. Then we set the scale a month ahead and weigh them up and put them back out again. This is not an unusual practice." In the same market some meat products come in with dates already stamped on them in ink. This calls for another solution—literally: "If these products get outdated there is this household cleaning solution that will remove the inked date so the customers don't know what the date is on it. If it is not possible to remove the ink, we just place the ticket over the date so people can't see it."

Another worker employed in a meat market in downtown Brooklyn observed that when meat spoiled, his boss would soak the meat in vinegar and salt for a few hours to remove the unpleasant smell. Such practices are apparently common, for a worker employed by a large supermarket chain described the same treatment in his store. "When the butcher detects spoiling meat he washes it in a salt solution, repackages it, and sells it. Also, some smoked meats develop a mold, and likewise they're also soaked in a salt solution, the mold is scraped off, and it's sold."

Mold is a four-letter word in some supermarkets. One woman worked in the delicatessen department—or what New Yorkers call the "appetizing" department—of a major supermarket. Because of what she observed there, she is now "wary about buying meats or cheeses at any appetizing department in any supermarket." Although the supermarket advertises that cold cuts and dairy products are fresh, she writes that "there is no attempt to throw out spoiled food." Once, when she noticed an entire pastrami with mold all over it and told the manager, he replied, " 'What mold? I don't see any mold,' he said while scraping the mold off the pastrami with his fingers. I was then instructed never again to say 'mold' or 'moldy' while working."

Another writer who worked in the delicatessen department of a major supermarket for four years wrote that meats are left in the poorly refrigerated deli display case overnight rather than stored in the refrigerator in the back room. Though naturally the meat spoils faster this way, it saves the store the expense of paying employees overtime to transfer the meat from display case to refrigerator each evening and back the next morning. A quick cosmetic job in the morning, cutting off the top slice of meat which has discolored, gives the product a fresh appearance once again.

The fish department in the same store also confronts the problem of perishability. The store assures its customers that "all fish which is marked fresh in the case has been delivered on the day it is being sold, because, as they say, 'Who would sell fish that is old? It's not safe to eat.' Nonetheless, it is done. I have seen them store the fish in the refrigerator and use the same fish day after day. Fresh fish is only delivered on Wednesdays and Fridays, which means if a customer buys fish on Tuesday he is purchasing something which was delivered to the store four days earlier."

One writer worked several summers for a caterer that

prepared thousands of sandwiches and meals each day for numerous summer camps. When the hamburger went bad, the caterer simply combined it with fresher hamburger meat to rejuvenate it. When cold cuts such as salami and bologna spoiled, they disguised it by going heavy on the lettuce and mustard to mask the taste and smell.

A supermarket stock clerk related a story which, though a single anecdote, seems typical of the deli manager's overriding concern for "efficiency"—that is, selling anything, regardless of condition. "Over the summer," the clerk writes, "while on a night crew, we accidentally left out a five-pound ham. By the morning it had turned brown and looked and smelled bad. Jim [the manager] came in and complained about how inconsiderate we were and said he would have to file a loss-of-inventory with the office so he would be reimbursed. However, the next day one of my colleagues told me that Jim had sold the ham as though there was nothing wrong with it. I rechecked the case and confirmed my friend's report."

The same worker mentions a recurring supermarket problem: What is to be done with abandoned carts of groceries? While shopping for groceries, some shoppers change their minds in mid-course. They take a shopping cart, fill it, then decide they haven't the time, money, or inclination to continue and simply abandon their carts and leave the store. In some stores abandoned carts are called "orphans," suggesting that they are common enough to have acquired a name. Supermarket managers are thus confronted with the problem of how to dispose of perishable food that has been left sitting in shopping carts for hours.

A cashier at a large supermarket chain in New York described the most typical procedure. "I have seen perishable items—fresh fish, frozen foods, meats, dairy items, appetizing items—returned to a refrigeration unit or freezer after having lain in someone's abandoned shopping cart *all day* [emphasis in original]." Others report the same practice. Almost invariably, workers say that abandoned perishable merchandise is simply restocked and sold.

Supermarket managers are adept at handling minor problems of perishability and by a practiced sleight of hand can restock the "orphans" or shift the contents of a broken freezer even after the food is thawed and spoiling. But the great New York City power failure of midsummer 1977 proved a particular challenge to at least one supermarket manager, according to one of his cashiers. With all the store's power out, the freezers naturally shut down and everything defrosted. The worker writes, "Since everything refroze when the power went on again, my ingenious manager, knowing the first question on every customer's mind, put signs all over the store, reading: 'DUE TO THE RECENT INSTALLA-TION OF OUR OWN GENERATOR, FROZEN FOODS AND DAIRY PRODUCTS HAVE *NOT SPOILED*.' It sounded very reassuring to the customers, but it had all the employees wondering where that generator was—all we saw in the basement were dead stock, rats, and roaches."

Fruits and Vegetables

The increasingly common practice of prepackaging fruits and vegetables provides many opportunities for supermarkets to conceal rotting produce from customers, besides forcing them to buy in larger quantities than they may desire. How frequent an experience it is for shoppers to buy what looks like good packaged produce at the supermarket only to find when unpacking it at home that a fair amount of it—usually hidden at the bottom—is sickly or worse. And most shoppers probably realize that the bad mixed in with the good is not the result of sheer chance.

One young man who worked packaging produce in a large New York supermarket reveals what most people suspect. He writes, "The most general rule my produce manager taught me was that I shouldn't make any packages which were all good. In other words I was told to put a rotten apple in every bunch. Specifically, when I was bagging potatoes, I was told to put some old green potatoes in every bag. I was also told to put the not-so-good-looking fruit on the bottom of the trays, the good-looking ones on top. This practice was especially common with strawberries—putting the soft ones on the bottom. Another general rule I learned was that I should put the bad side of any fruit down. This included items such as tomatoes, pears, or any item which had one side which looked better than the other."

An alternative to hiding or disguising decaying produce is to perform a little cosmetic surgery to create the proper appearance. A worker in a wholesale fruit and vegetable company reports that produce there was "doctored up" to bring a higher price and move the merchandise faster. Apples, oranges, tomatoes, and other fruits and vegetables were regularly sprayed with ethylene gas to improve their appearance.[1] And a woman who worked for two years in a chain supermarket wrote that in her store, when any green vegetable, such as celery, went bad or wilted, the manager had the produce worker soak the vegetable in water and freeze it. Thawed the following day, the vegetable would appear fresh.

Dairy Products

Deception in the sale of perishable dairy products goes beyond the innocuous practice of placing older merchandise toward the front of the display case, and may involve actual violations of the law. Altering expiration dates on perishable dairy products is a common practice. One worker employed by a large supermarket chain, for example, reported that when milk containers were labeled only by the *day* of the week, not the date, any milk expiring on a particular day was frozen and brought out a few days later and sold as fresh.

The dating of dairy products did not faze the owner of an independent grocery store for whom one writer worked.

When the date stamped on the products passed, the worker revealed, "my boss didn't throw them out as he should have. Instead, someone was assigned to erase dates, mark prices over the date in an effort to conceal it, or pour the milk out of dated containers into unsterilized, unmarked bottles."

What happened when a customer came back to complain about having been sold spoiled milk products reads a little like something out of a twentieth-century *Oliver Twist:* "If a customer ever brought something back and claimed it was spoiled, the boss would summon some hapless stock boy and in front of the irate customer go into this song-and-dance routine of how he's told the boy to remove all such products. By apologizing profusely and berating the boy for unreliability, the boss would ingratiate himself with the customer. The poor kid would dutifully nod his head in agreement and mumble something about having neglected to do it, and then go back to concealing expired dates."

In still another supermarket, one worker reported, the dairy department was well equipped for deceiving customers. Although everything sold in the dairy department had an expiration date on it, time's inexorable march was easily circumvented: "Our store had a little date stamp, so you could put any date you wanted on a dateless carton and repack the dairy goods into the newly dated cartons."

Baked Goods and Sweets

Even the wonders of modern preservatives cannot make breads and cakes last forever, which creates a predicament for sellers of bakery products. Restoratives, cosmetics, visual fresheners, and face-lifts are common in the bakery trade.

One young woman who worked as a pastry cook and salesgirl in an Italian bakery for about a year described the industry's problems and her shop's pragmatic solution to them. "Cakes, pies, and pastries were supposed to be made fresh daily, but do you think a good businessman would throw away all leftover cakes at the end of every day? Of course not! Only moldy cakes were thrown away. Everything else was saved as long as it was in salable condition. Different thing were done to the pies and cakes to make them look as though they were made that day. For example, the pies and danish were glazed with something called 'glaze and shine.' This glaze gave a shiny wet look to the pies so they never looked dried out. The pastry shells, too, were saved for as long as possible. When the cream got hard, we would take off the outside of the cream and put fresh cream in the old shells. Sponge-type pastries were resprinkled with rum to remoisten them and take away their dryness."

Another worker in a local bakery describes her employer's tactics when cakes became stale. She writes, "These items were not thrown away, but were disguised in various clever ways so that they could be sold as fresh. If a cake was not too stale, we would cut off the outside crust layer and sell it like that." In cases of advanced rigor mortis, however, "a cake would need a complete new look, so fresh whipped cream would be used to do the cover-up jobs."

Because large cakes are quite fragile and may crumble, it was often necessary to doctor them up with fruit or whipped cream. Sheet cakes present a special problem, for if they are not handled properly they can crack. In such a case, workers employ the following strategy: "It is the salesgirl's job to make sure the customer does not notice the crack, and this is done by holding the cake with the sides higher than the middle. This 'closes up' the crack until the cake is straightened out again after it's in the box. The girl must be sure the box cover is up and blocking the customer's view."

In the event a cake falls on the floor, the manager instructed the salespeople as follows: "If there are customers present at the time, one places the cake on the side somewhere and waits for the customers to leave. Then the cake goes back on the shelf."

Certain products become dated very quickly. Paradoxically, however, if they are kept long enough they become current again. For example, sweets and goodies for Christmas, Valentine's Day, Mother's Day, and so on become obsolete right after the holiday. Thanks to the annual revolution of the earth around the sun, however, these goods will become "fresh" again if one only has the patience. And apparently many merchants do. Several informants reported store owners selling last year's Christmas candy this year, last season's Valentine's candy this season, last year's chocolate Easter bunnies a year later, and so on.

Clothing

Clothing is not normally regarded as a perishable commodity, and indeed clothes do not spoil or rot. Nonetheless, frequent style changes in both men's and women's clothing imply a perishability of product just as genuine as the problems faced by the butcher, the baker, and the fruit and vegetable seller. One writer who worked in a clothing store reported that his employer and the salesmen were easily able to distinguish between customers who were style conscious and those who were not. With the latter, one could frequently unload clothing that had been sitting in the store for some time and had long gone out of style. The worker writes, "A person who is not style conscious is very easy to sell. An employer looks forward to seeing this type of customer. First of all it means money, and second and more important, it gives the employer a chance to sell clothing that dates back for years. We as salesmen know which was last year's clothing because it is labeled on the tag when it was purchased. I remember a few years ago selling a person five Nehru jackets when the style had gone out of date two years before."

Flowers

I noted earlier that workers employed in florist shops reported many deceptive practices there. This is partly because flowers are often sold to distracted customers who are preoccupied with other matters—weddings, funerals, graduations, love affairs in various stages of health or decay—and these persons are thus easily cheated. Probably the basic motive in whatever deceit the industry perpetrates is based on the perishability of the product and the need to move the product before it has to be thrown away.

One informant who worked for a florist reported a novel method by which his employer defied the laws of nature and delayed the inevitable mortality of the product: "Spray paint was used to make a dying bunch of flowers look fresh. If a customer ever came back to complain that their flowers died prematurely, the kindly florist would tell them that it must be due to the way they cared for them."

Apparently this practice is not peculiar to this florist, for some seven years later another young man who worked as a flower arranger and salesman in another local florist shop reported a similar technique. He begins with an anecdote. "A customer came over to me recently and asked me for a dozen red roses. I called in the back where they make the bouquets and they told me they only had white roses left. So what they did was dye the roses red."

Gertrude Stein to the contrary, it is apparently not true that a rose is a rose is a rose. The worker continues his account. "Whenever you dye or spray roses they don't last for more than a few hours. Sometimes the customers would come back and say the roses died or wilted. My boss would ask where the roses were kept, and the guy would say, for example, in the trunk of his car so his girlfriend wouldn't see them. My boss would then give him some bullshit line like if you keep roses in the dark for more than an hour that's what happens. . . . The idea of the spray can was very popular.

Whenever the bouquets looked like they were dying, an added touch of spray paint made them look very fresh."

So apparently, in the florist shop as well as the auto shop, a worker's best tool is his paint can.

Pets

When one thinks of perishable goods, one thinks first of food—meat, fish, dairy goods, and produce. Yet any product that is by its nature perishable tempts the seller to engage in dishonest tactics to sell the product before its noticeable demise. Pets are perishable, of course, and they age, sicken, and die at a rate that depends on the life span of the species and the care they receive.

One young man worked as a salesman for two years in a local pet store. Besides stocking the usual dogs and cats, the store handled more exotic animals, such as rare birds, hamsters, guinea pigs, fish, snakes, and other small reptiles. According to the salesman, the store cut all sorts of corners to reduce costs, and for that reason had more than its share of sickly animals.

Many of the animals were already sick when they arrived at the store. The worker claimed, for example, that if a shipment of twenty-five parakeets arrived one day, typically only about fifteen would still be in salable condition the following day. In addition, the store lacked proper facilities to care for the more exotic animals. Nonetheless, the manager's policy seemed to be move the product if the product is still moving. The employee writes, "Animals will be sold to customers even though they are known to be suffering from certain diseases that will eventually cause their death. If a tank of hamsters is infected with wet tail, for example, then all of the animals should be destroyed because the condition is very contagious. Instead, the animals displaying the symptoms are taken out of the tank and the others without the symptoms are sold. If a customer should see a dead hamster in the tank and is wary about purchasing an animal from that tank, they are told that the animal died because it had been attacked by the other hamsters. Nothing is mentioned about the actual cause of death, so the customer may then buy the hamster. To be sure, the customer returns very shortly with one very dead hamster."

The store offered no guarantee on its animals, something the customer was not told in advance. And, as with the case of the prematurely wilted flowers, the pet store manager sought to shift the blame for the animal's death onto the customer. By asking the customer how he handled the pet—especially true with exotic pets—the manager can always find something about the customer's care that could be blamed for the animal's premature death.

Such, then, are the pressures for deception on those trading in perishable goods. One worker, in fact, who had wide experience in all branches of a large supermarket, claimed that the grocery section of the store (canned goods, nonperishable items) was the *only* department where customers were not cheated.

In the context of the profit motive, the pressure on businessmen to get rid of perishable products occasionally drives them to endanger their customers' health and safety rather than endure the most meager financial loss. A cook who worked in a coffee shop in a Queens hospital, for example, reports that his manager "has served spoiled meats or salads without giving it a second thought. She figures that if she has it to sell, she will sell it whether it is safe to eat or not."

At least medical care is not far away.

CHAPTER 8

Filth

Of all the violations of public trust found in these essays, one of the most widespread is the pervasiveness of filth in establishments where food is either sold or served. In one account after another, workers employed in restaurants, cafeterias, catering establishments, ice-cream stores, fast food outlets, large supermarkets, small groceries, bakeries, fruit and vegetable stores, delis, nursing homes, and bottling plants report a level of filth that would give pause to even the least fastidious customer. It is not that the public is unaware of the problem; indeed, the conventional wisdom has it that most restaurants, for example, are probably dirty. This is confirmed by regular reports of local health departments, and is usually reckoned as merely one of the costs of eating out. Yet, though there is a great public awareness, I suspect that, while it is known in general, it is not overtly recognized with regard to the particular establishments one patronizes.

One of the most vivid testimonies in modern literature on restaurant fraud and filth is found in George Orwell's *Down and Out in Paris and London*. In chronicling his poverty adventures during the 1930s, Orwell described his job as a dishwasher, working up to fourteen hours a day at one of the most elegant hotels in Paris at that time—"Hotel X," as he called it, located near the Place de la Concorde. In his description of the hotel restaurant, Orwell highlights the contradiction between what customers thought they were getting and what they actually got. Such lucid prose is worth quoting at length.

The customer pays, as he sees it, for good service; the employee is paid, as he sees it, for the *boulot*—meaning, as a rule, an imitation of good service.

Take cleanliness, for example. The dirt in the Hotel X, as soon as one penetrated into the service quarters, was revolting. Our *cafeterie* had year-old filth in all the dark corners, and the bread-bin was infested with cockroaches. Once I suggested killing these beasts to Mario. "Why kill the poor animals?" he said reproachfully. The others laughed when I wanted to wash my hands before touching the butter. Yet we were clean where we recognized cleanliness as part of the *boulot*. We scrubbed the tables and polished the brasswork regularly, because we had orders to do that; but we had no orders to be genuinely clean, and in any case, we had no time for it. We were simply carrying out our duties; and as our first duty was punctuality, we saved time by being dirty.

In the kitchen the dirt was worse. It is not a figure of speech, it is a mere statement of fact to say that a French cook will spit in the soup—that is, if he is not going to drink it himself. He is an artist, but his art is not cleanliness.

Dirtiness is inherent in hotels and restaurants, because sound food is sacrificed to punctuality and smartness. The hotel employee is too busy getting food ready to remember that it is meant to be eaten. A meal is simply *"une commande"* to him, just as a man dying of cancer is simply *"a case"* to the doctor. A customer orders, for example, a piece of toast. Somebody pressed with work in a cellar deep underground has to prepare it. How can he stop and say to himself, "This toast is to be eaten—I must make it eatable"? All he knows is that it must look right and must be ready in three minutes. Some large drops of sweat fall from his forehead on to the toast. Why should he worry? Presently the toast falls among the filthy sawdust on the floor. Why trouble to make a new piece? It is much quicker to wipe the sawdust off. On the way upstairs the toast falls again, butter side down. Another wipe is all it needs. And so with everything.

Apart from the dirt, the *patron* swindled the customers wholeheartedly. For the most part the materials of the food were very bad, though the cooks knew how to serve it up in style. The meat was at best ordinary, and as to the vegetables, no good housekeeper would have looked at them in the market. The cream, by a standing order, was diluted with milk. The tea and coffee were of inferior sorts, and the jam was synthetic stuff out of vast, unlabelled tins. All the cheaper wines, according to Boris, were corked *vin ordinaire*. There was a rule that employees must pay for anything they spoiled, and in consequence damaged things were seldom thrown away. Once the waiter on the third floor dropped a roast chicken down the shaft of our service lift, where it fell into a litter of broken bread, torn paper and so forth at the bottom. We simply wiped it with a cloth and sent it up again.[1]

Now, our workers wrote about the 1970s and 1980s, not about the 1930s, and they wrote about restaurants in New York, not in Paris. Yet the similarities between Orwell's account and our own contemporary acccounts are remarkable indeed.

On affection for animals that contaminate the premises. One worker in a fruit and vegetable store described the little friends that hung about the premises: "Rats thrive on fruit," he writes, "and they enjoyed staying near the garbage compressor which is in the lot directly outside the store. The owners did nothing about this and thought of it as unavoidable. Sometimes they jokingly called them 'kittens.' When they told us to 'feed the kittens,' we knew that they wanted us to throw out the garbage. The deceit of the public was highlighted in an incident which happened over the summer. When we opened the store one morning, a watermelon was bitten into and half chewed. You could see the marks of the rat's teeth. Instead of throwing the melon away, they cut around the bitten part and sold the uneaten half."

In a small pizzeria, the pizza dough was made in the basement, the setting for an amusing sideshow. An employee there revealed that his co-workers "take pellet guns with them when they go down the basement, so they can take target practice at the rats as they streak across the floor. When there are no rats around, the real sharpshooters show off by shooting the cockroaches climbing up the wall."

On spitting. A waiter in the dining room of a mountain resort hotel reported that the silverware was often dirty. But better dirty than clean, for the waiters would spit on the silverware in the kitchen to clean it before bringing it to the dining room.

On being too busy to remember that the food is going to be eaten. A short-order cook who worked in a coffee shop says in words similar to Orwell's: "In a business such as this I would have to say that fairness is very seldom considered. The place just gets too busy at times to consider each and every customer. Things have to be done as quickly and as efficiently as possible. Tricks of the trade are used to speed things up and serve the general public instead of the individual customer." He describes how in a rush dishes and silverware are not washed but merely wiped clean, meats are cooked in advance, and money-saving techniques are used, such as stretching tuna and shrimp salad by adding egg salad, and occasionally serving spoiled meats and salads.

A waitress in a midtown Manhattan restaurant-bar confirmed Orwell's observation that you save time by being dirty. She writes, "Sometimes when it is very busy many shortcuts will be taken. At times workers will not have enough time to wash the dishes. If the plates are reasonably clean they will reuse them without washing them. If the glasses were just used for water and still appear clean they will just rinse them instead of putting them in the dishwasher to be washed thoroughly. The management feels that what the customers don't know won't hurt them. Management doesn't want customers to be upset by waiting for their food, even if it means serving their food on unclean plates."

A waiter at a fashionable resort hotel in New York's Catskill Mountains made a similar observation about the hotel's kitchen practices. He writes, "A constant in this hotel is the dirty dishes, silverware, and glasses. Some dishes are given the simple water wash (no soap); here the visible dirt is removed, but grease and film are not fully cleaned. Food is then piled back onto these dishes and served to people. In some cases silverware is not even cleaned. The forks and knives are just wiped off with a napkin and put back onto the tables. Water glasses aren't washed in most instances; they are just filled up again with fresh water. These are all shortcuts this establishment uses to cut down on costs and save time."

FRONTSTAGE APPEARANCE VERSUS BACKSTAGE REALITY

Two general observations should be made about filth. First, all the food establishments our informants discussed, even the worst violators of health department codes, sought to give the *illusion* of cleanliness. What is important is not cleanliness itself, but, as Orwell notes, the facade of cleanliness, the superficial and visible trappings of cleanliness. In almost no other business situation is there such a clear-cut division between frontstage pretense and backstage practice.[2] The areas of the store or restaurant visible to the public are clean and neat, while areas out of the purview of customers are dirty and neglected: dining room versus the kitchen, the display case versus the storeroom.

Time after time in these essays we encounter the contrast between frontstage cleanliness and backstage filth. A few examples suggest the magnitude and variety of the practice. A writer who worked at a franchised fried-chicken outlet reports: "As you enter the front door, the store seems fairly clean and neat; but if you dare venture past the counter, you will feast your eyes on such goodies as: filthy floors, chicken scattered around the floor (which, of course, gets resold to the public), roaches, and an occasional mouse here and there. At times the mashed potatoes and gravy may have a combination of paper and cigarette ashes in them. Of course, we're instructed to put more gravy on the potatoes to cover their discolored look. None of this is seen by the public, and the product is praised as the company's best. This is one of the many restaurants jobs I have had and this store is one of the cleanest. My advice to you: stay home and cook."

A waitress for two and a half years at a family restaurant in New York also stressed the importance of the appearance of cleanliness, but again there was a clear demarcation between frontstage appearance and backstage reality. She writes, "Everything has to seem clean and proper to the customer and be outwardly appealing." But, she noted, "the kitchen doors are the actual barrier between the world of customers outside and the world without customers inside."

The hypocrisy, formality, and pretense of frontstage etiquette in the restaurant occasionally creates a cynical mood backstage. The waitress continues, "One of the most blatant contradictions is that when we serve a customer we appear not to touch their food at all. But in the kitchen before we take it out, the food is touched by cooks, by yourself [the waitress], and by other waiters and waitresses. People steal your french fries and eat your peas until you have to fight them off so that there is still food on the plate by the time you bring it out to the customer. . . . Salad sits in a big bin in the kitchen, and you fill up a bowl by using your hands. . . . When we serve gravy, applesauce, or anything that goes in a dish and drips down the side, it would be disastrous to take it to a customer dripping, because it looks terrible. But instead of wiping the mess with a napkin, most waiters use their fingers and then lick their fingers clean. Next thing you know, their saliva-cleaned fingers are back in the salad, or the ice, or my customers' french fries. Little do the customers know that the drink they're enjoying was tasted by the bartender before he served it. Or for that matter that the chef stuck his finger (for the fun of it) in the cake they're eating."

The same contrast between frontstage cleanliness and backstage dirt appears in a report by a clerk employed in a bakery. She writes, "From all outward appearances (that is, to the unsuspecting public), the front of the bakery was always clean and swept. The back of the bakery (the part that no one saw, except, of course, the salespeople) was quite a different story. Everything was filthy, and I do believe that roaches bred incessantly back there, as I saw them in numerous spots." And the worker who described the "kittens" in the fruit and vegetable market reported that "the front of the store was always spotless. A floor polisher came in twice a week and the part-time help, like myself, swept up every few hours. The back of the store, the part that the customers didn't go into, was rat-infested, however."

Sometimes the effort to create the illusion of cleanliness paradoxically contaminates the premises, as the following cases indicate. A worker employed in the delicatessen department of a supermarket wrote that "as a rule the deli looks clean, the food looks fresh. That's where the efficiency of this department ends, in making things *look* good. For example, in order to make the window in the display case look clean and free of grease, the department manager uses Windex, both on the outside and on the inside of the case. The problem is that when he sprays it on the glass, the food inside is not covered and may get Windex on it."

In another deli, a worker reports a severe roach problem. The exterminator's visits are infrequent, and so between visits "the clerks are instructed to spray roach killer into the

cracks of the counters and under the floorboards every morning and night. It is impossible to do this without the spray
reaching the food, and when this is done twice a day, there is
quite a bit of contamination to the food. But do not fear, for
this is remedied by turning over the salads each morning and
cutting off the end slice on the meats." Thus the display case
looks clean and insect-free, but at considerable chemical cost
to the customer.

A second general point about filth is that it is not due
just to the sloth or sloppiness of the employees, but is more
often a consequence of the priorities of the employer. *Genuine*
cleanliness—apart from its facade—is expensive, for it requires
the use of hourly workers to do the cleaning, and it also requires throwing away food that is contaminated, dirty, or
spoiled. Not all businessmen are willing to make this investment in time and money for a kind of cleanliness the public
never sees; thus, because genuine cleanliness apparently pays
few dividends, it ranks low on the merchant's list of priorities. Much better to engage employees in the basic work of
the establishment, such as waiting on customers, preparing
food, unloading and pricing stock, than to use them in the
superfluous, time-consuming, and thus unrewarding activity
of cleaning up. One worker in the delicatessen section of a
supermarket confirms this view. "The amount of dirt behind
the counter is almost immeasurable. This may seem more the
fault of individual employees rather than the company, but
time is money and the manager is just not willing to allow
the time to be spent in any real cleaning jobs other than what
the customer might visually come in contact with." The
writer reports that he has worked in many branches of this
large supermarket chain, under many managers, department
heads, and supervisors, and alleges that this attitude toward
cleanliness is a general one, not peculiar to one particular
store.

A worker at a self-service cafeteria in a large New York
department store observed the disturbing contrast between

dining room and kitchen. She was distressed at her manager's priorities on cleanliness and resented the essential dishonesty of it. "One of the first things I noticed right away," she writes, "was my manager's inconsistent attitude about the cleanliness of the place. She was absolutely fanatical about how the place looked on the outside. The tables had to be spotless, the chairs all had to be pushed in place, all paper and garbage had to be picked up off the floor, the tops of the salt and pepper shakers had to shine, and she even had us clean the high chairs they had for babies. This wouldn't have bothered me so much if she had spent half as much time worrying about the cleanliness of the kitchen. The tables in the eating room may have been spotless, but that didn't mean there weren't any roaches and other insects creeping around in the kitchen. Once I opened the freezer where the ice cream was kept and I found a couple of dead flies stuck in the vanilla and coffee bins. The stoves and grills were full of grease and dirt that was so old it was already impossible to remove. I know it's hard to keep a large kitchen clean and free of insects, but I felt my manager didn't put as much effort into doing that as she did into keeping the outside of the place clean."

Simply because many restaurant managers do not seem to live by the credo that cleanliness is next to godliness, one should not assume that they do not abide by other trusted maxims. They certainly do subscribe to at least one time-honored aphorism—waste not, want not. Because it is expensive to throw food away, even if it is unfit to eat, many restaurateurs do not permit food that has fallen on the floor to be discarded, but insist that it be picked up and served to customers. What Orwell observed in Paris a half century ago is still common practice in New York City today, as the following accounts illustrate.

One waitress, after describing a number of hygienic horrors at her restaurant, remarked almost as an afterthought, "I shouldn't even have to mention that food dropped on the floor is always picked up, brushed off, and put back on the plate." Another waitress employed at one of a chain of well-known restaurants noted that "the uncleanliness of food preparation makes the restaurant employees hesitant to eat anything there unless they personally prepare it themselves. I have seen a whole side of beef thrown on the floor, pancakes that have fallen off plates onto the floor picked up and served, and the boss's fingers in the side dishes of vegetables that we serve, testing them for their warmth. It is known policy that in front of management one does not throw away anything that has fallen on the floor. Therefore, we must either put the rolls, butter, or lemons that have fallen on the floor back, or wait until management is not looking to throw them in the garbage pail."

In another account reminiscent of Orwell, a worker at an airport restaurant wrote that "when the cooks and short-order men prepare meals, they occasionally drop part of the meal on the floor, in which case they reach down and simply place it on the unsuspecting patron's dish. Whole steaks might be dropped from dishes, kicked and dragged across the floor, possibly tossed back into the oven in a feeble attempt to undo what had accidentally been done, and finally delivered to the table where a hungry customer would spend half an hour relishing it and another three regretting it."

Finally, one writer worked in a franchised ice-cream store that seemed to combine almost all the abuses mentioned here. She had worked in the store for three and a half years and thus knew its operations well. While countertops and equipment visible to customers were reasonably clean, the areas not visible to the public were filthy. Her account is detailed: "Flies and insects which were attracted by the sweet-smelling, sweet-tasting toppings and ice cream die when they become trapped in the containers from which the customers are served. The boss instructed us not to throw out a bug-infested topping well, but to pick the bugs out before scooping out the ice cream or topping. . . . The entire cleaning process was superficial, since the owner would not allow enough time in the day for it. Month-long intervals passed between the heavy-duty clean-up procedures. . . . Although the clerks waiting on customers were supposed to keep the store clean, the task proved impossible because, first of all, there were so many customers, and secondly, the cleaning cloths which were available were old, clorox-soaked rags which disintegrated in about a week's time. Unfortunately the boss refused to buy cleaning cloths more than once a month. . . . If a bag of sprinkles or nuts broke and spilled onto the floor, they would be swept up and placed onto the serving trays. I once was harshly reprimanded because the boss entered the store while I was throwing away a tray of sprinkles which I had knocked onto the floor. His verbal attack centered around my terrible wastefulness for not returning the sprinkles to the serving tray. . . . The final abuse is that the employer had a rule: no one will be allowed an absence. Even if you are sick and unable to get a co-worker to replace you, you had better show up or you will be fired. One girl lost her job because she failed to show up when she had infectious mononucleosis, and my best friend was fired because he failed to show up for work when he had a 104° fever. No customer in his right mind would want to be served by a person who should be home in a sick bed."

The worker noted that the parent company that owned this store boasted in its advertising of the cleanliness of each store, and claimed that all its facilities were regularly and strictly supervised.

While it is true that filth is generally a consequence of the employers' policies and priorities, occasionally filth is due to the negligence of employees as well. While it has been observed that too many cooks spoil the broth, one drunken cook may do the job all by himself. One worker in our study employed in a local hospital kitchen reported that the cooks and porters had a chronic drinking problem. And it is difficult to argue with her assertion that "a drunken cook does not always produce desired results." To illustrate this point, she recounted that a few months earlier, "one of the cooks was drinking before he began to prepare meat loaf. When he was mixing the ingredients he somehow got a tack mixed up in the meat loaf. The tack was baked in the meat loaf and ended up on a patient's dinner tray. Luckily I saw the tack before the tray was given to the patient."

FILTHY LUCRE

Let's face it, if you didn't have a health department, you couldn't eat out.

San Francisco restaurant manager

It is a fair generalization, then, that backstage a great many restaurants in New York City are dirty. But dirty restaurants are obviously not peculiar to New York City. At the other end of the continent, for example, San Francisco health inspectors have found an array of unsavory practices in some of that city's most elegant restaurants: food prepared on top of garbage cans; mouse droppings on bread boards and around salad coolers; flies in liquor bottles; grime and mold on refrigerator walls and shelves; poison pest strips kept close to food preparation areas; and so on.[3]

The New York City Health Department is charged with inspecting city restaurants. In 1984, over 5,000 restaurants in the city *failed* their initial Health Department inspections. And although fines for health code violations are small, in that year the city collected nearly $1.5 million in restaurant fines for these violations. Such a sum gives the term "filthy lucre" an entirely new (and literal) meaning.

While restaurant filth is unpleasant and potentially hazardous to public health, serious and widespread outbreaks of disease related to restaurant food seem fairly rare. On the other hand, health authorities generally estimate that only about 10 percent of food-related illnesses are reported and traced back to the culpable source.[4] If one hundred strangers eat contaminated food in a restaurant and later become sick, each victim, suffering alone, may not link his illness to the restaurant, or even if he does, will probably not report it. For that reason, most cases of publicized food poisoning involve caterers or hotels where diners are known to one another or are in physical proximity so their common agony becomes apparent.

Why, despite inspections, are restaurants dirty? As previously noted, cleanliness costs money but filth is dirt cheap. Moreover, in a large city, restaurant workers do not know most of their patrons. Customers form an endless stream of nameless strangers and thus ultimately become just a buzzing backdrop, morally irrelevant and invisible. Patrons become easy victims, therefore, both of a restaurateur's greed and of the alienated workers' indifference.

The New York City Health Department's restaurant program, while vital, is inadequate to ensure genuine cleanliness. By law the Health Department is required to inspect each restaurant once a year. Yet recent investigations suggest that even this schedule is not maintained. An audit of restaurant inspection by the city comptroller's office found major deficiencies in this area.[5] The audit found that during the 1984 fiscal year, over one-third of New York's restaurants had not been inspected as required by law.[6] Auditors visited a sample of these uninspected restaurants accompanied by a certified environmental health technician. The technician judged that over half the uninspected restaurants would have failed the Health Department's inspections because of such major health code violations as "insect and/or rodent infestation; dishwashing and other water-related violations; improper storage and refrigeration; and grossly unsanitary facilities and equipment."[7] The report charged that the Health Department's "failure to perform timely inspections may allow restaurants to operate for extended periods with numerous and serious Health Code violations. Exposure to unsanitary conditions in these establishments may jeopardize the health of patrons."[8]

The audit also charged that many of the restaurants that had been inspected and had passed Health Department checks still had serious health code violations. Auditors and the environmental health technician visited a sample of New York restaurants immediately after they had passed Health Department inspections. According to the technician, over 14 percent of the restaurants that had passed Health Department inspection should actually have failed because of "serious and blatant Health Code violations."[9]

In sum, the comptroller's audit argued that New York restaurants are not inspected as often as the law requires; that a high proportion of those that go uninspected for a long period have major health code violations; and that a substantial share of restaurants approved by the Health Department have unsanitary conditions that could endanger public health.[10]

Unfortunately, inadequate inspection of New York restaurants is not just a matter of inefficiency; it is also a matter of corruption. Over the years, rumors have occasionally surfaced about payoffs in the Health Department's restaurant inspection program. In the mid-1970s, the city's Department of Investigation chose twenty New York restaurants at random and sent out undercover investigators posing as restaurant inspectors. In 35 percent of these restaurants, the investigators were offered unsolicited bribes of either money or free meals.[11]

This was merely the tip of a very large iceberg. In 1988 the FBI and the city's Department of Investigation uncovered a major scandal in the Health Department's restaurant inspection program.[12] Fully one-half of the Health Department's restaurant inspectors and supervisors were arrested and charged with extorting hundreds of thousands of dollars from city restaurants. Over the years, hundreds of New York City restaurant owners and employees allegedly paid inspectors from $25 to $5,000 to keep their restaurants off the Health

Department's violations list. Since most New York newspapers regularly publish the names of restaurants that fail inspections, enterprising inspectors have considerable leverage over restaurateurs. Many clean restaurants had to pay to keep their names off the violations list. But more important for public health, many dirty restaurants paid to have violations overlooked and to have their names removed from the list. For a fee, inspectors allegedly overlooked cases of suspected food poisoning, rodent droppings, roach infestation, and so on. FBI authorities said the payoffs doubled the income of most inspectors and allowed a few to live "lavish life styles."

But old habits die hard. Even though the scandal got front-page coverage in New York newspapers, along with promises from the city to tighten its inspection procedures, less than two weeks after the scandal broke, some New York restaurant owners were back paying bribes to inspectors.[13] Payoffs are apparently so deeply ingrained in the industry's culture they are as hardy as the cockroaches in restaurant kitchens. In fact, the U.S. Attorney involved in the case called these practices "a systematic, institutional form of corruption that has existed for decades."*

GRESHAM'S LAW OF COMPETITION

Most filth involves food, but not all. Many workers employed in clothing, department, or drugstores noted that customers were allowed to return almost all cosmetics and clothing, which were then reshelved for sale. One young woman, em-

---

* While dozens of inspectors were arrested, restaurateurs were portrayed as innocent victims and none were charged. Could it be so one-sided? For every restaurant inspector who took money, there was a restaurateur or his representative who gave it. As noted earlier, in a small investigation in the mid-1970s, 35 percent of restaurant owners made *unsolicited* offers to undercover agents. And in this scandal, are we to believe that proprietors of dirty restaurants had to be coerced into having their violations overlooked and their names removed from the violations list?

ployed for three years at a large New York department store, wrote that the store has a very lenient return policy. In fact, "They will accept anything that the customers want to return. Old, washed, worn, and often damaged merchandise is returned to the sales floor as a result. Items such as bathing suits and wigs, which are not supposed to be returned, are taken back."

Similarly, a woman who worked in a dime store in Brooklyn for five years wrote that she couldn't understand "why the store took back certain products. For example, things like hair accessories and underwear are not supposed to be returned. Nonetheless, these items are taken back and later put back out for sale."

When buying a new pair of shoes, one has a right to assume that no one else has worn them previously. Yet a woman who worked for several years for a New York shoe store reports that shoes that have been worn are accepted for return. When this happens, the worker writes, "one of our managers routinely attempts to cover up worn marks by polishing the shoes, using Fantastik cleaner on the soles and heels, replacing laces with new ones, and various other tricks. The manager would then reticket the shoes and place them on the racks to be sold again."

Finally, a young woman who worked for three and a half years in a large department store chain in New York observed that once the customers survived the store's elaborate refund labyrinth, the store would accept for refund almost any item, including "pierced earrings and bathing suits," items not normally returnable.

According to staunch supporters of the free market system, economic competition is a universal blessing for consumers. Granted, when the system works according to the textbook model, genuine competition among firms does indeed bring consumers improved products and lower prices. But the cases just cited, however—the refund policy of various clothing stores—illustrate in microcosm that marketplace competition may often be detrimental to the public interest. Each store in the foregoing discussion competes with other stores for public favor. A store's image is enhanced by a lenient refund policy. No store can control the refund policy of any other, and thus competition in "service" escalates beyond the bounds of public welfare, ultimately leading stores to accept for return items which, for reasons of public health, should not be returned.

Examples abound demonstrating that competition among businesses often runs counter to the public interest. Frequently, in fact, a kind of Gresham's Law of competition takes over, in which bad competitive practices drive out good and ironically, sometimes companies compete to bring us the worst possible products and services.[14]

After World War II, when the U.S. automobile industry had successfully hooked Americans on speed and power, each manufacturer attempted to outdo the others in an unbridled horsepower race. There was a method to their madness, for the Detroit equation was: big car, big profit; small car, small profit. But ultimately, as each manufacturer attempted to surpass the others in producing bigger and more powerful cars, the situation escalated out of control. The result: a generation of road locomotives and automotive behemoths that bore no relation to public need and environmental realities. As one writer observed, postwar competition in the U.S. auto industry ultimately led to an absurd and utterly wasteful situation where Detroit was selling a 5,000-pound car to a 100-pound woman so she could drive one block to buy a one-pound loaf of bread. Such were the "efficiencies" of competition in the auto industry. Only the energy crisis of the early 1970s brought some sanity to the industry. But after decades of building huge gas guzzlers, Detroit had no experience designing sane, small cars, a fact which continues to explain the U.S. competitive disadvantage in small car production.[15]

For years the most popular fast-food chains in the United

States, which feed tens of millions of people every day, have
used highly saturated beef tallow for cooking and frying.
They have done so partly because it is cheaper than vegetable
oil, partly because the public had gotten used to it and each
chain was afraid to switch lest it lose sales to the others. So
much for competition. Only considerable publicity and public pressure in the mid-1980s convinced some to change their
practices.

Why are so many long-distance trucks rolling time bombs
on the highway? When the trucking industry was deregulated
to achieve the benefits of competition, the ensuing competitive struggle meant that only those truckers who could lower
their costs would survive. One effective way to lower costs is
to cut corners on safety and maintenance. Random roadside
inspections since deregulation have shown predictably high
rates of defective brakes, faulty steering, and dangerously
worn tires. In one national inspection during the mid-1980s,
30 percent of all trucks inspected were found unsafe and ordered off the highway; in New York and Connecticut, some
60 percent were ordered off the road.[16] In this competitive
environment, moreover, only those truck drivers willing to
push themselves—or be pushed—beyond fatigue to exhaustion
on the highway can survive and prosper.

Many airline passengers are getting edgy these days as
the intense competition in the deregulated airline industry
has forced each carrier to cut costs to the bone, adversely af-
fecting service, employee morale, maintenance, and possibly
safety. The competition encouraged under deregulation is
ironically creating greater concentration in the industry, as
those airlines which fail to cut wages and other costs sufficiently are being "merged, purged, or submerged." Shortly
before deregulation, the eight largest airlines accounted for
81 percent of the market. After a little more than a decade of
deregulation, the eight largest carriers control 95 percent of
the market. More important, many cities are now dominated
by one or two airlines, creating near-monopoly conditions.

Naturally, as oligopoly emerges from competition, air fares are beginning to rise.[17]

The chief benefit of deregulation is that it is becoming a contemporary case study of the potential for chaos when the free market is allowed to operate in its pure form and according to its own competitive logic. This new laissez-faire policy provides an ongoing object lesson demonstrating why regulation was necessary in the first place.

Why is commercial television still the "vast waste land" it was called a generation ago? Because competition in the context of mass culture is a perfect prescription for low-grade programming. All networks compete for the largest possible audience; the larger the audience, the greater the advertising revenue. And the formula for getting the largest possible audience is usually lowest common denominator programming. In the perpetual competition for viewers, there is relentless pressure to turn T.V. news into entertainment and entertainment into kitsch.

In New York City, 3,500 tow trucks prowl city streets waiting for accidents. According to the rules of this competitive game, the first tow truck at an accident gets the business. Hence, these radio-equipped trucks race to the scene of every accident in order to beat their competitors, creating a situation that caricatures the potential anarchy of market competition. In the three years between 1984 and 1987, tow trucks speeding to accidents were themselves involved in some 1,200 collisions causing 800 injuries and seven deaths. A classic example of Gresham's Law of competition.

Many workers in our study wrote of the deleterious effects of competition on the public. One, for example, worked as a waiter in an East Side coffee shop, an area where rents are high and competition for lunchtime trade is intense. To draw customers, the owner had to keep prices and thus costs low, a task he accomplished by wholesale deceptions on the menu. Orange juice described on the menu as "freshly squeezed" comes out of a carton. "Fresh, homemade soup" is

Campbell's. "Grade A Extra Large Eggs" are in reality medium. Canned fruit salad is billed as fresh. And a cheaper brand of cola syrup masquerades as Coke. Why these substitutions? Competition, which, according to the theory of the market system, is supposed to benefit the consumer actually harms him. Many of these shortcuts and deceptions are necessary in order to save money. If the owner didn't use cheaper substitutions, his prices would go up and his customers might go elsewhere. As the waiter in this restaurant writes, "Located in a competitive area, the restaurant has to employ these tactics to survive in this environment."

SOMETHING ISN'T KOSHER

Buying kosher food is a matter of faith in more ways than one. First, for Jews, kosher food is an expression of religious belief. But second, in a complex society where the production and preparation of food are increasingly separated from its consumption, the buyer of kosher food has faith that food advertised as kosher is in fact kosher, that is, has been prepared according to specific dietary laws and has passed inspection by the appropriate religious authorities. Those who have worked around kosher food often testify that this faith is unwarranted.

Because the Jewish population of New York is so large, a great many establishments serve or sell kosher food. About a dozen writers in our study worked for businesses that claimed to observe Jewish dietary laws, including butcher shops, a "kosher 'haute cuisine' caterer," a supermarket delicatessen, small grocery stores, two kosher resort hotels, and a nursing home. Of these dozen establishments, no more than two or three were kosher in fact as well as in name. The others, while maintaining a frontstage kosher appearance, consciously violated Jewish dietary laws and concealed it from their customers. After hours in a kosher delicatessen, for example, when no customers were present, workers sliced both kosher and non-kosher meats on the same slicer (a violation). In a kosher hotel, kitchen workers used regular dishes instead of special dishes during Passover if the hotel was crowded, used non-kosher dairy food which was cheaper, and mixed meat and dairy utensils in the kitchen (all violations).

The owner of one small grocery store was particularly resourceful in creating instant kosher foods. A cashier in his store recalls, "I can remember one year during Passover (when Jews can only eat food marked Kosher for Passover), all the cashiers had to stay and work overtime. The reason was so we could stick labels marked 'Kosher for Passover' on all the dairy products in the refrigerator. You see, 'Kosher-for-Passover' stickers are easily attainable by many merchants. To many people it may not seem so terrible, but to a religious Jewish person it is. It's sad to think how the public was so easily deceived." Apparently, selling non-kosher food as kosher is not limited to New York City. In the late 1980s, a Chicago judge ordered a nationwide recall of up to 376,000 pounds of poultry by a food company that had mislabeled its products as kosher.[18]

One of our writers worked as the maître d' at a catering hall that was advertised as strictly kosher. Yet he writes that he came to work one morning "only to be greeted by the scent of bacon and eggs frying on the stove, which obviously does not qualify as being kosher. If food is prepared on a stove which prepared unkosher food, the food is no longer kosher."

The most thoroughgoing violation of dietary observances occurred in a nursing home where one woman worked for two years. She reported many abuses in the operation of this "senior citizens' hotel," including neglect of patients and gross contradictions between the glamorous ads for the home and the actual state of physical disrepair. Knowledgeable in the laws of kashrut (Jewish dietary laws), the worker claimed that the home's most egregious deceptions occurred in the dining room. She writes that the home is "advertised as strictly kosher. Though most of the 190 guests don't care, there are about 40 or 50 who do. And certainly to most of the staff who eat there, it matters very much. Being pretty well-versed in the laws of kashrut, management has no excuse for letting things go as they do. They hire waiters who have no knowledge of the laws of kashrut, and in the kitchen the laws of the Sabbath are not observed. The food that comes in is not checked carefully, and the division between meat and dairy is not sufficiently observed. Indeed, there is not a *mashgiah* [a rabbi who certifies products as kosher] present and there should be one at all times. For Passover, when there should be a thorough cleaning and a special set of dishes and silverware, no such provisions are made. Of the three cooks, only one knows the laws well. . . . The old people involved are not able to understand or change these things, and they are successfully hidden from those outside."

These violations of dietary laws are not only more widespread than elsewhere, but are more callous, as they involve the aged, many of whom are near death and for whom religious observance, at this stage of their lives, is probably more important than for their children or grandchildren shopping at the local deli or vacationing at a resort hotel.

CHAPTER 9

Petty Bourgeois Tricks

GOING OUT for *BUSINESS*

Sign in the window of a
New York City shoe store

Although novelists from Balzac to Bernard Malamud have
given us vivid fictional portraits of petty bourgeois life, undoubtedly it is C. Wright Mills who, in our generation, has
written the most sensitive sociological account of the struggle
of the lower-middle-class businessman to survive. In *White
Collar,* Mills captures the dreariness of the "lumpen-bour-
geoisie," the midget entrepreneur who employs few workers
but sweats himself and his family year after year, struggling
to establish a secure economic foothold. Buffeted by forces he
can neither understand nor control, fenced in and pushed
around by big business, big labor, and big government, he is
so preoccupied with the scramble for gain that the pecuniary
motive infects every nook and cranny of his life, and he makes
his way by a combination of overwork and petty cost-cutting.
According to Mills, the social psychology of the lumpen bourgeoisie is shaped by their economic condition: "The whole
force of their nature is brought to bear upon trivial affairs
which absorb their attention and shape their character."[1]
Standing in the shadow of mighty conglomerates and multi-
national giants, the lumpen bourgeoisie is a frail twentieth-
century remnant of the old nineteenth-century American

144

hero, the self-reliant businessman confidently striding across economic frontiers.

Many of our informants worked for such tiny business-men, and the kinds of deceptions they practiced reflected the smallness of their business operations and the pettiness of their calculations. Petty bourgeois deceptions were generally designed either to: (1) cheat the customers in order to make or save minuscule amounts of money; or (2) give customers an exaggerated impression of the size and importance of the business.

The owner of a tiny sandwich shop in New York, for ex-ample, had learned to apply the maxim "waste not, want not" possibly at the expense of his customers' health. A counter man in the little shop explains: "Many of our customers would have a soda with their sandwich. A small cup of soda cost the customer 55 cents and a large is 75 cents. The 55-cent soda costs my boss 4 cents for the syrup and 5 cents for the paper cup; the carbonated water is produced by the fountain. So on a 55-cent Coke, my boss would make 46 cents profit. So, you say, what's wrong with that? Well, very often my boss would pick up the used paper cups that the customers left, bring them to the back of the store, and quickly rinse them out and serve them to the next customer."

One young woman, a cashier in a tiny grocery store in the Bronx, offers a humorous account of this hole-in-the-wall enterprise. She worked all day Sunday, when the owner's fifteen-year-old son gave his father a day off and played man-ager, ordering about both the elderly man who serviced the deli counter and the informant herself. This worker's de-scription of the store made it apparent that the boss's son had so prematurely internalized all the angles of petty bourgeois proprietorship that at age fifteen he was already a middle-aged cynic.

She writes of him: "I find Barney's way of manipulating customers quite obvious. When he weighs their appetizing order, he never fails to say, 'Is it okay if it's a little bit over?'

Some of the regular customers joke about his actions, but I can definitely see a customer being turned off to the whole situation. . . . When Barney brings out the days-old bagels from the basement he has to constantly remind me to try to push them off as being fresh. In other words, when the customers inquire, tell them that they are fresh. . . . One Sunday we hadn't received any of the magazine sections for the *New York Daily News.* Barney, knowing my tendency to be honest, insisted that I not inform the customers about the incomplete papers. . . . When we began selling caramel apples, Barney felt the urge to pick off some of the nuts and caramel. Obviously it was more fun than just tearing into a bag of peanuts or even eating his own apple; and, according to Barney, why should he waste his father's money by opening a package when the customer doesn't know what is taken from him. 'The customer buys it only if he wants it,' says Barney."

Ruthie, the young daughter of the co-owner of the store, escalated Barney's caramel apple ploy into what might be called the glazed doughnut gambit. Ruthie works as a part-time cashier after school during the week. According to our informant, Ruthie is friendly and courteous, a likable person, "but would her customers be fond of her if they knew her doughnut trick? Being weight conscious, Ruthie tries to keep her distance from all the delectable items in the store. Characteristic of many of the females that I know, myself included, she has a tendency to pick at certain foods. In other words, when Ruthie feels like eating chocolate, she will pick off the chocolate from the newly arrived doughnuts. I have been told by Barney that at times she licks the chocolate off, only to pass the doughnuts off as being glazed. Little do the customers know what the doughnuts are being glazed with."

Another writer worked for over a year as a secretary in a very small radio and television firm that solicits advertising for the stations it represents. The company acts as a middleman between the stations and the advertising agencies that seek to place commercials for their clients.

While most important media representative firms have many salespeople, this particular company was a tiny two-man operation that tried to pass itself off by mail and over the telephone as a big business. These delusions of grandeur backfired on at least one occasion. The informant writes: "My boss took one man from a radio station out to lunch to discuss representing the man's station. He thought the man had to catch a plane back home the next day, so he really laid it on, telling him we had five salesmen and many other untruths. Later that afternoon the man called up and told Jimmy [the boss] that he was not leaving until late the next day and that he wanted to stop up to the office and meet with all the salespeople. Naturally, there was nothing to do but find people who could pretend, so Jimmy had his brother, an accountant, come in, as well as his brother-in-law, a caterer, and a cousin, a former buyer for a department store. I must say it was rather an amusing situation."

Small businessmen frequently try to inflate the size and importance of their business to impress customers. One worker, for example, was employed by a CPA in Queens. She relates a typical incident: "I'll never forget the time a client called and wanted to check on something in his return which he had brought in the day before. One of the women who worked there used to bring a lot of the unfinished work home to complete, and that was where this particular client's file was at the time. I told the boss about it while asking the client to hold on. The boss said, 'Tell him his return was sent to our other office to be completed, so we can't refer to it at the moment.' Little did this man know that the 'other office' was an employee's living room."

Petty cost-cutting is endemic to small business operations, as, for example, in the case of the radio and T.V. company mentioned above. The owner cut costs in every conceivable fashion, for instance, by using office supplies that were unwittingly supplied by the New York Board of Education. "The boss rarely paid for office supplies," writes our informant. "His mother ripped off everything from paper clips to carbon paper from the school she worked in. It surprised me that we didn't get a typewriter from her." Though the boss couldn't get typewriters from his mother's school, he nonetheless discovered an equally effective angle. The worker explains: "While we're on the subject of typewriters, I must tell you that we had free use of various typewriters for approximately ten months. Jimmy would have me call up a typewriter company and tell them we might want to purchase one and that we would like to try it out for a while. After we had the typewriter for either a few days or a few weeks, the salesman would call back to find out if we wanted to purchase it. I would have to stall by saying either that the girl who uses it has been out sick or that the man who makes the decisions isn't in or that I haven't had enough time to get used to it. In this way we had each typewriter for a minimum of two weeks and sometimes as long as two months."

Another small firm also made good use of other people's property. This firm sold and rented closed-circuit television systems to department stores, hospitals, and factories and also serviced the equipment. When customers brought the equipment in for repair, the company kept it a bit longer than necessary. A bookkeeper for the company explains why. "When we get equipment for repair, we repair it but delay informing the customer that it's ready. We tell them, 'Oh, we're waiting for a part from the manufacturer and it will be another two weeks.' Meanwhile, we use their equipment for rentals or as loaner equipment."

A young woman who worked for several years at a small summer camp in upstate New York reveals how the owner saved money on food for the campers. "I think that parents of the campers would be shocked if they knew where [the owner] gets some of the camp food. Every so often in the middle of the night [the owner] gets into his truck and drives all the way into the city where he stops at a little secluded church. He drives around back and in the pitch black of night he loads cartons and cartons of food onto the truck. The food is donated to the church expressly for distribution to the needy, but the church sells it to him highly discounted. Therefore, the church makes money and [the owner] saves money!"

In another petty attempt to save money, the owners of a very small resort hotel in the Catskills so sharply limited the number of sheets, pillowcases, blankets, bedspreads, and towels they stocked that they simply didn't have enough to go around. A chambermaid in this hotel reports a constant merry-go-round game of musical beds, as rooms were made and then unmade, bedding shifted to rooms where persons were checking in and to those long-term residents demanding a change, inventing excuses why the bedding was not fresh, stalling guests, shifting them about, and generally borrowing from Peter to pay Paul. And just as the linen was frantically shifted about to try to please as many guests as possible with a minimum of inventory, so employees, never adequate in numbers or training, were regularly rotated on an ad hoc basis. To save money on a lifeguard's salary, other employees were given lifeguard duty on a rotating basis, regardless of swimming ability, chambermaids were occasionally asked to work as bellhops, and so on.

Other small enterprises also engaged in a miscellaneous array of practices to save or make insignificant amounts of money. One worker employed at a small independent variety store reported that "if any products come with free samples or bonus articles attached, they are removed if possible and sold separately." This is commonly reported in drug and variety stores.

Many small stores also squeeze a little extra profit out of manufacturers' incentives. It is not only consumers who eagerly cut out coupons from the Sunday newspaper for redemption; some small businessmen do the same. According to a clerk in a local pharmacy, coupon-clipping is an easy, albeit illicit, way for small merchants to make a little extra money. The clerk explains the scheme in general and describes how his employer worked it. "Owners of drugstores and supermarkets can easily cut out coupons for products they sell and then claim they received them from customers. Because the manufacturers have no real way of checking this, many small businesses can, without any difficulty, make hundreds of extra dollars annually. Although some companies will ask to see register receipts as proof, this can be easily overcome by 'fixing' the register tape. Since the owners of the store where I worked saw how easily they could make this money, they would often get carried away and buy twenty *Daily News* on a given day when coupons were plentiful. Sunday is a great day for coupons, and since buying twenty Sunday papers can be a bit expensive, the pharmacist would go to the corner candy store and offer the owners a small gift in exchange for these leftover papers. My job would be to rake through these papers and cut out all the appropriate coupons. This is an extremely boring and tedious job, but to the pharmacists it is quite essential."

A clerk in the cosmetics and drug department of a store in Brooklyn claimed that used merchandise was sold as new: "Sometimes children who roam around the department while their parents are shopping will spray aerosol cans and shaving cream all over the place. Customers don't really know how much they're getting in these cans, so what the stock boys do is wash them off and put them out again when they restock the shelves. If you buy a can of shaving cream that usually lasts you three weeks and you use it up in one, it's probably because it was used when you bought it."

Sometimes, however, the gremlins who deplete the merchandise are not children, but, as with Barney and Ruthie above, the employer or his employees. Several employees of small retail stores reported that workers used products off the shelves and then sold the unused portions to unsuspecting customers. A clerk in a small drugstore in Queens, for example, reported that the salespeople regularly used the stock and replaced it on the shelves to be sold as new. She writes that "All the help there used the merchandise at their convenience. The women used the nail polish, sprayed the hair sprays, and wore the perfume. The men also used any items which could not be visibly detected. If anyone got a cut, they used the iodine or Merthiolate and put it back on the shelf."

A supermarket worker reported that employees in his store devised similar self-help activities. "In the summer," he writes, "some of the employees would come back from the beach, use the shampoo, and then put it back on the shelf. When leaving the store they might take the deodorant off the shelf, use it, and then return it to its former position." An assistant manager in the same store apparently subscribed to the adage that half a loaf is better than none, for the worker reveals that "he would remove bread from the shelf, take a few slices out of a loaf for a sandwich or two, and then put the rest of the loaf back on the shelf and sell it at the regular price. He used to say, 'Nobody will notice that there are a couple of slices missing.' "

Similarly, in a small clothing store a worker reported that one of the three saleswomen, who was dubbed the assistant manager, appropriated stock for her own personal use: "When the assistant manager needed a new outfit, she would take home something new from the store, wear it, and bring it back when she no longer needed it. Then it was sold as brand new."

Of course, it is not only in petty bourgeois operations that merchandise is used by employees and then sold as new. During the 1980s, Chrysler Corporation employees disconnected odometers on tens of thousands of new cars and appropriated the cars for their own personal use for weeks or even months. Then Chrysler sold them to dealers as new cars, including many that had been damaged and repaired.[2]

Generally speaking, however, small-time business generates small-time swindles, as illustrated by a worker in a little variety and knick-knack store. Two salesmen worked out a simple scam to defraud naïve customers. One salesman pretended to be a little deaf. The worker describes how the scam operated. "One salesman wore a hearing aid and the other one did not. The salesman actually did not need the aid, it was just a gimmick to fool the unsuspecting public. They had a special plan. There was certain merchandise in the store that was not price-marked. When a customer came into the store and requested the price of an item, one of the men quoted a price, e.g., $33. The salesman then asked the man who was supposedly hard of hearing for corroboration of the price. This man in turn said, 'Yes, $23,' pretending he couldn't hear the first price quoted. The customer got the item for $23 and felt he was getting a bargain. In actuality, the merchandise really sold for, say, $17, and the salesmen split the extra money between them."

SMALL BUSINESS: PHONY REPAIRS, ADJUSTMENTS, AND SERVICES

Workers reported a wide range of imaginatively phony repairs, adjustments, and services piously offered to customers. A shoe salesman cited the case of a woman who came in to complain that the dye from the shoes she had just bought was coming off on her stockings. So, with the customer standing there, the manager told the salesman to write up a repair slip with the instruction: "Undye." Naturally, the shoes were never sent out for "undyeing" and remained on the shelf until the woman came to pick them up. She never brought them back, so either the treatment was effective or she just gave up.

A women's clothing store in Queens made equally illusory "styling" adjustments, according to a saleswoman. She writes: "Our specialty in the art of deception is called 'styling.' Styling is the simple practice of changing sizes. For example, if a customer comes over to the desk with a size small blouse and asks to see it in a medium, we would take the small to the back room and change the ticket to a medium, knowing we didn't have any mediums in stock. We even had a 'styling desk' set up in the back for just this purpose. However, there were times when we didn't want to be bothered changing the size, so we just gave the usual rap, 'This particular style runs very large.' In most cases we made the sale this way."

A salesman in a men's clothing store told a similar story of phony adjustments. The tailor shop in the back was the setting for a wide variety of deceptions, including one that might be termed the "alteration shortcut." On one occasion the salesman sold a suit to a customer, but the pants had to be lengthened. The customer needed the suit that evening, so the tailor told him he would do the alteration that afternoon and the customer could pick up the suit later that day.

After the customer left, "what the tailor did was hard to believe. He took a stretcher that he used in his work and stretched the bottom of the pants. He told me he was not going to let the length down; he did not like the particular customer and couldn't care less." But the tailor didn't reserve this technique just for customers he disliked; the salesman was often in the tailor shop getting merchandise for customers or "hiding from the boss" and had ample opportunity to observe the tailor at work. He writes that the tailor would "administer the same procedure on suits or sports jackets that needed additional lengthening after the initial alteration. There were other times when he would not do a particular alteration and the customer would not even notice it. What really hurt me inside with all these tricks of the trade and deceptions was that the employer was aware of most of them. Sometimes, he himself would go into the tailor shop and direct the tailor to cover up a mistake on a garment rather than do it the proper way."

Finally, a worker employed by a local veterinarian reported a number of petty bourgeois tricks designed to cut costs, cheat customers, and increase profits. The worker first describes the veterinarian's arithmetic. "When the doctor had me fill the bottles of medicine in the morning, he told me to fill them with ten pills, twenty pills, or in some cases ninety pills. He told the customers, however, that the bottles contained a dozen, two dozen, or one hundred pills, respectively, and he would charge for that amount. Surprisingly, quite a few people found the mistake with the ten and twenty pills and came back. I, of course, would tell the doctor and he would come out and apologize for the 'mistake.'* People believed him because he was the doctor and it was only a matter of a couple of pills and the doctor did seem very sincere. He made money on the one hundred pills, however, because no one seemed to keep track of such a large number." The worker also claimed that often the doctor would prescribe and charge for expensive medicines, but then would instruct the assistant to fill the medicine bottle with ordinary vitamins.

When the doctor's treatment was unsuccessful and the animals died, the vet often worked another, more cynical, deception on his customers concerning the disposition of deceased pets. "When I worked there," the worker writes, "many times the people would request that their dogs be buried at a local pet cemetery. There was an additional charge for this, a minimum of $60. From what I saw, 100 percent of the time this did not happen. The doctor took the money but he didn't send the pet off to be buried; he put the dead animals into large cartons with the other dead pets and the private sanitation department picked up the carcasses every morning. The sanitation company only charged a minimal fee compared to the fee the doctor had taken, so the profit was large."

---

* Here, as in many other cases cited earlier, unsuccessful attempts to defraud the public are immediately called "mistakes."

A POTPOURRI OF UNSAVORY PRACTICES

Bribery

Allegations of bribery were widespread in the essays. Several restaurant and supermarket workers reported—some based on direct observations, others stating with certainty but without giving the source of their information—that inspectors had been bribed to approve facilities that probably should not have been passed. A clerk who worked in a New York delicatessen in the 1970s noted that police from the local precinct came into his store and other stores in the neighborhood each holiday season for their annual "Christmas present." A number of workers for garment manufacturers alleged that buyers were commonly bribed.

The New York City construction industry is renowned for rampant corruption and has been for decades.[3] Corruption in the industry runs the gamut from labor racketeering to buying of political influence, bid-rigging, and extortion. In our study, four workers employed by four different construction companies each alleged that bribery of city inspectors, police, or union officials was commonplace. One worker, for example, was a relative of the owner of one construction company and had worked for him for three years in the early 1970s. He explained that "before any construction job is completed it must first be inspected and approved by the proper city inspector who testifies to its safety. If the job is not approved, it must be ripped up and redone—a great loss to the company. From my experience I have found out that a job can be of the highest quality and not pass inspection if the inspector is not 'rewarded' for his time. On the other hand, a poor, unsafe job can fly by with an 'A' rating just for the sole reason that an inspector has been 'justly rewarded.' The crucial point here lies in the fact that a poor construction job which has been approved results in a public hazard."

He then reports a practice that was described in detail by the Knapp Commission, which investigated police corruption in New York City in the 1970s. All construction jobs require permits, which are "under the jurisdiction of the police department. All permits state that sidewalks and roads cannot be blocked. However, because of the very nature of the job itself, this is an understandable impossibility—loading and unloading materials, tools, concrete, etc. As a result, when it comes to this provision, all construction teams deviate from the rules of the permits. A simple, unrealistic law is broken; and if you want to keep your job in operation, a 'donation' to the police is required."

Another informant worked in the 1970s as a laborer and carpenter's helper for a construction company. The worker alleged that for the right price inspectors "can be bought off and will overlook some discrepancies or shortcuts." Bribery of inspectors had become so institutionalized by the 1970s, according to this worker, that there was an "official" price list; various violations would be overlooked for a specified sum. "For about $25 an inspector will let you patch up a hole in a plaster wall with newspaper instead of wire lath. For $75 you can throw rubbish out of the window instead of chuting or carrying it down."

A woman who worked for five years in the 1970s as a secretary for a housing builder and developer alleged that payoffs were part of the initial costs of doing business. She noted that the first time the company built a housing development, her boss "refused to pay off any of the inspectors or union officials, and as a consequence the job was completely shut down. Not until each one received his envelope did it reopen. As an inspector is needed at many stages in the process of construction, 'envelope time' came often. These charges had to be figured in to costs as well, and so the customer also felt the pinch in the form of rising prices."

Racism

Several workers mentioned racist policies at work, either in hiring minority workers or in servicing minority customers, and although discrimination is not, strictly speaking, business deception, it is unlawful and hence relevant here. One young man observed what appeared to be discrimination at the employment office of a well-known restaurant chain where he applied for work. He writes, "Most of the people waiting ahead of me on line were either black or Puerto Rican, and they were told the only openings were for porters and busboys. But when I, a white, got to the window, I was told I could have a clerk's job in a restaurant on the Upper East side. And though I noticed the sign on the wall, 'An Equal Opportunity Employer,' I took the unequal opportunity."

Another worker employed at a drive-in restaurant observed a similar situation. He writes, "Although the restaurant claims to be an equal opportunity employer, the truth of the matter is there are only three blacks working there. One is a large man of about forty who is the restaurant's private policeman. The other two are men who sweep the floors after the restaurant is closed. Never has the management trusted a black man behind the counter, working with the cash register."

A clerk in a small pharmacy in Brooklyn described his boss's attitude toward minority customers: "This drugstore was the epitome of racism. The store's secret motto was, 'If a customer is colored, whatever they want we don't have it.' There are a great many Spanish-speaking people in my neighborhood, and when they came into the store and knew little English, my boss would not have the patience to try to understand what they wanted."

Finally, one worker wrote of his experience in a Wall Street area employment agency, where he worked interviewing job applicants. His essay was straightforward, revealing no particular dishonesty in the firm, and he wrote mainly about the techniques of making quick, perceptive inferences about job applicants, how to conduct an "exit interview" with someone obviously unqualified, and the like. Some time after writing his essay, he came to my office and said there was one company practice he had hesitated to reveal but which he wanted to mention. He said that when a black applicant was present in the office, the agency used a simple code when speaking to a prospective employer on the phone to convey that the applicant was black. The employment agent might phone an employer and remark toward the beginning of the conversation, "We have a *new applicant* here." As arranged beforehand, this was the code for blacks. The employer could then say the job was filled without fear that this violation of fair employment laws would be recognized.

Passing Counterfeit Bills

One might not be surprised to learn that a small business of dubious reputation occasionally passed counterfeit bills to hapless customers. This, in fact, was reported by a worker at a Long Island retail store that handled cheap, imported goods.

What is more astonishing, however, is that in the shoe department of one of the country's most illustrious women's shops, it was store policy that cashiers were to pass on to customers whatever counterfeit bills they accidentally received. At one period, according to the writer who had worked as a part-time cashier in the store for two years, the store found itself receiving a great many counterfeit bills. The firm called in the FBI, which questioned the regular cashiers and a few of the salesmen. "After the investigation died down," she reports, "I was informed to check for counterfeit bills, and if we do get stuck with one, not to let it get down to the security office—in other words, I am to give it to a customer as change."

"Ecopornography" is the term once given to that genre of advertising in which companies that are major environmental polluters publicize in prose and photograph their efforts to clean up the environment. One writer worked for three years driving a forklift truck at a major company in upstate New York that produced a full line of well-known beverages. In conjunction with two manufacturers of cans and glass bottles, ABC Beverage launched an ecological awareness campaign by embossing environmental hints on can tops and bottle sides. "Unfortunately," according to the worker, "ABC Beverage doesn't practice what it preaches. The company dumps raw waste products directly into the lake on which the company is located. The nature of this waste is decomposed paper labels and caustic acid solution which is used to sterilize returnable bottles."

CHAPTER 10

Honest Business:
Neighborhoods and Saints

Many writers in our study, in fact about 30 percent, reported working for honest businesses. Or, more accurately, 30 percent of our writers said they were *unaware* of any deception in the businesses they worked for; there were undoubtedly many swindles hidden from many workers.

Nonetheless there were in fact a large number of firms workers described as scrupulously honest. How did these firms differ from the dishonest ones? Not coincidentally, honest firms had the opposite characteristics of dishonest firms. Honest businesses, for example, normally do not deal with ignorant or helpless customers, nor with scarce or perishable goods.

Consider the principle of ignorance. While the ignorant customer is easily cheated, the knowledgeable customer rarely is. One writer, for example, worked in a sporting goods store specializing in ski equipment for aficionados. The worker reports that the store rarely cheated its customers, because most of them knew as much about the merchandise as the salespeople. In fact, the private market system can work honestly and efficiently when buyers have what economists call perfect information. The system works as it should, for example, in industries where knowledgeable hobbyists buy specialized products in a competitive market. Firms making the best products at the best price are the most successful because informed customers choose and buy wisely. While the best and most honest firms thrive, the worst and most dishonest die out. The state of the art in such industries advances quickly because alert customers recognize and buy innovative products. This situation is rare, however, for as noted previously, in an economy of increasingly complex products, most consumers are likely to be poorly informed.

Honest businesses have other distinctive characteristics. Some kinds of businesses tend to be honest by default, one might say; they have little or no opportunity to cheat even if they might want to. Criminologist Donald Cressey once noted that illegal behavior is as much a function of opportunity as of desire. Blacks, for example, are rarely convicted of insider trading and stock fraud, not necessarily because they are financially more reliable than whites, but because few blacks are in positions where they could commit these crimes. Likewise, General Motors and Boeing are far less likely than meat packers to violate food and drug laws, simply because they have little opportunity to do so.[1] Honest firms are thus not necessarily more virtuous than dishonest ones; they may just have less opportunity to deceive.

In this study, many businesses were honest by default. Either their product or service was easy for customers to evaluate, or else it was so standardized that no lucrative alterations could be made. One informant, for example, worked in a bowling alley and reported that his employer did not deceive his customers in any way. And indeed, it is difficult to imagine how he might have done so. In a bowling alley, as in so many businesses where customers are not cheated, what the customer sees is what he gets. Another worker, employed by a local printer who printed up wedding announcements, business cards, letterheads, and the like, also reported that customers weren't cheated. Customers can evaluate the product easily: either the printing is done as ordered or it is not; and if it is not, the customer can normally recognize it immediately.

Still another writer worked for a large manufacturer of greeting cards. Although her description of working conditions was reminiscent of the mills of early nineteenth-century England, she could think of no specific way in which the public was deceived. How, in fact, could a greeting card company cheat the public? Consumers can easily judge the product for themselves, and there is virtually no way greeting cards can be defective. Likewise, a worker in a small stationery store in Greenwich Village, which sold the usual array of standard, prepriced stationery products, reported no deceptive practices.

A liquor store clerk reported that, aside from a little exaggeration about having the "lowest prices in town," the store was basically honest, selling standardized bottles of alcoholic beverages. In fact, in a liquor store, the perishability principle applies, only in reverse. Not only does the product not perish over time, but some products, such as wines, may actually become more valuable. Thus there is no particular urgency to get rid of the product as quickly as possible.

Aside from these considerations, one of the most important conditions determining whether a firm is honest is its social setting, specifically whether it is rooted in a close-knit neighborhood or community rather than floating in an impersonal urban sea of strangers.

Generally speaking, when a merchant's business is built on a steady flow of familiar neighborhood customers whose satisfaction spreads the reputation of the firm by word of mouth through the community, he is less likely to cheat than merchants whose business depends on fleeting encounters with strangers. Sociologists use the term *Gemeinschaft* to refer to such neighborhoods and small communities where relationships are based on personal face-to-face association and shared values. A *Gemeinschaft* milieu alone does not absolutely guarantee honesty in the marketplace, however, for in some cases neighborhood businesses deceived their customers, and some businessmen effectively used techniques of pseudofriendliness or pseudo-*Gemeinschaft* to charm their customers while lifting their wallets.*

On the whole, however, a *Gemeinschaft* environment discourages dishonesty, because in a small community or neighborhood a businessman's reputation travels fast. Conventional wisdom has it that small-town businesses are more honest than their big city counterparts, and most evidence confirms this. A study of new car dealers' service departments, for example, found that dealers in small towns performed far fewer unnecessary repairs than dealers in big cities. One consumer advocate in the Midwest said, "In the rural communities a crook is not going to survive."[2] And the owner of an auto repair shop in a tiny Michigan town commented, "Everything here is word of mouth. If you get a bad reputation, no amount of advertising can change it."[3]

A great many of the essays confirmed the importance of neighborhood in discouraging business deception. One young woman worked as a waitress for three years at a small diner on Long Island. Primarily serving people who lived and worked in the area, the restaurant had become an integral part of the community. The waitress testified that the diner served good food from a clean kitchen and at reasonable prices. Her employers were honest with their customers and generous with the community to which they had many social ties. She writes that the owners of the restaurant "would never close the door to the kitchen, and no one would hesitate to walk through the kitchen. The diner never hides anything. Everything is always fresh or thrown away. They never try to sell pastry the next day even though they would be able to. My bosses have always been courteous and honest. They contribute to most functions in the town, such as the fire department, boy scouts, church functions, and sports in the local schools. All the stores in the town patronize each other and the owners are all very good friends."

* On pseudo-*Gemeinschaft*, see p. 199.

The diner had many regular customers who were on friendly terms with the employees. The waitress describes the *Gemeinschaft* atmosphere in the restaurant and its implications for how the restaurant is run. "If a regular customer doesn't come in, I always inquire to make sure everything is O.K. If I won't be working on a Sunday [her regular work day], I always let the customers know it because they too would be concerned. I think it is so important to have a cup of coffee waiting for the customer and a friendly smile because that is more important than money, and my bosses have taught me that in the last three years."

Another writer illustrates the importance of personal relationships with customers. She had worked for three and a half years for an interior design firm in Manhattan that catered to a wealthy clientele. The firm does no advertising, but depends for its business solely upon word of mouth recommendations. The company's relationship with its clientele is continuous, not transient, for often the firm will decorate room by room over a period of years. Relations between the decorators and their customers are often personal, transcending the business relationship. According to the writer, the decorators are frequently invited to their customers' cocktail parties and even to their children's weddings. In such a milieu, obviously, there is strict adherence to ethical standards. The worker writes of the company: "There are very few, if any, tricks of the trade. The firm is noted for being trustworthy and honest, and upholds this position in all transactions. It should be understood that since this firm gets its business through recommendations, such images must be upheld in order to remain in business."

A saleswoman wrote of her experience working for two years in a shoe store in Brooklyn. The owner had been in business for thirty-five years at the same location and had built a neighborhood reputation for reliability. He took an active interest in community affairs, sponsoring such local projects as parades, art exhibits, and Little League baseball, besides contributing substantially to various charities and organizations. He also served as president of the merchant's block association. In the context of this obvious *Gemeinschaft* milieu, it is not surprising that the worker reported no contradiction between what the public observed and what went on behind the scenes. The owner guaranteed his products unconditionally and repaired at his expense any shoes that were defective in material or workmanship. An unsatisfied customer could also get a full refund or exchange any pair of shoes within a reasonable time after purchase.

Another essay described a small men's and boys' clothing store, where the writer was employed part-time: "The store had been in operation about fifty years and through this relatively long period of time had developed a good family trade. I think one of the reasons for this was the open honesty and frankness that everyone who worked there had in their dealings with the customers. We [the employees] were specifically instructed to be honest with the customers."

Still another worker wrote of her experience working in a small housewares and variety store that had been operated by the same proprietor for twenty-five years. Describing the honesty and integrity of the establishment, she writes that in an era of large, impersonal department stores, "this housewares store serves as a link to the past. People enjoy coming into the store just to browse. They know they get what they desire, personal attention. A store like this depends upon its reputation to survive. Customers of twenty-five years still flock to the store, as do the young people in the neighborhood."

Other essays describing a local restaurant, two local liquor stores, a local optometrist—all in business for decades—testify to the same point: the old-fashioned neighborhood has not been excessively romanticized, but does, in fact, exert a significant ethical force on the operation of business enterprise.

If it is true that the small, stable neighborhood is an important restraining force on business fraud, then contemporary social and economic trends do not bode well for the future. The urbanization and metropolitanization of America continues, and rural America continues to wither. Today, over three-quarters of Americans live in metropolitan areas, compared to only about half in 1940. Within the cities themselves the Howard Johnsonization of America proceeds. Large corporate chain stores take over retail activity once dominated by small businesses. Fast food franchises, with their impersonal service and rapid employee turnover, blanket the landscape, homogenizing communities and whole cities, offering little possibility for the kind of community roots the small independent businessman once provided. Neighborhoods—intimate social and economic networks—disappear, replaced by suburban shopping centers. Young people who once called the familiar neighborhood their home ground now drift and wander about the malls. Stable urban neighborhoods are uprooted by massive population shifts within the city and by large-scale real estate development. Such changes inevitably diminish whatever cohesiveness and community spirit remain in the American city.

There is one final type of honest business that, paradoxically, indicts the market system as much as dishonest business. In a number of cases, writers described the firms for which they worked as scrupulously honest mainly because of the extraordinary integrity and character of the owner. Workers portrayed these businessmen as virtual saints, resisting temptation on all sides to cheat, swindle, shortcut, and maximize profit at their customers' expense. One writer who worked in a fruit and vegetable market wrote an eloquent tribute to his employer's sterling character. The worker writes that his employer could have tampered with his scales to cheat his customers, as did the produce store down the street, but he wouldn't. He could have bought cheaper grapefruit at wholesale and sold it for the same price as the more expensive grapefruit he stocked, but he wouldn't. In fact, the worker argued with his boss, urged him to buy cheaper fruit, told him the customers wouldn't know the difference. But his boss refused, and took pleasure in giving customers better quality produce, even at the cost of reducing his profits.

The message we get in these sorts of accounts is that a businessman's honesty represents an unusual triumph of human integrity, character, and will over the built-in temptations of the system to cut corners and deceive. This is certainly admirable, and these honest men and women are in many ways the heroes of the business system. Their honesty often costs them money. But they nonetheless stand up and assert their freedom *not* to be simple by-products of a system that says buy cheap and sell dear. In short, they assert their free will not to be corrupt.

But while these good deeds say something noble about the character of these individual businessmen, they say something else about the way the market system is set up. In brief, it is that an economy which is arranged so that it requires a saint to be honest is an economy that is going to have a great deal of dishonesty. For most people are not saints, nor can we expect them to be. Neither are most people martyrs, heroes, or idealists. The costs are too high. The heroes are notable because they are unusual. Most people are understandably just trying to get by, trying to pay the bills and meet the financial and material demands of their lives. Most people, therefore, follow the rules of the market game in which they find themselves, and if the rules of the game are such that dishonesty pays, so be it.

In the final chapter, I turn to a general consideration of the rules of the game.

CHAPTER **11**

Morality and the Marketplace

RECAPITULATION: THE PARADOX OF CAPITALISM

Twentieth-century critics of capitalism have directed most of their fire on the system's economic weaknesses rather than on its moral deficiencies. Radical critics have focused on such economic problems of capitalism as inflation and depression, poverty and unemployment, waste and inefficiency, and the general anarchy of production. While some of these problems have moral components, most critics have not gone much beyond their economic significance. In their analysis, furthermore, most radicals have accepted Marx's assumption that capitalism will inevitably fail and have repeatedly predicted that the system cannot long endure. In 1850 Marx gave capitalism a life expectancy of fifty years; subsequent Marxists have been reading from similar actuarial tables. Accordingly, radicals describe our era as one of "late" capitalism, suggesting a system near the end of its time.

It is true that since the inception of capitalism, even the system's most fervent supporters have been alarmed at how unpredictable and unstable the system seems to be, with its disconcerting alternations of boom and bust. Even these ardent admirers have had the uncomfortable feeling that at any moment of crisis capitalism might collapse.

But radical critics have not merely wondered *if* the final cataclysm is coming, but *when*. Like doomsday prophets atop the mountain, they regularly predict the end of the old world,

168

noting this or that sign of impending doom, and the birth of the new. Big trouble is always just around the corner. Each problem becomes a crisis. Each crisis becomes *the* crisis. Thus, an American conservative chided a radical economist for having "predicted twenty-four of the last three recessions."[1] But when the system rides out the storm, as it has managed to do, radical critics must retreat and explain again how the system has been able to escape calamity once more.

More dogmatic Marxist critics have not only forecast a growing crisis of capitalism, but have tried to stay with many of Marx's other predictions—the continuing growth of the working class, its relative or absolute immiseration, increasing working-class consciousness, and the like—forecasts whose relevance and validity seem to be receding as rapidly as the nineteenth century when they were made.

Nowhere is the dual nature of social theory better illustrated than in Marxism. On the one hand, the power of theory lies in its explanatory architecture, its ability to organize and illuminate what previously seemed like random facts, and to bring order out of the chaos of social reality. Marxism has done this. Theory's greatest danger, on the other hand, is that used dogmatically, it becomes a set of blinders, obscuring inconvenient facts and ignoring inconsistent events. Marxism has also done this.

Aside from the arguments about the eventual collapse of capitalism and the destiny of the working class, for generations the central argument of radical critics has been that capitalism could not, over the long haul, solve society's fundamental economic problems—the problems of production and distribution. Whether this is true in the long run no one knows; economists can scarcely predict with any accuracy the state of the economy six months hence. But assessing the question from the perspective of the capitalist world since World War II, it does seem that capitalism in the industrialized countries, aided by enormous strides in technology, great gains in productivity, and decades of welfare state legislation, has in fact been solving the economic problems for most people in most of these countries.

In America, to be sure, the "solution" to the nation's economic problems comes at the price of great enclaves of poverty, great and growing inequality, irrationalities and waste, decay of the public infrastructure, and the decline of urban amenities. Yet such is the wealth and abundance—and easy credit—of the society that even with extraordinary waste and inequality, the economic needs of most people are being adequately met. Capitalism may be unstable and unpredictable, but over time it has proved enormously resilient and adaptable to changing circumstances.

Ironically, then, radical critics of capitalism have directed most of their criticism toward the system's greatest achievement—its ability to produce. At the same time they have given far less attention to the economy's moral foundations which are far shakier. Why this relative neglect of the moral dimensions of capitalism? Compared to the hard political and economic issues, moral questions may seem too softheaded or too self-righteous in an age of moral relativism. Then, also, there is the long shadow of Marx who denounced and ridiculed the moralizers of his day. A contemporary of Marx once commented that "the moment anyone started to talk to Marx about morality, he would roar with laughter." Moralizing can play no role in advancing a science of society, Marx believed, and in fact undermines the enterprise. Moralizing and preaching are useless as instruments of social change; people cannot be shamed into making a revolution. Morality is simply a reflection of changing material conditions and economic relations. And yet, despite his withering criticism of moralizers, Marx was actually, in spite of himself, a great moralizer; his writings burn with outrage at the historic evils and cruelty of capitalism. As historian E. P. Thompson has written, "Marx, in his wrath and compassion, was a moralist in every stroke of his pen."[2]

Because an economy shapes the quality of life in society,

it is important not to overlook the social and moral consequences of an economic system. Here I share the viewpoint
suggested in the U.S. Catholic Bishops' recent pastoral letter
on the American economy: "Every perspective on economic
life that is human, moral, and Christian must be shaped by
two questions: What does the economy do *for* people? What
does it do *to* people?"

The question, then, should not just be whether capitalism works. It does, in its own anarchic way. The question
should not just be whether capitalism is productive. It is, in
its own wasteful way. The important question is one that was
asked centuries ago by the Catholic church and generations
ago by nineteenth-century social critics and early socialists: Is
capitalism moral? What does it do to personal ethics of honesty and integrity? What does it do to human relationships
and to the tenuous ties of human solidarity and community?

In addressing these questions, I want to repeat that central paradox of the private market system mentioned in the
Introduction—the great dual nature of capitalism. On the
one hand, the profit system stimulates ambition, production,
and innovation. On the other hand, it often generates greed,
mendacity, and deception. In any economic system where the
prosperity of the seller depends on how much he can sell and
at how high a price, the seller has enormous built-in incentives to deceive the buyer when it is profitable to do so. As
the workers in this study have amply illustrated, the seller
has a powerful incentive to deceive, because doing so often
brings him greater rewards, and honesty often brings him
fewer. Such are the imperatives of commerce in the private
marketplace.

Needless to say, capitalism has no monopoly on crime
in the workplace. In the Soviet economy, bribery, *blat* (influence), black-market operations, profiteering, and the like
have long been common.[3] While entrenched bureaucracy and
inflexible totalitarian methods obviously play a part, a central factor in Soviet workplace crime is the endless material

shortages that have plagued the Soviet economy for decades. Thus scarcity plays its accustomed role.

In our own study, a number of writers worked in the public sector. Most said their workplace was honest; it is difficult to cheat patrons in the public library, for example.* Several workers, however, had part-time or summer jobs in the city's Parks Department, which has at times been called a model of an ossified government bureaucracy: inefficient, inert, and occasionally corrupt.[4] Our writers observed the following Parks Department practices: (1) workers who stretched thirty-minute lunch breaks into two hours; (2) workers who slept, played cards, or took drugs—all while on city time; (3) workers who arrived very late for work and left very early—and had other workers sign them in and out; (4) supervisors who hired relatives for jobs in the department for which they collected paychecks but who never showed up and in fact held other jobs at the same time; (5) supervisors who did not supervise, who themselves disappeared during the day, and who, by example, contributed to the overall climate of cynicism and futility in the department. As a consequence, many writers reported that actual work accomplished was but a fraction of what might have been done.

Though these practices differ from business deception in the private sector, where people are cheated individually for gain, here the entire public—whose taxes pay the Park Department's budget—is cheated and badly served. Apathy, negligence, and malfeasance are clearly afflictions of the public sector, especially one already demoralized by public indifference and chronic fiscal neglect.

While no economic system has a corner on misbehavior

---

* Although deception of the public was not directly involved, two library workers in two different branches each reported that supervisors occasionally told employees to check out dozens of books and then return them in order to increase the library's circulation figures, which, presumably, would increase the budget of their branch.

in the workplace, my primary focus here is the private market system and the specific pressures for deception built into it. Consider, for example, some of the cases reported earlier. When a customer brings her car with a loose ignition wire into a gas station, why does the owner tell her she needs a new starter? The question is naïve: merely compare the charge for connecting an ignition wire with the charge for replacing—or better yet, painting—a starter. Why does the owner of a fish store sell shredded halibut as crabmeat? Obviously, because halibut is cheaper than crab, his profit is accordingly increased, and if his customer can't tell the difference, so much the better. Why do the caterers we discussed fill name-brand bottles of liquor with cheaper, inferior liquor? Simply because it cuts costs and boosts earnings. Why, in a case not previously discussed, does a garment manufacturer show buyers a garment made of one fabric and then, after an order is placed, instruct the mill to supply the same garment in a cheaper fabric? Because it reduces costs and raises profit margins. Why do so many retail stores mark prices up before marking them down for a sale, thus misleading the public? Obviously, customers are more likely to buy if they feel they are getting a bargain.

Why do supermarkets, in prepackaging fruit, pack spoiling fruit and conceal it from the customers? Clearly, because it raises costs to throw away rotting produce. Why is spoiling meat cosmeticized and sold to the public? Why does a florist spray-paint his dying flowers and pass them off on unsuspecting customers? Why does a veterinarian charge his customers for one hundred pills and then instruct his receptionist to put only ninety pills in the bottle?

We could, of course, go on and on, but the point is clear: in each case, honesty is discouraged because it contradicts the logic of the enterprise; dishonesty is rewarded because it cuts costs or increases earnings. Thus, the built-in pressures of the market system take their toll, and a businessman who starts out with the very best of intentions frequently finds his integrity worn down by the inexorable temptations of the system.

Of course, if this structure of deception operated within the framework of a larger moral order that stressed such values as collective welfare, the social good, and cooperation, then much deception might be inhibited. After all, the 1960s spawned a kind of counterculture capitalism of artisans, craftspeople, and small shopkeepers that was essentially honest because it was based on a moral foundation of communal values, social consciousness, and environmental concern. But the moral order of the larger market system today only reflects and reinforces what occurs in the marketplace itself and overruns moral concerns fostered by the church and other social institutions. A moral order whose central credo is "Take care of number one" is not going to be a restraining force on the pressures for deception built into the system.

Moreover, what all this deception reveals is not that human nature is evil or greed innate, but merely that people behave rationally and logically in response to the imperatives of a system. In a different game with different rules, behavior changes, and what is often assumed to be innate greed may become innate altruism.

Conservatives, of course, disagree. They argue that the ultimate cause of marketplace deception lies not in the larceny in our institutions but in the larceny in our hearts, that marketplace swindles have more to do with evil people than with evil social arrangements. Thus, a contemporary American conservative, discussing the moral transgressions of capitalism, argues in great conservative tradition that "we have to start by accepting the pervasiveness of human corruption and the limitations inherent in all systems."[5] Of course, it is true that we are dealing with human beings in the real world, not angels in heaven, so it makes no sense to argue that people are everywhere pure and good and only corrupted by their institutions. But to explain social evils in terms of the "pervasiveness of human corruption" is too easy; it is at once a sweeping and unverifiable theological indictment, and an apology for contemporary social arrangements. A more sociological and less metaphysical proposition might be that most people have powerful impulses of self-interest and somewhat weaker impulses of altruism. That being so, social institutions can be designed to try to bring self-interest into harmony with public interest, so that the inevitable pursuit of self-interest will yield the common good. On the other hand, institutions can be arranged to set the powerful impulses of self-interest in direct conflict with public interest, so that the pursuit of self-interest will frequently produce antisocial behavior.

A simple illustration: The butcher may put his thumb on the scale while weighing your meat, suggesting "the pervasiveness of human corruption"; but why then will the postal worker most likely *not* put *his* thumb on the scale while weighing your package? The explanation lies not in human nature but in social institutions. The butcher, operating according to the logic of a profit system, may put his thumb on the scale because he may gain personally by doing so, while the postal worker, operating according to the logic of a nonprofit system, gains nothing from the same act and thus has no reason to do so. The culprit, then, is not innate human corruption or even self-interest, but simply the rules of the market system, which often reward people for acting indecently and punish them for acting decently.

Is honesty or dishonesty, then, the natural state of things? It seems reasonable to assume that normal people tend to be honest unless it is in their self-interest to be dishonest. If this is true, then a system in which dishonesty brings no rewards will be a system in which most people will be honest.

Naturally, conflicts between individual self-interest and the larger social interest can never be eliminated altogether, and in the choice between them, most people will most often favor themselves. But the moral defect of our economic system, as Einstein noted in a classic essay, is that capitalism takes a person's egoistic drives, which are already stronger by nature, and gives them additional social sanction and encouragement, while a person's social and altruistic drives, which are weaker by nature, are neglected and allowed to deteriorate.[6]

While conservatives blame social evils on the eternal corruption of the human soul, liberals are more optimistic and place greater faith in people's ability to improve themselves and their institutions. Education is one of the most popular liberal remedies for a variety of social ills. So, in the wake of the extraordinary insider trading scandals of the 1980s, many suggested, as one approach, more ethics courses in our business schools. A former chairman of the Securities and Exchange Commission donated millions of dollars to the Harvard Business School for a program in ethics, and many other business schools strengthened their ethics course offerings. Although well-intentioned, this remedy rests on the dubious assumption that the reason people lie, cheat, and steal is because they never learned in school that it was wrong. Moreover, the problem with trying to prevent business crime by teaching ethics courses in college is that there are many forms of education besides what goes on in the classroom. An economic system that day after day demonstrates that deception can be made to pay is likely to be a far more effective teaching instrument than a few abstract lessons taught in the classroom.

Aside from liberals and conservatives, moralists often blame social evils on individuals who simply choose to behave badly in a world of free choice. Orwell, for example, once characterized Charles Dickens's moral vision of evil in nineteenth-century England as follows: "If men would behave decently, the world would be decent." While that is obviously true, it places responsibility for an indecent world solely on people freely choosing to behave badly, regardless of the weight and influence of the institutions bearing down on them. Certainly Dickens's vision is an accurate moral judgment; people may choose to behave decently regardless of the larger circumstances and pressures acting on them. Yet it is a naïve sociological judgment, for it neglects the ways in which the pressure of institutions, the rules of the game, and the logic of the system inevitably shape ordinary people's behavior.

Take an example from the American marketplace: a new car dealer's service department. When a customer brings his car in for repairs, the person he sees is the service writer, the familiar man in the white smock with a clipboard who writes up the work order. Service writers are renowned for talking customers into more repairs than they need. Does this demonstrate a kind of basic human corruption or indecency? There is a simpler explanation. In most dealerships, the service writer is paid partly on commission; the more repairs he sells the customer, the higher his own income. Is it any wonder then he tries to sell customers unnecessary repairs? How could it be otherwise? Self-interest has been set up in direct conflict with the public interest. The service writer is not inherently corrupt, but it's likely that the system has corrupted him.

CONSUMER COOPERATIVES: ALTERNATIVE TO THE PREDATORY MARKETPLACE

Consider another example. Compare two pharmacists and how they dispense over-the-counter medication. The first is a self-employed businessman whose income depends on maximizing sales. We encountered this pharmacist in Chapter 4, when a drugstore worker described how the pharmacist made extra money when doctors wrote out prescriptions for over-the-counter medications. The worker wrote: "Many items which could be sold over the counter are prescribed by doctors. When the pharmacist receives a prescription from a customer which is for, say, Vitamin 'X', Donnagel, or Emetrol, he sees it as a chance to get more money out of the customer. In my time working in the pharmacy, many liquids, tablets, and capsules have been transferred from their original bottle to a dispenser used only for prescriptions. This way the pharmacist earns that extra profit and the customer is none the wiser. I'm surprised that customers don't look at the prescriptions before they hand them to the pharmacist."

Contrast this now with the practices of a pharmacist working for a nonprofit consumer cooperative. The prime function of consumer cooperatives is to serve the needs of their members, not maximize profits. Employees are on salary and do not gain by cheating customers, and the larger organization itself has no incentive to cheat the customers because the customers collectively own the enterprise and set its policy through their elected representatives on the board of directors. In a news story on the pharmacy at the Consumers Cooperative of Berkeley, California, the resident pharmacist stated his view that "protecting the consumer should be a goal for pharmacists, especially on over-the-counter drugs." He often advises customers not to buy them, for he believes that this saves Co-op members money and is better for them in the long run. Instead, the pharmacist tries to "suggest how customers can heal themselves without the over-the-counter remedies. But if they can't, and they have to have something, I recommend the least noxious remedy and the one I believe is most effective. I try to be more person-oriented than product-oriented." As name-brand prescription drugs are usually much more expensive than their generic equivalents, the Co-op pharmacist says he "always informs patients of the generic alternative, except at times when the cost difference is insignificant or in rare cases where the brand name is known to be more effective."[7]

The Co-op illustration is pertinent here. Adam Smith argued that when everyone pursues his own individual self-interest, the general interest will be served. Ironically, that principle more aptly depicts consumer cooperatives than the private capitalist sector he was purportedly describing. Self-interest in cooperatives does indeed promote the general interest.

When consumers, pursuing their self-interest, own their own supermarket, for example, and run it themselves or through their representatives, it is highly likely that this self-interest will assure quality goods, honest merchandising, fair prices, and, in short, will serve the general interest. Because in this situation one is essentially buying from oneself, ordinary self-interest promotes honest business. This suggests that deception in the marketplace is not an iron law born of some conservative notion of a selfish, weak, or evil human nature, but is a consequence of the design of social and economic institutions.

While in the typical private firm there is a potential conflict of interest between buyers and sellers that frequently leads to deceptive practices, the chief virtue of consumer cooperatives as they have developed over the last century and a half is that there is an inherent identity of interests between buyers and sellers, thus minimizing the incentive for deception.

For this reason, consumer co-ops have generally been able to maintain their social integrity and original cooperative purpose more successfully than have producer-co-ops, that is, enterprises owned and run by workers. Because of the structure of producer cooperatives, their goal can easily drift from cooperative service to profit maximization for the worker/owners at the expense of customers, and thus can fall victim to the predatory practices of ordinary private firms.

Founded during the Great Depression, the Consumers Cooperative of Berkeley has grown to be the largest retail food co-op in the country.[8] At its peak in the 1970s, it operated twelve supermarkets in the San Francisco Bay area, and its flagship store in Berkeley sold more goods per square foot of floor space than any supermarket west of the Mississippi. In its long history, the Berkeley Co-op has launched a wide variety of enterprises besides its supermarkets, including a credit union, a hardware and variety store, gas stations, natural foods stores, delicatessens, bakeries, a wine shop, bookstores, pharmacies, and a travel agency. At its height, Co-op enterprises formed a virtual alternate economy in the Bay area.

For years, the Berkeley Co-op has been a leader in honest merchandising and consumer education. Compare the differences, large and small, between the Co-op and conventional supermarkets. Since 1955, the Berkeley Co-op has had full-time, in-store home economists on staff, providing advice to shoppers on nutrition and food preparation, and arranging informative store displays. The home economists also have input to the Co-op's quality control department and to the buying staff.

The weekly Co-op newsletter mailed to members carries articles on nutrition and health, food economics, and environmental and consumer issues, along with the stores' advertised specials. As far as can be discerned, the Co-op runs no deceptive ads or phony sales. The same cannot be said of conventional supermarkets, if the testimony of our workers and other independent studies are accurate. Many of our supermarket workers reported phony sales in supermarket fliers. And in a study of several conventional supermarkets in one city, researchers found that of all the advertised sales, up to 25 percent of the items actually had not been reduced in price at all.[9]

The Co-op has long been a supporter of truth-in-packaging laws and other consumer and environmental legislation. Their merchandising policy states that they will sell "only the lowest hazard pesticides and/or those known to be non-persistent, in order to protect the health and safety of the community at large." As early as 1975, the Co-op stopped selling aerosol cans with freon propellants, which deplete atmospheric ozone.

The Berkeley Co-op, in 1967, was the first store in the country to adopt unit pricing, enabling shoppers to compare prices on items in a variety of sizes. Unlike the situation in many other stores, larger sized packages are always less expensive per unit than smaller sizes of the same item. Years ago, the Co-op began translating suppliers' dating codes on perishable goods into a form that shoppers could understand. Co-op stores stock Co-op brand food products, which are less expensive than comparable brand-name merchandise because they do not require huge advertising and promotional budgets. Labels on Co-op brand products are straightforward and supply information on ingredients, nutrition, and quality beyond what the government requires. A "Lifeline Foods" program at Co-op stores offers a variety of basic foods on sale each week to help low-income consumers keep their food costs down.

In American supermarkets, front end-aisles are ambiguous territory. According to supermarket culture, most shoppers assume that whatever is stacked up on the front end-aisles is on sale, and managers often pile hundreds of cans, boxes, or bottles there in eye-catching displays and prominently post a price. Many supermarket workers in our study reported, however, that their stores took advantage of the shoppers' assumption and displayed merchandise there at its regular price, intentionally creating the illusion that those products were reduced in price. At Co-op supermarkets, merchandise on the front end-aisles is always genuinely on sale. Moreover, according to Co-op merchandising policy, managers choose sale items for front end-aisles based on quality, value, and nutrition; junk foods, as defined by the store's home economist, are not displayed there.

For years, many Co-op supermarkets had supervised child care "Kiddy Korrals" in the stores where parents could leave their children while shopping. Drugs or vitamins designed to entice children are kept on upper shelves. Cereals are stocked on color-coded shelves that indicate sugar, salt, and fat content. Checkout stands are clear of impulse items, such as cigarettes, gum, and candy. One amusing innovation reveals the Co-op's culture of scrupulous integrity. For a short time, in a burst of consumeristic zeal, the Berkeley Co-op packaged their meat with the good side *down* so shoppers would know exactly what they were getting. Such an oasis of fervent honesty stands in symbolic contrast to the rampant deception chronicled in these pages.

Unlike private supermarkets whose only purpose is to sell merchandise, the Co-op, owned by some 90,000 people in the community, is itself a community institution. The Co-op often sponsors community events and festivals on various themes. And within the framework of the Co-op, there has always been a wide variety of activities for members. At one time or another there has been a Co-op chorus, a baseball team, a camera club, music and dance instruction, a single's group, classes in home decoration, investment advice, foreign languages, and so on.

Consumer cooperatives are important to consider as alternatives to the predatory marketplace, but not as vehicles of fundamental social change. Marx was essentially correct when he argued that because cooperatives normally lie outside the major battlegrounds of political power and exist on the margins of the economy, they play little or no role in transforming society. But he noted that cooperatives are significant, nonetheless, for they can serve as practical working models demonstrating that social and economic alternatives to capitalism are possible. In these already existing forms one can see the future as an embryo in the present. Of cooperative factories in nineteenth-century Europe, for example, Marx wrote that they "represent within the old form the first sprouts of the new."[10]

Consumer cooperatives are extremely weak in America, reflecting the larger failure of communal and socialist forms here. Yet, paradoxically, like many socialist ideas, co-ops embody some of America's most important political and cultural values. Co-ops are decentralist and pluralistic; they are locally controlled; they are voluntaristic; they avoid the bureaucratic rigidities of central control; they are democratic and self-governing in the best American tradition (one member, one vote) and in fact extend political democracy into everyday economic life. In short, they are all-American. The weakness of consumer cooperatives in the United States says more about the economic and ideological strength of capitalism than it does about the incompatibility of co-ops with American values.

SOCIAL CONSEQUENCES OF THE MARKET SYSTEM

> Sometimes I wonder, since this policy of deception works so well in my line of work, am I getting equally deceived in all the financial transactions of my own?
>
> Restaurant waiter's essay

> Oh, them big bugs have bigger bugs
>   That jump on 'em an' bite 'em,
> An' the bigger bugs have other bugs
>   An' so—*ad infinitum.*
>
> WILL STOKES

While economists naturally study the economic effects of the market system, they often completely overlook the social consequences of that system. What, for example, are the social, as opposed to the strictly economic, implications of the so-called law of supply and demand? That law tells us, for instance, that during a power failure the price of flashlights may rise from $2 to $10. While that kind of exchange might be good economics, it is dubious morality. What does the rising price of flashlights during a blackout say about the social relations among citizens in such a system? It seems to say much about the exploitation of weakness and vulnerability and the assertion of power and advantage for personal aggrandizement, and suggests a predatory social as well as economic environment. And what, then, may we reasonably infer about the impact of that predatory relationship on our sense of moral community in city and nation?

In the present frenzied corporate merger and takeover movement, the images and language are clearly those of either a jungle or a society that resembles one. Some favorite terms employed by those on the corporate battlefield: headhunter, hired gun, hostile takeover, takeover by rape, Saturday night special, cyanide pill, hot pursuit, running into flak, siege, throwing up barricades, ambush, shootout, wounded list, pirates, raiders, sharks, shark repellent, big game hunting, mankillers.[11]

Two centuries ago, Adam Smith explained how the private market system works:

> It is not from the benevolence of the butcher, the brewer, or the baker, that we expect our dinner, but from their regards of their own interest. We address ourselves, not to their humanity but to their self-love, and never talk to them of our own necessities but of their advantages.[12]

Now, while that arrangement might make for an efficient *economy*, it does not always make for an enviable *society*. For if the butcher, the brewer, and the baker provide us our dinner only because it serves their interests, self-love, and advantage, you may be assured that when their interests diverge from ours, which, as we have seen, happens often, then we shall all be frequently deceived. True, Adam Smith himself was not particularly enamored of the ethics arising from self-interest, but he believed—erroneously, for the most part— that competition in the marketplace would be sufficient to keep businessmen honest.

Certainly buyers and sellers do have some common harmony of interests; one wants to buy what the other seeks to sell. Yet it is quite obvious that the "social contract" between them repeatedly breaks down and often produces the kinds of tactics the workers in this book have documented at length.

The growth of the welfare state in the last century demonstrates, in fact, that an unregulated market system, existing in its pure form, cannot be counted on to work for the common good. The expansion of the welfare state in advanced capitalist countries is a historic admission that the market system must be constantly watched, monitored, and modified by statute and by regulatory bodies in order to try to keep the system honest, or at least within bounds.

As we have seen in earlier chapters, business deception is not universal; there is enormous variation in its amount and extent. Deception may occur only infrequently and then only marginally in most firms. Yet even if it occurs only occasionally, it acts as a kind of guerrilla warfare against public trust. Repeated deception of consumers in their day-to-day encounters with business firms may be a powerful corrosive force undermining the quality of life in the American city, depleting whatever sense of community, solidarity, and fellowship remains in American society, leaving only such negative social bonds as national chauvinism.

When people are routinely or even occasionally cheated by the auto mechanic, deceived by the T.V. repairman, sold a bill of goods by the furniture salesman, ripped off by the used car dealer, and short-weighted by the butcher, such experiences may erode social cohesion and create a hostile and suspicious mind-set where people expect to be deceived and exploited in many encounters and accordingly respond in kind. Their own moral restraint is loosened by the example of those around them, and public morality declines to the lowest common denominator.

Consider, for example, the *social* implications of the following. An expert on automobile repair rip-offs describes the best strategy for taking a cross-country trip in America.

The first step in protecting yourself on out-of-state trips is to have your car completely inspected before you go and have all needed repairs taken care of. That way, any repair the gas station attendant recommends can be viewed with suspicion.

The next step is never to leave your car unattended in the service area of a gas station and to watch the station employees like a hawk. If the attendant opens your hood or checks your tires, be looking over his shoulder. It's best to use restrooms in restaurants whenever possible so that you don't have to leave your car unattended at a gas station. If you must use a service station restroom, park your car far away from the gas pumps and service bays. To avoid being sold extra oil, keep a rag in your car and check the oil yourself.

If you do get repairs done at an unfamiliar gas station, be sure you get an itemized written estimate, your old parts back and an itemized receipt which clearly identifies the name of the station and its location.[13]

This passage makes it seem that one is traveling in an alien and hostile land, not one's own. The Hobbesian jungle did not have automobiles; aside from that, the similarities between that world and this are striking. Besides what this passage says about auto repair, consider what it says about the level of trust and trustability in this country, and how the need to behave in such a guarded manner in one's own country may undermine a sense of national unity and fellowship.

IN DEFENSE OF CAPITALISM

The problem with the argument made here—that incentives for deception are built into capitalism—is that it runs counter to the generally accepted theory of the market system. That theory has two components. First, a complex capitalist economy does *not* engender deception and distrust, but, on the contrary, actually requires a high level of trust in order to function.

In the haggle of a preindustrial bazaar, the seller gets as much as he can for his goods, regardless of their quality, and then disappears. A modern economy functions very differently, so the argument does. Modern business depends on long-term contracts and continuous business relationships among manufacturers, wholesalers, retailers, and customers. In a stable, rationalized capitalist system, the relationship between buyer and seller will presumably "continue beyond the individual transaction," and hence trust, regularity, and dependability are essential. Without it, agreements would not be honored or honored unpredictably, no one could count on anyone else, and the system would simply break down.[14]

This argument is obviously valid in part. No long-term economic relationship can survive without some basic minimum of trust. But as the innumerable accounts in this book demonstrate, while an essential nucleus of trust must exist in any continuing economic exchange, this still leaves enormous room for massive, secretive, undisclosed deception. Trust, in fact, may *secure* the relationship so that deception is more easily perpetrated.

A second element in the defense of the ethics of capitalism requires a more extended discussion. The argument is often made that capitalism actually rewards honesty, not dishonesty. The honest firm builds a reputation over the years for integrity and reliability. It consequently wins a large circle of loyal customers who return again and again. Loyal customers spread the word to others. Hence, honest firms become successful while dishonest firms lose out to their honest competitors.

To be sure, this does occur. Many firms do in fact operate this way; they are successful because they are honest and their customers recognize it. When it succeeds, this strategy of enlightened self-interest vindicates the system; private interest coincides with public good. A waitress in our study who worked in a well-run, honest, and successful restaurant testified to the validity of this ideology. She writes that her employer "realizes that honesty and friendliness will always win out in the long run. If you serve good food at a moderate price in a clean, friendly atmosphere, you will have regular customers which keeps a business going strong." In short, honesty pays.

If the system actually worked this way most of the time— where honest firms thrived and dishonest ones disappeared— there would be very little business deception in America, very little business crime, and very little need for consumer legislation to protect the public. Yet we know that none of this is true. Unfortunately, there is more than one way to run a profitable business, and the flat generalization that business crime never pays and honesty is always rewarded is both naïve and simplistic.

Businessmen continue to find deceptive practices profitable for a number of reasons.

1. The concept of deception itself implies that the customer being deceived is not fully aware of it. Successful deception thus not only increases one's earnings but also keeps the goodwill of the customer. Consider again the case cited by a service station attendant in Chapter 4. He writes, "Mrs. H. comes into the station upset because her car won't start. Being a true gentleman, my boss will send someone to bring it into the station. The mechanic finds that an ignition wire is loose, but tells Mrs. H. she needs a new starter. The mechanic, being an expert painter, takes the old starter out, paints it, replaces it, and charges Mrs. H. $85. *As a crowning joy for the mechanic, Mrs. H. tips him for his kindness and good work* [emphasis added]." This kind of deception is doubly effective because the customer leaves not only her money but her gratitude as well. The fraud, therefore, is not disadvantageous to the business but highly beneficial.

Business deception continues to flourish because many sellers believe they can deceive buyers without their knowledge. In the relationship between seller and buyer, the seller usually has a crucial edge. The seller knows his product and sells it all day every day; he thus has the advantage of both expertise and experience over the customer who might shop for that product only occasionally.

A car dealer who confessed his stratagems for outwitting his customers year after year writes that while the auto industry has changed in many ways in recent decades, "one terribly important thing has not changed in the car business, and that is the absolute ignorance of the average car buyer. While improvements have made the selling of cars a more accountable process, the customer's knowledge of how dealerships function, of financing, of dollar value has remained back in the Dark Ages."[15]

The point here is that because of the seller's often crucial advantage both in knowing the product itself and knowing how to sell it, he may believe he can deceive the buyer and get away with it. Thus, the seller can have the best of both worlds—the goodwill of the naïve customer and the immediate pecuniary benefits of deceiving him.

2. According to the ideology of the private market system, the honest businessman will make more money in the long run than the dishonest one because loyal customers will return. But honesty often requires a seller to give up a quick profit now for the mere possibility of a gain later on, something many sellers are not willing to do.

Consider another automotive example. A motorist with a dead battery asks a gas station owner what ails his car. The car needs a $5 battery charge, not a $65 battery. The owner makes more money selling a new battery, however, than charging the old one. If he resists the temptation to sell the customer unnecessary parts and tells him he needs only a battery charge, the owner hopes his honesty will win him a steady customer. Perhaps it will. But only perhaps. Hence his honesty requires a willingness to defer immediate gain for the possibility of gain later on. But, as we know, the willingness to defer gratification is by no means universal. Some people will, some won't. Some businessmen will, some won't. Many sellers have a short time perspective. They would rather make a sale now, even a deceptive one, than forego it for the possibility of a sale in the indefinite future when a grateful customer might return. A customer in the shop is worth two on the street.

3. The theory of the market system, which claims that honesty is rewarded by loyal customers who return, ignores the fact that many firms, especially in an anonymous urban environment, don't depend on repeat business at all. They get a steady stream of new customers who buy once and are gone. The classic example is the gas station on the highway; such firms care little about long-term customer loyalty. They have one shot to sell you the whole store, which is why the writer cited earlier on auto repair fraud recommends that on the road, when the gas station attendant opens your hood, you stand there and look over his shoulder.

THE SOCIAL PSYCHOLOGY OF URBAN LIFE

Early sociological observers of the urban scene, writers such as Ferdinand Tönnies, Georg Simmel, Robert Park, and Louis Wirth, sketched what they believed were the fundamental features of the modern urban personality.[16] These nineteenth- and early twentieth-century writers argued that in the modern city the bonds of trust, neighborliness, and open friendliness decay. In an urban world of strangers, personal aggrandizement and mutual exploitation undermine social solidarity. Compared to small town or rural peoples, city dwellers are aloof, blasé, detached, uninvolved, distrustful, potentially hostile. Their relationships to most others are instrumental and impersonal, superficial and transitory.[17]

Many of these early writers assumed that destruction of the bonds of community were inevitable by-products of city life. They often explained urban social psychology in terms of a kind of demographic determinism. Louis Wirth, for example, defined cities as large, dense, and heterogeneous agglomerations of people. And in Wirth's view, these three demographic characteristics—size, density, and diversity—generated the stereotyped urban personality.

There is some truth to this. Increasing the size of any group changes the nature of social relations in that group. Social relations in a village are very different from social relations in a city. While one may know personally everyone in a small village, that is clearly impossible in a large metropolitan area, where most people are inevitably strangers, which invariably alters the nature of social interaction. Quantity has a quality all its own, as the dialectic tells us.

Nonetheless, I want to argue that if much of the sense of community has been lost among strangers in the modern city, it is only partly because of the size, density, and diversity of those cities. It is also a consequence of the structural and cultural characteristics of those cities themselves.

Specifically, what Wirth and others seemed to be describing was not so much the universal social psychology of urban life, but the unique social psychology of cities with the structure and culture of Western industrial capitalism. Urban sociologist Manuel Castells has made the same argument, writing that "the fundamental point is this: everything described by Wirth as 'urbanism' is in fact the cultural expression of capitalist industrialization."[18]

Nearly a century and a half ago, Friedrich Engels described the social psychology of city life as it was being shaped by the forces of capitalist industrialism. Observing London in the 1840s, he condemned the "brutal indifference" with which Londoners "ignore their neighbors and selfishly concentrate upon their own private affairs." He continues:

> We know well enough that this isolation of the individual—this narrow-minded egotism—is everywhere the fun-

damental principle of modern society. But nowhere is this selfish egotism so blatantly evident as in the frantic bustle of the great city. The disintegration of society into individuals, each guided by his private principles and each pursuing his own aims has been pushed to its furthest limits in London. Here indeed human society has been split into its component atoms.

From this it follows that the social conflict—the war of all against all—is fought in the open. . . . Here men regard their fellows not as human beings, but as pawns in the struggle for existence. Everyone exploits his neighbor with the result that the stronger tramples the weaker under foot.[19]

Recent studies of Chinese cities reveal patterns of social relations far different from what we in the West often assume are universal urban characteristics.[20] Despite the paranoid atmosphere created by the Cultural Revolution and its ensuing witch hunts, life in Chinese cities seems to have retained a far more communal quality than Western sociologists might have thought possible in an urban environment. Much of this the regime consciously created after the 1949 revolution.

When the communists came to power, they inherited a legacy of urban crime, disease, and poverty. To treat these problems and to assure political control, the government created comprehensive urban political organizations permeating every neighborhood and household. The regime sought to replace a society of isolated urban families with a comprehensive cellular structure organized from top to bottom; to accomplish this it established residents' committees in every urban neighborhood (overseeing from one hundred to eight hundred families) and small group units (supervising fifteen to forty families). These organizations provide an elaborate set of neighborhood services, including nurseries, medical facilities, welfare, "cleanliness inspections," as well as regular political study groups.[21] Although they help maintain political orthodoxy by transmitting policy and ideology downward, they also foster *Gemeinschaft* relations in urban areas.

Neighborly relations in Chinese cities are also strengthened by the extremely low rates of residential mobility. Severe restrictions on urban in-migration from the countryside and limitations on movement within cities have created unprecedented urban stability. One study found, for example, that the average urban resident had lived in the same house or apartment for *eighteen years*. Kitchens and bathrooms are often shared. Unlike the West, where neighbors—especially in apartment houses—are mere transient acquaintances whom one often does not greet or even recognize on the street, in China neighbors are long-term intimates. In Chinese cities, moreover, residence is commonly integrated with the workplace, so people live close to work and among co-workers. This creates stronger social bonds than in Western cities, where after work people scatter to their homes in all parts of the city and surrounding suburbs.

Political theorists have often noted that in totalitarian societies, everything, even one's private life, becomes politically relevant. In Chinese cities, the government encourages, in fact requires, neighbors and co-workers to be actively involved in each other's personal lives so as to smooth out the social structure at the bottom. Neighbors and co-workers mediate marital disputes, resolve quarrels with children, and help solve other personal problems. Such enforced involvement in one's private life by neighbors and co-workers is unheard of in the West and would be resented as a gross violation of privacy. The personal privacy Westerners take for granted is unknown in Chinese cities, but so apparently is the individual isolation, long thought by Western sociologists to be intrinsic to urban life. Isolation is, after all, a dimension of privacy.

Other features of Chinese society also foster urban *Gemeinschaft*. The rough egalitarianism of Chinese society poses few barriers to interaction. The familiar communal slogan, "Serve the people," long a motto of the regime, unites rather than atomizes society. Low levels of occupational mobility assure that workers remain at the same job and with the same co-workers far longer than do Westerners. And on the job, as at home, communal relations are strong. The work unit is especially influential in structuring the lives of its members. Among its activities,

> work units may run nurseries, clinics, canteens, and recreational facilities; they convene employees to hear government decrees and for political study; they organize campaigns for birth control and to send down youth [to the countryside]; they approve marriages and divorces and mediate disputes; they hold meetings to discuss crimes and misbehavior off the job by their members; they distribute rations and carry out cleanliness campaigns; they supervise untrustworthy employees and organize patrols to guard the area; and they may employ family members of employees in subsidiary small workshops or vegetable farms.[22]

Undoubtedly, the workplace in China creates stronger social bonds than does its counterpart in the West.

The object here is not to praise Chinese urban policy—the population is obviously highly regimented—but merely to make a theoretical point. For good or ill, Chinese cities seem to possess a far greater *Gemeinschaft* structure than those in the West. This suggests that social structure and cultural values may be at least as important in determining the nature of social relations in the city as population size and density. If so, then possibly what has subverted the communal spirit in Western cities may not be just the imperatives of urban demographics—as the classic urban theorists believed—but certain features of industrial capitalism itself.

I am not arguing that Western city dwellers are merely isolated atoms floating anonymously about the urban environment. Primary groups obviously remain strong in the city; we have family, friends, associations, and so on. But it is

the overall sense of urban community and solidarity, our ties
to fellow citizens and fellow city dwellers, that seems to be
extraordinarily weak. Engels's depiction of the frantic egotism and callous individualism of mid-nineteenth-century
London seems just as true today. In New York City, for example, human encounters
often take the form of the war of each against all. This can
be seen in many places, but perhaps best on the streets and
highways. Motorists come equipped with a permanent chip
on their shoulders, ready to explode in anger and abuse at
the slightest provocation from other drivers. The horn is
used as a plow to clear the way. Most drivers only slowly and
reluctantly make way for ambulances and fire trucks. Many
ignore them completely, continuing serenely on their way
while sirens blare behind them, refusing to pull over or stop,
calculating, one can only imagine, that a minute of their
time is worth more than someone else's life.

What are some of the larger social and economic forces
underlying urban anomie and its relentless individualism?
As the urban public infrastructure decays and as growing
numbers of people compete for space to live, to drive, to
park, to walk—people's behavior is reduced to an individual-
istic struggle to make room for themselves. As writer Tom
Wolfe observed, the key to survival in New York City is
"insulate, insulate, insulate."

The economics of competitive individualism also tends
to set each against all. The cash nexus, a by-product of the
market system, reduces human relationships to a system of
pecuniary advantages.† Capitalism and its great voice, advertising, stress private material accumulation, while public
goals and collective welfare are ignored. The market system's
central credo, "Take care of number one," builds a wall of
indifference and noninvolvement outside the nuclear family
and helps undermine whatever solidarity remains in city life.

In an ironic twist, the affluence of Western societies has

† On the cash nexus, see p. 207.

also become a privatizing force. Poor people need one another. They are often dependent on family, friends, and neighbors to borrow this, to share that, to help out during frequent emergencies. Necessity creates interdependence and mutual aid.

Affluence, on the other hand, implies self-sufficiency. The affluent nuclear family, secure and isolated in its well-stocked home or apartment, requires little help from friends, neighbors, or extended relations; it can simply purchase all the good and services it needs. Moreover, the affluent family's home today doubles as an electronic recreation center. Television has always been a privatizing medium, but VCRs are even more so. With these and other sophisticated electronic paraphernalia, there is less and less reason to leave home for outside entertainment. There may come a time when going out to a play may seem like the ultimate communal experience.[23]

Another possible key to understanding urban alienation in the capitalist West is that most people have no control over the institutions in which they live out their lives—apartment house, workplace, market. Day in, day out, people are immersed in institutions that do not belong to them, over which they have no jurisdiction or influence. There is no sense of proprietorship, no comfort in knowing that "this is mine—this is subject to my will, my control, my influence." Powerlessness becomes a form of isolation. In the typical urban apartment house, for example, the landlord not only owns and controls, but has a vested interest in keeping tenants isolated, alone, and unorganized. Any kind of community among residents poses the immediate danger of a tenant's organization, which threatens the landlord's interests. Without any institutional or organizational bonds among them, each tenant is alone and subject to the control of others with power and property. Landlord-tenant relations are more primitive, more medieval, more unequal in terms of power than any other set of relationships in modern society. Even the term, landlord—lord of the land—is a medieval relic. Compared to landlord-tenant relations, management-labor relations are light years ahead. Urban cooperative apartments, of course, suggest that communal ties can develop when people control and run their own institutions. In apartment co-ops, there are meetings, elections, a governing board. Decentralized self-governing cells in the city can create a structure that fosters social interaction, cohesion, and *Gemeinschaft* relations in an otherwise anonymous urban environment.

At work, the typical city dweller is again involved in an institution that belongs to someone else and over which he has little control or influence. He is again subject to the will of others. But this, of course, is an old and well-understood story. After work, in the market, the city dweller enters stores and shops that also belong to someone else, and over which he or she has no conceivable control or jurisdiction. In the market the individual consumer has only one power: the power to continue to shop or not to shop there, a decision which, however symbolic the statement, has virtually no impact on anyone else.

In small-scale, self-governing organizations, even in the largest, most impersonal city, one can in some sense feel, "I am home. This belongs to me. These people are my partners." In a consumer cooperative market, for example, even among strangers in the store, one can feel linked to the other shoppers by the knowledge that "we own this enterprise and it works for us."[24]

A final element in the destruction of urban *Gemeinschaft,* and what is central to this study, is deception in the marketplace, which takes its toll on any lingering sense of urban fellowship. Repeated deception in the market breaks down solidarity instead of building community. Day-to-day personal contact with marketplace fraud helps create a world of isolated people operating in a social and economic mine field where, unless one watches one's step, one can be taken. In the marketplace in one's own community, an individual encounters potential adversaries, not friends, people one has to watch out for. The ambience for any sense of community is all wrong.

For nearly two centuries conservative thinkers have mourned the spirit of community that has been lost in urban, industrial society. Ironically, what conservatives fail to realize is that the very sense of community they cherish and whose loss they lament has been undermined by the possessive individualism of which they are the staunchest defenders. The invisible hand promised the collective good. But just as often we get the invisible sleight of hand, which yields not the collective good but anomie.

Sociologist Robert Merton made a similar argument many years ago. In his book *Mass Persuasion,* written in the mid-1940s, Merton analyzed singer Kate Smith's enormous success during World War II in raising hundreds of millions of dollars in war bonds during marathon radio drives. What explained her charismatic appeal? In his interviews, Merton discovered that a key to Kate Smith's effectiveness was the public perception of her as a person of great integrity and honesty. Here at last was someone who could be trusted. The public perceived her radio appeals for war bonds as selfless devotion to the war effort, untainted by motives of personal gain, a refreshing change from a world of self-promotion and deceit. Merton writes that his informants contrasted Kate Smith's honesty with

> the pretenses, deceptions and dissembling which they observe in their daily existence. On every side, they feel themselves as the targets for ingenious methods of control, through advertising which cajoles, promises, terrorizes; through propagandas that, utilizing available techniques, guide the unwitting audience into opinions which may or may not coincide with the best interests of themselves or their affiliates; through cumulatively subtle methods of salesmanship which may simulate values common to both salesman and client for private and self-interested motives.[25]

In an elegant phrase, Merton concluded that for many Americans, *"Society is experienced as an arena for rival frauds* [emphasis added]."[26] And here he introduces for the first time his important concept of pseudo-*Gemeinschaft:* "In place of a sense of *Gemeinschaft*—genuine community of values—there intrudes *pseudo-Gemeinschaft*—the feigning of personal concern with the other fellow in order to manipulate him the better."[27]

Despite sociological revisionists who have rediscovered community in the American city, urban loneliness continues to be a stark reality for many.[28] And in the face of urban loneliness, the marketplace exploits for its own profit the need for belonging by offering pseudo-community as a substitute. Selling the product is made easier by manipulating the urban dweller's need for belonging. How often the informants in this study reported the casual use of pseudo-*Gemeinschaft* with customers. Make the customer feel you care, tell him he's got a friend, tell him he's going to be treated like family, tell him he's special; it's easier to sell him that way. And as these workers often noted, the glad hand and the faked emotions often mask not only indifference but contempt for the customer as well. If, in the 1940s, Merton found that many Americans experienced society as an arena for rival frauds, that sense must be even greater today, for though consumer protection laws are stronger now, techniques of public manipulation in politics, the marketplace, advertising, and the media are far more pervasive today than they were then. And indeed, recent opinion research reveals a widespread climate of public distrust and even cynicism toward major institutions in American life. This distrust manifests itself in many ways.

"THE BUSINESS OF AMERICA . . ."

It may be true that the business of America is business. It may be true that America is unfettered capitalism's last and best hope in the world. It may be true that socialist ideas have had less influence in the United States than in any other advanced capitalist nation. It certainly appears true that capitalism enjoys near universal public support. In recent surveys, at least 80 percent of Americans agree that freedom itself is inseparable from the free enterprise system, and only a tiny minority—little more than 10 percent—expressed any sympathy for socialism.[29]

This is not the whole story, however. Despite the overwhelming legitimacy of capitalism in the United States, an underlying strain of hostility toward business runs through American history. The public has always harbored a deep-seated suspicion that business in this country is too big, too powerful, too self-interested, and too free from ethical constraints. Periodically this hostility to business bursts to the surface in political protest—Populism, the Progressive movement, the New Deal. Most often public suspicion of business simmers just below the placid surface of general support for the system. On the one hand, the public generally credits American capitalism with impressive technical and material achievements. On the other hand, Americans often detect a conflict between private profit and public good, between business pursuit of its own pecuniary self-interest and public morality.[30]

However much Americans support capitalism—and they do—at some level of consciousness they do not trust the profit motive and the profit system. However much Americans support the economic status quo—and they do—they are at some level radical critics of the system. It is not a criticism based on politics, ideology, or theory. It is based solely on a kind of populist suspicion of big business derived from common stereotypes of business greed and validated by personal anecdotes and periodic news stories of business crime. Survey research of many kinds reveals this underlying public distrust of business.

In the 1970s and 1980s, for example, the Roper organization surveyed public attitudes toward American business and industry. Despite general public praise of capitalism for its economic performance, large majorities were highly skeptical of the ethical performance of American business. In a 1984 survey, 70 percent of respondents agreed that American business and industry "is far too often not honest with the public," and 68 percent said that American business and industry "has lost sight of human values in the interest of profit." Over half the public (55 percent) agreed that American business and industry had become too big and powerful for the good of the country.[31]

Other opinion research organizations have found similar public criticism of business ethics. In 1977, Cambridge Reports, Inc. found that two-thirds of its respondents agreed that "businessmen—big and small—put profit ahead of morality."[32] In four Cambridge surveys taken between 1969 and 1979, up to 79 percent of the public agreed with the strong statement that "big business doesn't care whether I live or die, only that somebody buys what they have to sell."[33] In the mid-1970s, Peter D. Hart Research Associates found that nearly three-fourths of Americans—72 percent—agreed that "profits are the major goal of business even if it means unemployment and inflation."[34] In a Louis Harris poll taken in the mid-1970s, 71 percent of Americans agreed with the statement that "businessmen will do nothing much to help the consumer if that reduces profits—unless it is forced to do so." Only 11 percent disagreed.[35]

In 1978, although the House of Representatives had killed the proposal for a federal Consumer Protection Agency, the public continued to favor it by a margin of 58 percent to 28 percent, according to a Louis Harris poll of the period. And two-thirds of Americans at that time agreed that "big business has so much power with the government that, unless the consumer has someone in government to argue his case and make business give better quality, the consumer will continue to be shortchanged on products and services."[36]

Public support for a consumer protection agency and the consistently positive public attitudes toward the consumer movement in this country suggest that Americans do not believe that business can be trusted to protect the interests of consumers.[37]

In five surveys taken between 1973 and 1981, the Opinion Research Corporation found that between 65 and 72 percent of the public agreed that "Businessmen do everything they can to make a profit even if it means ignoring the public's need." And in the same surveys, even when a question about business was phrased positively ("Business today has a moral conscience—it is motivated by more than just the profit motive"), only about two out of five agreed, while about half disagreed.[38] Finally, in surveys taken between 1975 and 1981, about two-thirds of the public agreed that "American business and industry has lost sight of human values in the interest of profit."[39]

In sum, beneath the bedrock of public support for capitalism lies the deep and recurrent suspicion that the profit motive is often incompatible with the public interest.[40]

PUBLIC CONFIDENCE IN BUSINESS
AND BUSINESS LEADERS

There are other measures of public ambivalence toward business. Though Americans unquestionably support capitalism as an economic system, they seem to have little confidence either in business or in business leadership, as many surveys taken over the years clearly indicate.

Since 1973, for example, the Gallup Organization has measured public confidence in major American institutions (Table 11.1). In nine Gallup surveys, the proportion of Americans reporting either "a great deal" or "quite a bit" of confidence in big business in America has averaged only 29 percent, and has ranged from a low of 20 percent to a high of

Table 11.1. Confidence in American Institutions

"I am going to read you a list of institutions in American society. Would you please tell me how much confidence you, yourself, have in each one— a great deal, quite a lot, some, or very little?"

	Percent saying "great deal" or "quite a lot"								
	1986	1985	1984	1983	1981	1979	1977	1975	1973
Military	63	61	58	53	50	54	57	58	*
Church, organized religion	57	66	64	62	64	65	64	68	66
U.S. Supreme Court	54	56	51	42	46	45	46	49	44
Banks & banking	49	51	51	51	46	60	*	*	*
Public schools	49	48	47	39	42	53	54	*	58
Congress	41	39	29	28	29	34	40	40	42
Newspapers	37	35	34	38	35	51	*	*	39
Organized labor	29	28	30	26	28	36	39	38	30
BIG BUSINESS	28	31	29	28	20	32	33	34	26
Television	27	29	25	25	25	38	*	*	37

SOURCE: Gallup Poll, various years
* not asked

only 34 percent. Big business, in fact, is one of the least trusted institutions in American life.[41]

As Americans express little confidence in business institutions, it is not surprising that they have little confidence in the persons who run them. In 1966 and then annually after 1971, the Harris poll surveyed public confidence in the leadership of major American institutions (Table 11.2). While over half the public expressed "a great deal of confidence" in business leadership in 1966, confidence in business leaders fell dramatically after that and in recent years has consistently remained under 20 percent. And Americans express less confidence in leaders of business than in the leaders of most other American institutions.

As these figures reveal, public distrust is not restricted to

Table 11.2. Public Confidence in the Leadership of American Institutions

"As far as people in charge of running [each institution] are concerned, would you say you have a great deal of confidence, only some confidence, or hardly any confidence at all in them?"

	Percent saying "great deal"																
	1986	1985	1984	1983	1982	1981	1980	1979	1978	1977	1976	1975	1974	1973	1972	1971	1966
	%	%	%	%	%	%	%	%	%	%	%	%	%	%	%	%	%
The military	36	32	45	35	31	28	28	29	29	27	23	24	33	40	35	27	61
Major educational institutions such as colleges and universities	34	35	40	36	30	34	36	33	41	37	31	36	40	44	33	37	61
Medicine	33	39	43	35	32	37	34	30	42	43	42	43	50	57	48	61	73
The U.S. Supreme Court	32	28	35	33	25	29	27	28	29	29	22	28	40	33	28	23	50
Television news	27	23	28	24	24	24	29	37	35	28	28	35	31	41	*	*	*
Organized religion	22	21	24	22	20	22	22	20	34	29	24	32	32	36	30	27	41
Congress	21	16	28	20	13	16	18	18	10	17	9	13	18	*	21	19	42
Local governments	21	18	23	18	*	*	*	*	19	18	21	*	*	28	*	*	*
The press	19	16	18	19	14	16	19	28	23	18	20	26	25	30	18	18	29
The White House	19	30	42	23	20	28	18	15	14	31	11	*	28	18	*	*	*
State governments	19	16	23	18	*	*	*	*	15	18	16	*	*	24	*	*	*
The executive branch of the federal government	18	19	*	*	*	24	17	17	14	23	11	13	28	19	27	23	41
MAJOR COMPANIES	16	17	19	18	18	16	16	18	22	20	16	19	21	29	27	27	55
Law firms	14	12	17	12	*	*	13	16	18	14	12	16	18	24	*	*	*
Organized labor	11	13	12	10	8	12	14	10	15	14	10	14	18	20	15	14	22

SOURCE: Harris poll, various years
*not asked

business alone. There appears to be a generalized lack of confidence in most American institutions and their leadership. In recent Harris surveys, for example, none of the leaders of fifteen major organizations and institutions commanded great confidence from as much as 40 percent of the public.

PERCEPTION AND REALITY

Perhaps these surveys slightly exaggerate public distrust of business and other major institutions. Some distrust may be a form of "ritualized cynicism," a response based on the feeling that cynicism is a more sophisticated attitude than exuberant faith or trust.[42] Yet if it were no more than that, cynicism would be expressed toward all institutions equally across the board. But this is not so; the public clearly expresses more confidence in some institutions than in others.

Public suspicion of major political and economic institutions may stem in part from the natural American inclination to distrust large concentrations of power, and distrust of leadership may flow from traditional American values of egalitarianism and anti-elitism.[43]

While there is obviously some truth to this, it seems more likely that distrust of American political and economic institutions and its leadership stems from long-term public experience with the *realities* of political malfeasance and business crime. In other words, public distrust may be well-founded. A recent survey, for example, found that 84 percent of Americans believe that corruption and payoffs are common among government officials. There is a genuine basis for that perception. Consider recent history.

Between 1970 and 1981, federal convictions of local government officials increased 1,219 percent. Altogether in 1981 some 436 government officials were convicted of federal crimes, up from 32 in 1970, 155 in 1975, and 303 in 1980. Sometimes the people involved are central operatives in the political system. In the Watergate scandal alone, more than 75 individuals and corporations, including some of the biggest names in corporate America and a good portion of the White House staff, were found guilty of lying, spying, obstructing justice, tampering with the electoral process, or other violations of elementary morality and democratic values.[44]

Business fares no better in public estimation. Most Americans believe that business crime is widespread and increasing, that the majority of corporate executives are dishonest, and that most white-collar criminals either get away with their crimes or are inadequately punished. In a 1985 *New York Times*/CBS poll, for example, 59 percent of Americans expressed the view that business crime was very common, and an additional 34 percent said it occurred occasionally. Only 3 percent said business crime was rare. While one-third of the public thought most corporate executives were honest, over half—55 percent—believed most executives were not honest. Only 23 percent of respondents believed the government was making sufficient effort to catch business criminals, while 68 percent thought the government's efforts were inadequate, reflecting the traditional double standard in the enforcement of business crime compared to street crime. And, as most people thought the government's efforts to prosecute business criminals were insufficient, not surprisingly 85 percent said that most white-collar criminals get away with their crimes, and 65 percent said that those convicted received too lenient a punishment.[45] In 1987 a Harris poll found that fully 90 percent of the respondents viewed white-collar crime as either very common or somewhat common; less than 10 percent said it was not very common. Only 2 percent of Americans rated the ethical standards of business executives as excellent, while 58 percent rated executive ethics as only fair or poor.[46]

Again, these perceptions are not simply empty public imaginings having no connection with the actual state of affairs; they reflect the reality of widespread business crime.

In the 1970s, criminologists Marshall B. Clinard and Peter C. Yeager conducted the first comprehensive census of business crime since Edwin Sutherland's classic study of white-collar crime in 1949. For the years 1975 and 1976 Clinard and Yeager investigated all federal court actions against the 582 largest industrial, wholesale, retail, and service corporations in the United States. In these two years alone:

> A total of 1,553 federal cases were begun against all 582 corporations . . . or an average of 2.7 federal cases of violation each. Of the 582 corporations, 350 (60.1 percent) had at least one federal action brought against them, and for those firms that had at least one action brought against them, the average was 4.4 cases.[47]

In the mid-1980s, a survey of business crime found that within the previous decade 115 (23 percent) of America's 500 largest corporations had been convicted of at least one serious crime or been assessed civil penalties for serious misbehavior. The crime rate of the twenty-five largest corporations was even higher.[48]

No estimate of the total cost of business crime can be accurate, of course, because so much is hidden. But we get at least a sense of its possible magnitude from the Senate Judiciary Subcommittee on Antitrust and Monopoly, which estimated in the 1970s that business crime of all kinds costs Americans between $174 and $231 billion annually.[49] By contrast, current estimates put the direct cost of violent crime at about $11 billion annually.

THE CASH NEXUS

> What good is the moon if you can't buy it and sell it?
>
> IVAN F. BOESKY

Earlier in this chapter I argued that the erosion of communal values in the city is not merely a product of such demographic characteristics as population size, but is also a consequence of industrial capitalism itself. And if there is a system of *social* relations that tends to grow out of the *economic* relations of capitalism, it is best described in terms of the concept of the cash nexus.

In a society dominated by the cash nexus, all things are reduced to their pecuniary value and judged accordingly. The phrase is Thomas Carlyle's, but its most well-known expression appears in that passage in *The Communist Manifesto* where Marx and Engels describe the transformation of social relations under capitalism. The pecuniary calculus carried by capitalism has triumphed everywhere, obliterating values, tradition, and sentiment.

> The bourgeoisie, where it has got the upper hand, has put an end to all feudal, patriarchal, idyllic relations. It has pitilessly torn asunder the motley feudal ties that bound man to his "natural superiors," and has left remaining no other nexus between man and man than naked self-interest, than callous "cash payment." It has drowned the most heavenly ecstacies of religious fervor, of chivalrous enthusiasm, of Philistine sentimentalism, in the icy water of egotistical calculation. It has resolved personal worth into exchange value.

The concept remains valid. Nearly a century after Marx and Engels wrote these words, the German sociologist Karl Mannheim observed that in contemporary society governed by the cash nexus, "men will tend to look at every relationship through a tradesman's eyes. They will tend more and more to picture natural objects as commodities and look at personal relationships from a mercenary point of view. In this process those much-discussed psychological phenomena, self-estrangement and dehumanization, will develop, and a type of man is born for whom a tree is not a tree, but timber."[50]

(Despite its dreary effect on human relations, the cash

nexus can be seen as having at least one redeeming feature. In a society where money is the measure of all things, considerations of race, color, creed, gender, sexual orientation, and so on are all largely irrelevant. Money is a universalistic instrument. Everyone's money is green—capitalism's favorite color; everyone—with money—is equal, and the market is at your service. All minorities are welcome. Capitalism is inherently an extremely tolerant economic system—for those with the ability to pay.)

Today the cash nexus appears in strange new forms, including in our language. What better expression of the cash nexus than the term "bottom line," which has come to mean in all areas of life that which is the most crucial, the ultimate, the most important. Certainly the most dramatic contemporary manifestation of the cash nexus in America is the extraordinary propensity of Americans to sue one another. Many people today see strangers not just as fellow citizens but also as potential defendants in negligence suits. America's favorite three little words no longer seem to be "I love you," but "Sue the bastards!" And in a variation on the biblical injunction, Americans are now of the predisposition to sue thy neighbor.

It is an elementary sociological fact that as the social fabric of a society unravels, shared values and norms that once guided behavior break down and are replaced by formal codes, regulations, and laws. As the sense of community withers further, social conflict intensifies and litigation proliferates as each person seeks advantage at the expense of others. In his book *The Litigious Society*, legal scholar Jethro Lieberman writes:

> Litigiousness is not a legal but a social phenomenon. It is born of a breakdown in community, a breakdown that exacerbates and is exacerbated by the growth of law. . . . But until there is a consensus on fundamental principles, the trust that is essential to a self-ordering community cannot be.[51]

If litigiousness is a symptom of the ascendance of the cash nexus and the decline of community, then it is perhaps an indicator of the state of things here that with only 5 percent of the world's population, the United States has two-thirds of the world's lawyers. The Chief Justice of the Supreme Court observed in the late 1970s that "we may well be on our way to a society overrun by hordes of lawyers, hungry as locusts, and brigades of judges in numbers never before contemplated."[52]

Legal experts disagree over whether America has in fact undergone a "litigation explosion" recently or whether rates of litigation have held relatively constant; data have been marshaled to support both arguments.[53] But the question is irrelevant. Whether the propensity of Americans to sue one another has increased in recent years or just held constant, America is almost certainly the most litigious society in the world.[54]

In some ways litigiousness is both desirable and necessary—in making corporations that sell hazardous or defective products accountable, in making companies that pollute the environment accountable, in making negligent physicians accountable. But in America it has gone beyond that. On a deeper level it reflects the underlying cash nexus psychology in American society, that state of mind that makes one poised to cash in whenever there is "the merest whisper of an insult," to try to profit from the inevitable misfortunes of life.[55] The social psychological foundation on which this fury of litigiousness is based is the predatory notion that if your neighbor makes a mistake at your expense, enrich yourself at his. In a society where the cash nexus is the prevailing social equation, lawyers are eager to demonstrate—for a substantial contingency fee—how pain and suffering can be turned into dollars and cents. The American dream of rags to riches can be achieved in many ways.

Meanwhile, in the 1980s the cost of liability insurance soared and thousands of policies were canceled outright. Insurance companies placed the blame for this on rising rates of litigation and astronomical settlements. Others charged insurance companies with poor financial planning over the years or outright conspiracy to manipulate the cost of liability insurance. Whatever the reason, small businesses, local governments, and professionals were paralyzed by the mounting cost of insurance or by the loss of their policies altogether. Thousands of doctors in such high malpractice-risk fields as obstetrics and neurosurgery abandoned their specialties. The substantive irrationality of the system is clearly demonstrated when trained doctors refuse to treat their patients, when obstetricians refuse to deliver babies for fear of being sued or because they cannot afford malpractice insurance.

In all this, the behavior of the American people mirrors the behavior of their corporations. In an age of American industrial decline, U.S. corporations are devoting more and more resources to mergers and acquisitions, toward rearranging wealth instead of creating it. Likewise, on a personal level, in the litigious society many Americans seek to enrich themselves by rearranging wealth instead of creating it.

While the penchant for lawsuits and the cash nexus psychology that underlies it stem ultimately from the market system, these things are not just automatic by-products of capitalism, for cultural and social factors also play a role. The litigiousness of capitalist America is not duplicated in the capitalist countries of Western Europe, nor certainly in Japan. The social foundations of litigiousness in the United States go beyond the cash nexus of capitalism to two distinctive features of American life: the adversarial nature of American culture and the traditions of American individualism.

The United States has twenty-five times as many lawyers per capita as Japan—650,000 here compared to only 10,000 in Japan. Predictably, after a plane crash in the United States come the lawsuits. But lawsuits after a plane crash are still rare in Japan. More common are highly ritualized apologies by airline executives, visits to survivors' homes, religious atonement, and private out-of-court consultations to determine fair compensation—all reaffirmations of the bonds of community.[56]

ADVERTISING: THE "PERMISSIBLE LIE"[57]

A society trained to accept the preposterous claims, the deceptions, and the vulgarities of American advertising can perhaps be manipulated into accepting anything.

HENRY STEELE COMMAGER

In June 1970, just a year after the first landing of men on the moon, the Knight newspapers conducted an informal survey of Americans in a half dozen cities, asking some 1,700 persons whether they believed U.S. astronauts had actually been to the moon and back. The survey did not use standardized sampling techniques, so the percentage of disbelievers probably did not reflect public opinion exactly. Nonetheless, the study did reveal that an astonishingly large minority of persons actually believed the moon landing had been faked and that what they had seen on television was an elaborate hoax. Many thought the government had staged the show to deceive the Russians or the Chinese. A few thought the government did it to deceive the public in order to justify the space agency's budget, or simply to make people forget their troubles.[58]

This is a rather extreme form of cynicism, but it actually reveals the strong predisposition of Americans to believe that much of what happens in the public arena is rigged, faked, exaggerated, passed off for what it isn't—whether in the marketplace, on T.V., in the White House, in Congress, or on the campaign trail. It is no accident, as Marxists are wont to say, that two recent and now widely used additions to the American vocabulary are the words "hype" and "scam."

Certainly public cynicism has been raised in recent years

not only by business deception, but by the political deceptions of the Vietnam War, Watergate, and the scandals of the
Reagan administration. National opinion surveys show that
a majority of Americans believe that government officials and
even the president of the United States regularly lie to the
American people.[59] What is extraordinary is not just that the
public believes that their elected officials routinely lie to
them, but that it seems to be accepted with no sense of moral
outrage or even surprise and does not provide a reason for
judging these officials adversely. During the Reagan years,
over one hundred administration officials or appointees faced
charges of illegal or unethical behavior. Yet, so apparently
inured had Americans become to deception, that Reagan's
claim that his administration represented a return to old-
fashioned morality went largely unchallenged, and his public approval rating remained high throughout most of his
presidency.

The predisposition of Americans to discount as hype so
much of what they observe around them has many deep roots,
but probably none so deep as the pervasive deceptions of advertising. The usual case against advertising is that it is a
genre dominated by half-truths, puffery, exaggeration, mis-
information, distortion, outright lies, and the exploitation of
carefully researched human needs, fears, and insecurities.[60]
In a society that prides itself on science, knowledge, precision,
rationality, and careful measurement, advertising represents
a huge island of the irrational where reason is intentionally
obfuscated and decisions based on intelligent measurement
and comparison are deliberately sabotaged. Granted that the
following are particularly irrational examples, consider the
copy of some recent cigarette ads. What is the literal meaning
of these words? Newport Lights: "Alive with pleasure";
Marlboro: "Come to where the flavor is"; Vantage: "Performance counts"; Salem: "The Refreshest"; Kent: "The
experience you seek." What do these words actually say about
the product? Nothing.

To be sure, occasionally one encounters an ad that is scrupulously honest. Mark Twain heard of one from a man in Hannibal, Missouri, who had the habit of reading his daily newspaper sitting in front of the local hotel. One day the man saw a small patent medicine ad in the paper that said, "Cut this out. It may save your life." He cut out the ad and continued reading his paper, but then through the hole in the paper he saw an assailant coming toward him with a knife. He threw the paper down, grabbed a chair, and knocked out his attacker.[61] This may have been the world's most honest ad.

While the usual charges against advertising are generally true, I want to go beyond that and argue that much advertising, especially T.V. advertising, is by its nature inherently deceptive, even when it is not intentionally so. This can best be seen by comparing the genre of advertising to the genres of nonfiction and fiction as presented on television and stage.

In a nonfiction work—a T.V. documentary, for example—we assume that the people, places, and events are all indeed real and that the things described have in fact occurred. In a fictional drama, on the other hand, we assume that the people, places, and events have all been invented, contrived. In a play, the audience knows that the people on stage are acting, that the stage is not a living room, that the poison in the vial is not actually poison. No one is deceived, everyone knows it is a play. The actors merely hope the audience will suspend its disbelief *temporarily,* and pretend the play is reality for the moment for the sake of entertainment.

Compare now a typical T.V. commercial. A woman appears on camera. She is standing in a kitchen wiping a spill with a paper towel. She says to the audience that she always uses X paper towels because they are twice as absorbent as the leading brand.

Now, as everyone knows, or should know, the woman in the kitchen does not actually use this brand of paper towel at all, or if she does, it is irrelevant to the situation. She is an actress playing a housewife who says she uses X paper towels because she has been paid money to say so. That seems obvious. Like fiction, there is no deception here. It is evident that she is an actress, standing on a stage set, not in her own kitchen, and merely speaking lines she has been paid to memorize.

There is an important difference between the T.V. commercial and a fictional drama, however. Unlike fiction, the intent of the advertiser is to convince viewers to suspend *permanently* their knowledge that this is a contrived dramatization. For after all, what would happen if every viewer thought during every commercial, "These people aren't using this product because it's better; they're only paid to say so"? If viewers consciously thought that, commercials would be totally ineffective. Although commercial dramatization is patently phony, advertisers implicitly seek to convince viewers to believe, at some level of consciousness anyway, that "Yes, she is a housewife who uses X paper towels because they are better."

I am not arguing that advertisers are trying to convince us that the Jolly Green Giant really exists; I am arguing that in real-life depictions advertisers do indeed try, at some level, to pass these dramatizations off as genuine. One might counter that advertisers are just seeking to get the product before the viewing audience and the dramatization is merely a harmless vehicle. This reasoning is not convincing, however, for a commercial's effectiveness depends on how believable the dramatization is, that is, the extent to which viewers believe that the actors really are using and genuinely endorsing the product.

After all, what is the purpose of a celebrity endorsement? A professional athlete is paid $500,000 to appear on camera and say he uses a particular shaving cream. The advertiser clearly does not want viewers to think each time they see the commercial, "He was paid a half million dollars to say he uses that shaving cream." If viewers believed that the commercial would be worthless. Rather, the advertiser seeks to convince the viewer to believe, at least at some level, that the celebrity is singing the praises of this shaving cream simply because he loves the product and wants to share his enthusiasm with others. But even though this is not true, the effectiveness of the commercial depends on the extent to which viewers are convinced that it is true. In fact, the persuasiveness of a commercial rests on how convinced viewers are of the veracity of a lie. In sum, then, much T.V. advertising is a genre which is fiction but which implicitly masquerades as fact and can only be successful if it is accepted as fact at some level. As a strange, hybrid genre of fiction pretending to be fact, much advertising is *inherently* deceptive.

And yet Americans *do* understand the deceptions of T.V. advertising. An ABC News/Harris survey of public attitudes toward T.V. advertising in the late 1970s found that most Americans believed that T.V. commercials regularly attempted to deceive them.[62] Interviewers asked respondents to estimate how much of T.V. advertising was, in their view, seriously misleading. Over half—52 percent—said that *most* or *all* T.V. commercials are seriously misleading, and another 40 percent said *some* of it was seriously misleading. Just 5 percent said not very much was seriously misleading, and only 1 percent said none of T.V. advertising was seriously misleading.

Asked whether "the claims for most products in TV advertising are generally accurate or are exaggerated," 81 percent of the public said that advertising claims were exaggerated, while only 15 percent said they were generally accurate. A 1984 Roper survey found that 70 percent of Americans agreed that business and industry in this country "hoodwinks the public through advertising," supporting the general conclusions of the earlier survey.[63]

The industry often claims that one of advertising's chief benefits is to provide a source of information about products and services. Yet, only a bit more than one-third of the respondents in the ABC News/Harris survey said that they found T.V. ads informative, while nearly 60 percent said they did not. And although by the mid-1980s American business was spending about $100 billion annually on advertising, most people feel that the most honest source of information about products in the United States is *Consumer Reports* magazine, with a budget minuscule by comparison.

Corporate advertising saturates American society as nothing else does. If T.V. can be seen as a revealing window on the power structure in society—on the prevailing ruling ideas in that society—then there is no doubt where the power lies. No other idea, form, impulse, theme, or worldview is as ubiquitous as advertising. The voice of America is the voice of advertisers hawking their wares. What is not deceptive is inane and insulting. The evening's national news is interrupted every few minutes by commercials for hemorrhoid preparations, constipation remedies, and false teeth paste. And yet we are told by intelligent people with great conviction that this is the only rational way to fund a national communications system.

Aside from advertising's essential vulgarity and aggressiveness, so much of it is inherently misleading that it is unquestionably the most widespread form of business deception in America. As such, it has been a major influence in fostering that climate of distrust, fraud, hype, and deception observed here. The whole culture of advertising helps create a culture of manipulation in the larger society generally and in world of business particularly. The manipulation of the T.V. viewer through commercials becomes the manipulation of the customer in the store. Along with the routine political deceptions the public has been exposed to in our generation, advertising helps deplete the shallow reservoir of trust still remaining. It projects a babble of individual voices urging private acquisition instead of appealing to the community of interests in society. During the age of Reagan, in fact, there was almost no voice in America that spoke for the nation as a whole, for the commonwealth. The one institution that represented the collectivity and that could speak for America as a community, the government, was disparaged by the prevailing conservative philosophy as alien and parasitic. As Ralph Nader remarked, the conservative message is "Hate your government."

Unfortunately, as has so often been observed, the techniques of advertising, the most irrational and deceptive subculture in America, have been appropriated by politics in the packaging and marketing of candidates, thus contaminating the institutions of democracy with the deceptions of the marketplace. In this we find a peculiar contemporary validation of Marx's theory that the economic substructure finds its echoes high up in the social and political superstructure.

A century ago Edward Bellamy published his memorable utopian novel, *Looking Backward,* contrasting life in a classless, cooperative America at the end of the twentieth century with the sordid realities of late nineteenth-century urban America. His description of the advertising of the 1880s is noteworthy because, with remarkably few changes, it accurately describes the advertising of our own age.

Bellamy's protagonist has just returned from the utopian world of the year 2000 to the Boston of 1887 where he had spent much of his life. He is shocked by what he sees:

> Another feature of the real Boston, which assumed the extraordinary effect of strangeness that marks familiar things seen in a new light, was the prevalence of advertising. There had been no personal advertising in the Boston of the twentieth century, because there was no need of any, but here the walls of the buildings, the windows, the broadsides of the newspapers in every hand, the very pavements, everything in fact save the sky, were covered with the appeals of individuals who sought, under innumerable pretexts, to attract the contributions of others to their support. However the word-

ing might vary, the tenor of all these appeals was the same:

"Help John Jones. Never mind the rest. They are frauds. I, John Jones am the right one. Buy of me. Employ me. Visit me. Hear me, John Jones. Look at me. Make no mistake. John Jones is the man and nobody else. Let the rest starve, but for God's sake remember John Jones!"

Whether the pathos or the moral repulsiveness of the spectacle most impressed me, so suddenly become a stranger in my own city, I know not. Wretched men, I was moved to cry, who, because they will not learn to be helpers of one another, are doomed to be beggars of one another from the least to the greatest! This horrible babel of shameless self-assertion and mutual depreciation, this stunning clamor of conflicting boasts, appeals, and adjurations, this stupendous system of brazen beggary, what was it all but the necessity of a society in which the opportunity to serve the world according to his gifts, instead of being secured to every man as the first object of social organization, had to be fought for.[64]

How little things have changed in a century. Except, as technology has advanced, so have the means and methods of selling. Today, unlike Bellamy's time, advertisers have learned to use the sky.

SOME OBJECTIONS

I have argued that the kind of business deception chronicled in this book may create a climate of distrust and undermine the social cohesion essential to a sound society. While I believe this is generally true, it is important not to weaken the argument by overstating it. The marketplace is undoubtedly a mixed experience for many Americans, full of paradoxes and contradictions. In the absence of a systematic body of research on consumer responses to business deception, it might be advisable to assess some alternate hypotheses.

1. While most Americans are suspicious of business ethics and practices, it cannot be denied that many, perhaps most, Americans love to shop. Since the end of World War II, shopping has become not only a national pastime and a secular religion, but a popular means of psychic healing as well. When upset, Americans often seek a little "retail therapy," as Karen Kersnar has called it. And motorists whose bumper stickers proclaim that they are "Born to Shop" and that "A Woman's Place Is in the Mall," do not betray symptoms of the estranged consumer.

In a Marxist framework, of course, this might all be dismissed as a kind of false consciousness. In the Swedish consumer movement, for example, radical activists had always assumed that older citizens were alienated by the problems and deceptions in the marketplace. But when surveys indicated that most older consumers were satisfied with most of their purchases, the activists did not concede that these consumers were apparently unalienated after all; instead they concluded that the aspirations of the elderly were simply too low. Consumers had never known a completely honest marketplace, the activists argued, and so they probably assumed that the present arrangement was all one could ever expect. According to the radical activists, consumer consciousness had been blurred by business ideology and hence needed to be sharpened by education and consumer legislation. Thus, the activists asserted that it was indeed possible for consumers to be objectively alienated while claiming to be subjectively satisfied.

They supported their position with a clever analogy. Most peoples the world over seem subjectively satisfied with their diet. Yet objectively, in terms of established standards of good nutrition, most people's diets are actually deficient and unwholesome. Likewise in the marketplace, they concluded, people may seem quite content, but this may only mask more objective alienation.[65] This view—that consumers may not be aware of their own best interests, and that consumer activists may know the public interest better than the public itself—has obvious elitist elements.[66] Yet it does not seem necessarily elitist to suggest that the social arrangements under which people live can distort their outlook in ways they do not fully realize, limit their imagination of alternate possibilities, and impoverish their aspirations by creating the comforting illusion that the way things are done now is the only way to do things ever.

In Chapter 1, I noted that over 70 percent of the writers in this study reported that the firms they worked for engaged in some deceptive practices. This is an impressively large number, but it does not mean that all these firms were deceptive all the time in all of their transactions with customers. Some were; but for many firms the swindle was but an occasional supplement to the whole enterprise of selling. This suggests that even though most firms engage in deceptive practices at some time, the experience of deception in the marketplace may be a marginal rather than a central one for many consumers. Moreover, even when they are being deceived in one way or another, many consumers may be totally unaware of it, for as noted earlier, business deception is successful only if it goes unrecognized. In this sense, certainly, consumers may be said to be objectively alienated even if subjectively content.

In any case, while Americans may love to shop—and thus appear to be subjectively satisfied—they do not love to be seriously swindled in the marketplace, nor do they wish to be harmed by the products they buy. We must separate out the joys of shopping from the sorrows of being grievously cheated. As Robert Reich has written, "Ask the average consumer whether he wants unsafe cars, carcinogenic drugs, adulterated foods, dangerous toys, or advertising intended to exploit the gullibility of his four-year-old child, and he will answer with a resounding 'no.' "[67] And despite public ambivalence toward government regulation, that resounding "no" explains the widespread support for consumer legislation in this century.

2. Although people obviously resent being grossly swindled, one might argue that many people may not really care if they are cheated in small ways at the margins of their marketplace experience. In an affluent society, some people may simply not mind paying a few extra dollars here and there, and may regard most business deception as a petty annoyance, especially when measured against the glittering abundance of the contemporary marketplace. They know that a sale is not always what it appears to be, but so what? They bought the product anyway, and enjoy it. They know their auto mechanic cheats them now and then, but that is the price one has to pay, and at least the car is repaired. In an affluent society, most business deception is a minor nuisance which one's pocketbook can easily handle.

This may indeed be true for wealthy families for whom monthly bills are harmless little arithmetic problems in their checkbooks. It may even be true for middle-class families in an expanding affluent society where income is constantly rising. But it ought to be clear now, after fifteen years of stagnating living standards, that ours is an affluent society in crisis, where millions of families are struggling to hold on to their accustomed living standards and millions of others are sinking.

If it were true that in a predatory society everyone has his hand in everyone else's pocket, then everyone might come out roughly equal—cheating others and being cheated in turn—with little net cost to anyone. But many people in contemporary society are unable to pick other people's pockets, even if they were inclined to do so. The vast mass of wage and salary workers are unable to cheat others in the marketplace, and they are consequently the big losers at the hands of those in business more advantageously situated. For these people, business deception is expensive; it costs them money, and lowers their living standards because they are being overcharged or underserved. In a dynamic affluent society, business deception is a tolerable expense; in a society of declining affluence and growing inequality, business deception is an expensive luxury most people can no longer afford.

3. Despite widespread business deception, many people may believe that caveat emptor is the natural state of things in this and all markets. Bluffing, cheating, and haggling have gone on since the first marketplace in ancient history, and many people may not be offended by it or regard it as harmful or even undesirable. Business, after all, is business. Deception is the essence of trade. Everyone expects it; no one takes it too seriously. One set of customs governs the market, another governs life elsewhere. The rules that apply in the market do not apply at home, at the club, with friends, associates, relatives, neighbors, or even strangers outside the market. In other words, predatory relations in the marketplace are encapsulated there and quarantined from the rest of society.

But one can just as easily suggest the opposite, as I have done earlier. Without making a strict Marxist argument about the inevitable reflection of the economic base in the larger superstructure, one can still reasonably assert that the marketplace and its great voice, advertising, are so powerful in contemporary society, so dominant, so ubiquitous, that they inevitably place their stamp on the entire society. Predatory relations in the market cannot be simply walled off from the rest of society; their contamination inevitably spreads. The power of the market is more than economic; it extends into other institutions and into the larger realm of morality and social relationships.

BUSINESS DECEPTION: EXCESS OR ESSENCE
OF CAPITALISM?

Consumer advocates are not usually concerned with social theory. They direct their energy to correcting business malpractice in this industry or that product. If one were to infer the theoretical position of most consumer advocates, however, it would probably be that business deception is basically an occasional abuse of the system instead of a central feature of the system itself, and that it is possible to correct such abuses by legislation, regulation, and judicial action.

What I have suggested in these pages, however, is that business deception, though certainly not universal, represents the chronic essence rather than the occasional excess of the system. In short, we have come full circle: medieval church doctrine was correct. There are strong corrupting forces in the marketplace, and these corrupting forces can undermine personal morality and poison social relations. True, there are many sellers in the marketplace who act on the belief that in the long run honesty is not only the most ethical policy but the most profitable one as well. Nonetheless, the structure of the system itself and the inherent enticements of profit maximization always tempt those in the market to break through the fragile boundaries of ethical behavior, regardless of law and public policy.

Consider, for example, the legal setting in which this study took place. While no local department of consumer affairs is particularly powerful, the New York City department purports to be the strongest urban agency of its type in the United States. In its own words, the department possesses "the most effective, comprehensive set of remedies against abuses in the marketplace available to any jurisdiction in the country."[68] Beyond that, New Yorkers have the protection of federal and state consumer protection laws. And yet, despite all this, look what deceptions this one study has uncovered.

Nonetheless, I am not taking the doctrinaire position

that reform is impossible. On the contrary, with public support, many gains in consumer protection have been made over the years. Yet, these gains have come very slowly and laboriously, for in the recurrent battles between business and consumers, it is an historical axiom that business wins most of the time.[69]

On the surface this may seem surprising and ironic. After all, everyone is a consumer, and in the unity of all consumers pursuing their common interest in an honest marketplace lies enormous political leverage. In fact, amid the many theories of postindustrial society, one can spin out the following postindustrial scenario. In the twentieth century we have moved from an age of production to an age of consumption. And with this change, the locus of class conflict tends also to change. In an age of production, the major class battles are fought between employers and workers; in an age of consumption, the battles are increasingly fought between sellers and buyers.

There is at least a shred of truth to this. As early as 1914, Walter Lippmann wrote that "we hear a great deal about the class-consciousness of labor. My own observation is that in America today consumers'-consciousness is growing very much faster."[70] And certainly consumer issues have become more important in the United States since World War II, in part because America entered an unprecedented age of consumption, with new and complex products available for the first time to an enormous number of people.

Yet, those who see consumers as a new, militant, and united class—a substitute proletariat for the declining proletariat proper—are mistaken for two reasons. First, by any reasonable definition consumers do not form a class; and second, consumers are not consistently militant in defense of their own interests.

Although consumers may have common interests, this does not necessarily mean they will recognize that fact and develop any meaningful solidarity. Marx himself observed that for class consciousness to develop, potential members of a class must share a common living or working environment where they are involved in continuous and ongoing social relations. In close proximity to others, each recognizes that his predicament is shared by all, and that their common interests can best be pursued by collective action. On the other hand, persons who share similar objective conditions but whose lives isolate them from others will rarely develop a solidarity on which genuine class consciousness is based. For that reason, Marx believed that the working class, concentrated by its very nature in factories where communication among workers was inevitable, was far more likely to develop a militant class consciousness than were the peasantry who were scattered and isolated across the countryside.[71]

In many ways consumers resemble Marx's peasantry. Consumers are isolated, unorganized, scattered, privatized, unknown to one another, and without any permanent institutional ties connecting them. The solitary shopper drifting through a suburban shopping mall is no one's model candidate for class consciousness. While in modern society production is a collective enterprise, which facilitates solidarity among workers, consumption is essentially an individual enterprise, which undermines a common consciousness.

Not only do consumers in general lack solidarity and class consciousness, they normally lack the militance and motivation necessary for sustained and significant political action. For although everyone in society is a consumer, the *role* of consumer tends to be less important, less salient, for most people, than the role of worker.[72] As Anthony Downs pointed out many years ago, because people spend their money in many different areas but earn their money in only one, the role of consumer is normally less vital than the role of producer. Moreover, because consumers spend their money in so many different places, and have the option to change where they shop or what they buy, their interest in any one product or industry is likely to be diffuse and limited.[73] Even though business deception may be widespread, it often takes a scandal, disaster, or dramatic publicity about a major business violation to awaken public interest and temporarily arouse public ire. Thus, for example, Upton Sinclair's revelations about the atrocities in the meat-packing industry helped generate support for the Pure Food and Drug Act of 1906. The thalidomide scare in 1962 led to public sympathy for legislation strengthening drug safety. Ralph Nader's book, *Unsafe at Any Speed,* and General Motors's well-publicized and clumsy investigation of Nader helped mobilize support for auto safety legislation.[74]

Actually, however, while the public has generally supported consumer legislation in this century, that support has typically been passive. In fact, what has popularly been called the "consumer movement" in the United States is, in terms of any precise sociological definition, not a social movement at all. Michael Pertschuk, former head of the Federal Trade Commission under President Carter, has argued that "if we understand a [social] movement to reflect not only widespread support but, like the 'populist movement' of the late nineteenth century, an organized grassroots effort that, for its members, transcends all other political identity or involvement, it cannot be said that a consumer movement has ever existed."[75] The so-called consumer movement in America, therefore, has actually consisted of a small number of consumer organizations, some unions, consumer activists, other liberal organizations, sympathetic journalists, and congressional consumer advocates who can muster widespread but largely passive public support.

While consumers have a real but limited stake in any one area of consumer reform and are thus likely to commit only limited resources to the political battle, businesses that might be affected by reform have an enormous and total interest in the outcome. While consumers are half-committed and half-informed on pending legislation or regulation, business will marshal its formidable array of forces—wealth, in-

fluence, consciousness, singleness of purpose—into the legis-
lative and regulatory battlefield.

Another circumstance also weakens public resolve on
issues of consumer protection. Citizens whose knowledge of
current affairs is acquired from the superficialities of T.V.
news and a cursory reading of newspapers are apt to be
poorly informed about the details of government and thus
more likely to respond to political symbols than to political
substance.[76] Statutes and regulatory agencies have reassuring
titles. But because most people know little more about them
than their names, slogans, and a few stereotypes, they often
assume that laws and regulatory agencies work as intended or
promised and feel that their interests are accordingly pro-
tected. Because there is something called the Consumer
Product Safety Commission, it is assumed that all consumer
products must be safe. Consumers are thus politically and
psychologically pacified by laws which may be impotent and
regulatory agencies which have long ago been captured by
the industries they are supposed to regulate.

No wonder then that in the battle with consumers, business wins most of the time. Most, but not *all* the time. In a
capitalist society, the political deck is stacked in favor of
business, but the outcome of the game is not a foregone conclusion. Labor and consumers can win an occasional hand.
And in the accumulation of small victories by labor and the
left lies the hope and the key to incremental reform. Against
great and powerful odds, there has been reform, and once
achieved, reform is hard to take away. It is difficult to imagine the political and social circumstances that would have to
exist in this country before the legal rights of workers to
organize collectively could be revoked, child labor restored,
the civil rights laws of the 1960s repealed and segregation
reinstituted, the legal gains of women abolished, the social
security system eliminated, Medicare repealed, the Food and
Drug Administration terminated, and so on.

The age of Reagan ushered in one of the most powerful and sustained conservative onslaughts in twentieth-century America. His administration successfully slashed the budgets of social programs and weakened business regulation; his appointees everywhere undercut enforcement of labor, civil rights, environmental, and consumer protection laws. Yet despite this assault, the institutional structure of the welfare state remains intact. What Reagan has done can be undone by one progressive administration. True, if we were to have several more consecutive national administrations as conservative as Reagan's, the structure and ideology of the welfare state would indeed be in jeopardy. But given the typical pendulum swings of American politics, this seems unlikely. And even if we were now to have several moderately conservative administrations, the social programs achieved heretofore would probably be revived.

Social reform seems to operate like a wheel with a protective ratchet. The wheel of reform does not turn at a constant speed; sometimes it doesn't turn at all. But there is some kind of social ratchet that prevents us from slipping back too far.[77]

Although I have argued that much in capitalism remains the same as in earlier periods, much has changed. Capitalism is not the same today as it was in the grim satanic mills of Manchester in 1820, nor even as it was in 1920, not only because of rising living standards but also because of the gradual, painstaking success of social reform.

As for the reforms historically pushed by labor and the left, the role of business has generally been to obstruct, delay, and weaken them. The major social consequence of this has been to put social change into permanent slow motion and to stretch out into decades or even generations what might have been achieved, with less formidable opposition, in a few years. The major *personal* consequence is that social change which might have comfortably fit within a lifetime stretches out beyond it so that during one's life one may never see what might easily have been.

Though slow in coming, twentieth-century gains in consumer protection have been genuine and valuable. As noted earlier, consumers do have more rights of redress than ever before. Over the long haul, capitalism has turned out to be far more able to absorb reform than its critics realized, however sluggishly that change has occurred.

Yet, as I have argued, the gains in consumer protection so far may have reformed the system but do not seem to have altered its essence. Ultimately, the effort to make the system intrinsically honest will have to come up against the imperatives of the structure, the inherent pressures for deception built into it.

On the other hand, social reality almost always works out to be more complex and nuanced than even the most profound social theory.* Should we not, then, at least consider the possibilities of thoroughgoing reform, however unlikely it is? Is it not conceivable, therefore, that over the very long run, capitalism may be so incrementally reformed, so hedged about with consumer protection and growing consumer awareness, so infused with economic innovations, so enveloped with civilized values of ethical practices, so gradually modified and altered that sellers will have little choice but enlightened self-interest and honest dealings, and that the system, almost unnoticed, will at some point no longer be what it once was? Is it possible that gradual quantitative reform may eventually, almost imperceptibly, transform the market system into something qualitatively different? Is it possible that gradual, evolutionary change may turn out to be the most revolutionary change of all? Such slow, almost undetectable, change, which cumulatively adds up to enor-

---

* Consider how simplistic were the predictions of even the genius Karl Marx compared to the actual developments of capitalism and communism in this century. On the capriciousness of social change, no observation is better than that of the nineteenth-century British socialist William Morris: "Men fight and lose the battle, and the thing they fought for comes about in spite of their defeat, and when it comes turns out not to be what they meant, and other men have to fight for what they meant under another name."

mous transformation, is not unusual either in the maturation of individuals or their societies.

Whatever the scenario, the book ends where it began. One of the major struggles of the twenty-first century—in both East and West—will be, in my view, to build a system that combines some of the powerful economic incentives of capitalism with the more socially responsible motives of co-operative and communal forms.[78]

APPENDIX

Business Ethics
and Research Ethics

In a book on business ethics, it is legitimate to ask about the ethics of research based on students who, it might be charged, were used as forced whistle-blowers and unwilling collaborators.

Several points should be made. First, the participants in this study were not forced whistle-blowers. Over the years I made it clear that if anyone felt uncomfortable writing an essay about his or her job for any reason whatsoever (for reasons of privacy, for example), I would welcome an alternate essay on another subject. Virtually no one chose that option.

Second, the participants did not have to be whistle-blowers at all. These essays were wide open in content, and writers were just as free to sing the praises of their honest employers—as many did—as to damn them for their dishonesty.

Third, I did not design the study so that participants were unwitting or unwilling collaborators. I collected these essays over a fifteen-year period. At the beginning, and for many years thereafter, I had no clearly formulated plan to use them in a book at all; I was merely curious to see how young workers would describe their experiences on the job. In later years when the idea of a book began to take shape, I told students at the end of each term that I might eventually want to write something based on these essays, and if I did I would attempt to contact each person whose essay I wished to use. I mentioned this after they had written their essays rather than before for obvious methodological reasons. In much social science research, investigators are faced with the dilemma that if they reveal the explicit purpose of the study to their subjects beforehand, that disclosure may alter the results of the study. In this case, for example, if I had told the workers beforehand that I was writing a book on business honesty and deception and that I might want to use excerpts from their essays, that might have distorted or biased their essays in unknown ways. Some writers might have tried to make sensational claims or to exaggerate what they had observed. Others might have been more conservative in their claims. Some might have been more self-conscious and stilted in their writing, rather than natural and informal, as most were.

After the book was finished, I sent letters to every writer whose essay I have used here, describing the book, assuring them of anonymity for the people and companies they described, and requesting permission to reprint excerpts of their work. Because these essays were written as long as a decade and a half ago, during a period in these young people's lives when they were highly mobile, it was difficult to locate many of them. But of the dozens who received my letter and responded, not one asked that I delete their material. A great many, in fact, wrote that they were pleased to be able to contribute to the book.

Notes

Introduction: the Paradox of Capitalism

1. John Gilchrist, *The Church and Economic Activity in the Middle Ages* (New York: St. Martin's Press, 1969), p. 51.
2. Thomas Aquinas, "On Fraud Committed in Buying and Selling," from *Summa Theologica* in Arthur Eli Monroe (ed.), *Early Economic Thought* (Cambridge, Mass.: Harvard University Press, 1930), pp. 60–61.
3. Ibid., p. 62.
4. John W. Baldwin, *The Medieval Theories of the Just Price* (Philadelphia: American Philosophical Society, 1959), p. 67.
5. Quoted in Robert Heilbroner, *The Making of Economic Society* (Englewood Cliffs, N.J.: Prentice-Hall, 1985), 7th ed., p. 24. On the views of Plato and Aristotle, see Baldwin, *op. cit.,* pp. 12–13. Heilbroner also notes Aristotle's distaste for the quest for gain in the marketplace, pp. 25–26.

Chapter 1. A Bit of Bolshevik Sociology: Workers Write About Their Jobs

1. As this study is based on the use of workers' personal essays, it falls within the sociological tradition that employs a wide variety of personal documents—letters, diaries, essays, memoirs, and autobiographies—as a rich source of social testimony. This tradition goes back to the early years of the twentieth century, to W. I. Thomas and Florian Znaniecki's classic study of the Polish peasant. See Thomas and Znaniecki, *The Polish Peasant in Europe and America,* 5 vols. (Boston: Richard Badger, 1918–20). The first systematic discussion of the use of personal documents in the social sciences appears in Louis Gottschalk, Clyde Kluckhohn, and Robert Angell, *The Use of Personal Documents in History, Anthropology and Sociology* (New York: Social Science Research Council, 1945). For

a contemporary account, see Ken Plummer, *Documents of Life: An Introduction to the Problems and Literature of a Humanistic Method* (Boston: Allen & Unwin, 1983).

2. Georg Simmel, "The Stranger," in Kurt Wolff (ed.), *The Sociology of Georg Simmel* (Glencoe, Ill.: Free Press, 1950), pp. 404–5.

3. James Murtha, William Protash, and Barry Kaufman, "Persistence and Achievement: The June 1981 Graduates from the City University of New York" (New York: Office of Institutional Research and Analysis, The City University of New York, 1983). Thanks to Audrey Blumberg for bringing this study to my attention.

4. Henry Campbell Black, *Black's Law Dictionary* (St. Paul, Minn.: West Publishing Co., 1968), 4th ed., p. 788.

Chapter 2. Selling It:
The Seamy Side of the Marketplace

1. For the title of this chapter, I am grateful to *Consumer Reports* magazine, which features a monthly column, "Selling It," documenting the "excesses" of the American marketplace.

2. Bryan Miller, "How Restaurants Are Monitored for Food Safety," *New York Times,* May 11, 1983.

3. New York City Department of Consumer Affairs, press release, "Consumer Affairs Finds: Shoppers at Meat Warehouses May Not Get All They Pay For," August 4, 1983; press release, "Consumer Affairs Follow-Up Sweep of Discount Meat Warehouses Reveals Significant Short-Weighting," October 5, 1983; cf. "Weight Violations on Meat Uncovered," *New York Times,* August 10, 1983.

4. "Consumers Pay for Short Weight," *New York Times,* May 4, 1983.

5. Selwyn Raab, "Talks Are Held on Settling Backlog of Violations Against Supermarkets," *New York Times,* May 15, 1988.

6. Office of the District Attorney, Kings County, New York, press release, "M.A.D.C.A.P. Investigation [Malfeasant Activities of Department of Consumer Affairs Personnel] Bags Scores in Supermarket Sting," November 6, 1980; cf. Joseph P. Fried, "City Inspectors and Food Stores Charged with Bribery," *New York Times,* November 7, 1980.

7. Federal Trade Commission, "Guides Against Deceptive Pricing," (Washington, D.C., 1964), pp. 1–2. See also New York City Department of Consumer Affairs, *Consumer Protection Law of 1969,* Administrative Code, Chapter 64, Title A, Regulation 13, " 'Sales and Discounts.' "

8. Isadore Barmash, "The Retail Battle in Chicago," *New York Times,* December 12, 1981.

9. See New York City Department of Consumer Affairs, *loc. cit.*, paragraph 13.15, p. 11.

10. Remar Sutton, *The Insider's Guide to Buying Your Next Car: Don't Get Taken Every Time* (New York: Penguin Books, 1983), p. 9.

Chapter 3. Ignorance: Dumb Customers and Distracted Customers

1. Studies show that women, in fact, are more likely to be cheated by auto mechanics than men. See, for example, Arthur P. Glickman, *Mr. Badwrench: How You Can Survive the $20 Billion-A-Year Auto Repair Ripoff* (New York: Wideview Books, 1981), p. 7.

2. Personal account told to the author by Hua Ji.

3. Fred Ferretti, "Three Mexican Visitors Are Charged $167 for a Taxi Ride," *New York Times,* September 12, 1974.

4. New York City Department of Consumer Affairs, press release, "Consumers Pay Handsomely for Hansoms: Commissioner Aponte Cites Drivers and Owners for Overcharging," December 15, 1987.

5. See, for example, New York City Department of Consumer Affairs, press releases, "Consumer Affairs Charges Midtown Camera Firm with Deceiving New Yorkers and Tourists," June 9, 1987; "Aponte [Consumer Affairs Commissioner] Urges Caution for Last-Minute Shoppers; Cites Results of Recent Cases Against Electronics Store," December 21, 1987.

6. New York City Department of Consumer Affairs, press release, "One-Third of Stores Checked Caught Misrepresenting Reconditioned TV's as New," September 1, 1987.

Chapter 4. Ignorance in the Knowledge Society: The Technically Uninformed Customer

1. Robert Heilbroner made a similar argument in "Economic Problems of a 'Postindustrial' Society," *Dissent* 20 (Spring 1973), pp. 163–76.

2. George Bernard Shaw, *The Intelligent Woman's Guide to Socialism and Capitalism* (London: Constable, 1929), p. 162. Smith himself, of course, made the same observation in the *Wealth of Nations*. While praising the division of labor for its efficiency, he also notes that "the man whose whole life is spent in performing a few simple operations . . . has no occasion to exert his understanding, or to exercise his invention. . . . He naturally loses, therefore, the

habit of such exertion and generally becomes as stupid and ignorant as it is possible for a human creature to become."

3. Ibid., p. 163.

4. Ibid., p. 164.

5. True, Durkheim considers some pathologies of the division of labor in modern society that create conflict rather than solidarity. Nonetheless, he feels these are temporary and unusual aberrations that can be overcome. For a sharp critique of Durkheim's *Division of Labor* and other works, see Tom Bottomore, *Sociology and Socialism* (New York: St. Martin's Press, 1984), Chapter 6 and pp. 167–68.

6. This is the so-called Monroney sticker, named after the law's Senate sponsor. See Brock Yates, *The Decline and Fall of the American Automobile Industry* (New York: Empire Books, 1983), p. 219.

7. For a dazzling array of deceptive sales techniques, see Remar Sutton, *The Insider's Guide to Buying Your Next Car: Don't Get Taken Every Time* (New York: Penguin Books, 1983).

8. *Business Week,* June 2, 1986, p. 66.

9. Arthur P. Glickman, *Mr. Badwrench: How You Can Survive the $20 Billion-a-Year Auto Repair Ripoff* (New York: Wideview Books, 1981), p. 6.

10. Roger William Riis and John Patric, *Repairmen Will Get You If You Don't Watch Out* (Garden City, N.Y.: Doubleday, Doran and Co., 1942).

11. Ibid., p. 54.

12. Robert Sikorsky, "Highway Robbery: The Scandal of Auto Repair in America," *Reader's Digest,* May 1987, pp. 91–99. For other recent investigations of automotive repair fraud, see Glickman, *op. cit.,* Chapter 1.

13. Sikorsky, *op. cit.*

14. See, for example, Frances Cerra, "11 of 24 Auto-Repair Shops Pass a Test of Honesty," *New York Times,* December 8, 1975; Ralph Blumenthal, "15 Vehicle Repair Shops in Queens Accused of Fraud in Needless Work," *New York Times,* October 17, 1980.

15. *New York State Repair Shop Registration Act,* 1975.

16. Iain McLellan, "You Pay High-Octane Prices for Regular Gasoline," *The National Examiner,* November 25, 1980.

17. New York City Department of Consumer Affairs, press release, "Aponte Announces Suit Against Brooklyn Service Station with Worst Enforcement Record in 1986; Schumer Calls for Congressional Investigation of Octane Misrepresentation," February 11, 1987. For a general discussion of gasoline manufacturing and re-

tailing, see David Owen, "Octane and Knock," *The Atlantic Monthly,* August 1987, pp. 53–60.

18. *Report of the New York State Interagency Task Force on Motor Fuel Quality to Governor Mario M. Cuomo,* March 27, 1986.

19. Ibid., p. 3.

20. Ibid., p. 4. Some new car owners remove or defeat their catalytic converters in order to use leaded fuel, which is usually cheaper than unleaded gas. But here the 11 percent figure included only those owners who did not knowingly purchase leaded fuel.

21. Riis and Patric, *op. cit.,* Chapter 5. On deception in watch repair, see also Fred L. Strodtbeck and Marvin B. Sussman, "Of Time, the City and the One-Year Guarantee: the Relations Between Watch Owners and Repairers," *American Journal of Sociology* 61 (1956): pp. 602–9. Reprinted in Marcello Truzzi (ed.), *Sociology and Everyday Life* (Englewood Cliffs, N.J.: Prentice-Hall, 1968).

22. Riis and Patric, *op. cit.,* Chapter 6.

23. Ibid., Chapter 4.

24. "15 of 21 TV Repairmen in Study Distorted Prices for Services," *New York Times,* July 26, 1976.

25. Suffolk County (New York) Department of Consumer Affairs, press release, "Consumer Affairs Goes Undercover with VCR: Violations Issued," November 29, 1987.

26. On the conflict between pharmacist as professional and pharmacist as businessman, see Richard Quinney, "Occupational Structure and Criminal Behavior: Prescription Violations by Retail Pharmacists," *Social Problems* 11 (Fall 1963), reprinted in Gilbert Geis and Robert F. Meier (eds.), *White-Collar Crime* (New York: Free Press, 1977).

27. City of New York, Department of Consumer Affairs, "Drug Dollars and Nonsense: The Availability and Cost of Pharmacy Products and Services for Elderly Consumers in New York City," November 1985; cf. William R. Greer, "Prices for Drugs Vary Widely, Study Finds," *New York Times,* December 28, 1985.

28. See, for example, Grace Lichtenstein, "Fraud Complaints on Health Spas Rise," *New York Times,* December 26, 1972.

Chapter 5. Helpless Customers and Potemkin Villages

1. Grigori Potemkin, a minister in the eighteenth-century government of Catherine the Great of Russia, supposedly constructed charming, prosperous—but fake—villages along a country route Catherine was

to travel in order to conceal from her the sordid realities of Russian peasant life. Thus, a Potemkin village has come to mean "an impressive facade designed to hide an undesirable fact or condition." On Potemkin villages in modern institutional settings, see, for example, Erving Goffman, *Asylums* (New York: Anchor Books, 1961), pp. 101ff.

Chapter 6. Scarcity

1. See Daniel Bell, *The Coming of Post-Industrial Society* (New York: Basic Books, 1976), p. 456.

2. C. B. Macpherson, *The Political Theory of Possessive Individualism* (London: Oxford University Press, 1964), pp. 23–24.

3. Karl Marx, *The German Ideology* (New York: International Publishers, 1970; orig. 1846), p. 56.

4. Ibsen's *An Enemy of the People,* a play Miller adapted for the American theater, has a similar theme.

5. Kermit Vandivier, "Why Should My Conscience Bother Me?" in M. David Ermann and Richard J. Lundman (eds.), *Corporate and Governmental Deviance* (New York: Oxford University Press, 1987), 3rd ed., pp. 103–23.

6. Richard Halloran, "Pentagon Calls 'Product Substitution' a Key Fraud Problem," *New York Times,* October 18, 1987.

7. Ibid. For another defense contractor who put profit before patriotism, see Leonard Buder, "Two Are Indicted for Faulty Part for Warplanes," *New York Times,* April 3, 1987.

8. J. Patrick Wright, *On a Clear Day You Can See General Motors: John Z. De Lorean's Look Inside the Automotive Giant* (New York: Avon Books, 1979), Chapter 4, "How Moral Men Make Immoral Decisions"; Mark Dowie, "Pinto Madness," in Mark Green (ed.), *The Big Business Reader* (New York: Pilgrim Press, 1983), 2nd ed., pp. 32–45.

9. Paul Brodeur, *Outrageous Misconduct: The Asbestos Industry* (New York: Pantheon Books, 1985).

10. Mark Dowie and *Mother Jones,* "The Dumping of Hazardous Products on Foreign Markets," in Green, *op. cit.,* pp. 362–73.

11. Leah Margulies, "Babies, Bottles, and Breast Milk: The Nestle's Syndrome," in Green, *op. cit.,* pp. 353–61.

12. Leonard Buder, "Beech-Nut Is Fined $2 Million for Sale of Fake Apple Juice," *New York Times,* November 14, 1987; Chris Welles, "What Led Beech-Nut Down the Road to Disgrace," *Business Week,* February 22, 1988, pp. 124–28.

13. Daniel Egger, "Chernobyl's Cup Runneth Over: West Germany Pours Hot Milk," *The Nation,* March 28, 1987, pp. 392–96.

14. Stanley Milgram, *Obedience to Authority* (New York: Harper Torchbooks, 1975), Chapter 4.

15. Ibid., pp. 8–9.

16. Clyde H. Farnsworth, "Survey of Whistle Blowers Finds Retaliation but Few Regrets," *New York Times,* February 22, 1987.

17. On the employee as functionary, see Marshall B. Clinard and Peter C. Yeager, *Corporate Crime* (New York: Free Press, 1980), pp. 63ff.

Chapter 7. Perishability

1. On the use of ethylene on common foods, see Alley E. Watada, "Effects of Ethylene on the Quality of Fruits and Vegetables," *Food Technology* (May 1986), pp. 82–84.

Chapter 8. Filth

1. George Orwell, *Down and Out in Paris and London* (New York: Berkley Books, 1959; orig. 1933), pp. 58–60.

2. It was, of course, sociologist Erving Goffman who pioneered the analysis of frontstage and backstage behavior in his dramaturgical analysis of social relations. See his *Presentation of Self in Everyday Life* (New York: Doubleday/Anchor Books, 1959).

3. James A. Finefrock, "Famed San Francisco Restaurants Were Among Dirty Dozens," *San Francisco Examiner,* October 29, 1985.

4. Bryan Miller, "How Restaurants Are Monitored for Food Safety," *New York Times,* May 11, 1983.

5. Office of the Comptroller, City of New York, Bureau of Management Audit, "Audit Report on the Restaurant Inspection Practices and Procedures of the New York City Department of Health Through April 30, 1985."

6. The Health Department's major defense in the light of this finding was that "the audit period encompasses Fiscal Year 1984, which was the lowest point in terms of initial inspections of food establishments . . . in recent history." Ibid., p. 8.

7. Ibid., p. iv.

8. Ibid.

9. Ibid., p. 22.

10. Ibid., p. 23.

11. Miller, *loc. cit.*
12. Selwyn Raab, "Inspectors Seized in Extortion Plan in New York City," *New York Times*, March 25, 1988; Todd S. Purdum, "15 More Arrested in Restaurant Inspection Bribes," *New York Times*, July 8, 1988.
13. Michael Marriott, "City Investigates New Restaurant Bribes," *New York Times*, April 14, 1988.
14. See Mark Green and John F. Berry, "White-Collar Crime Is Big Business," *The Nation*, June 8, 1985.
15. For an elaboration of this thesis, see my essay "Snarling Cars," *The New Republic*, January 24, 1983.
16. Robert Hanley, "60 Percent of Trucks Inspected in New York Area Fail," *New York Times*, October 8, 1986.
17. "The Big Trouble with Air Travel," *Consumer Reports*, June 1988, pp. 362–67.
18. "Judge Orders National Recall of Much Nonkosher Poultry," *New York Times*, November 8, 1987.

Chapter 9. Petty Bourgeois Tricks

1. C. Wright Mills, *White Collar* (New York: Oxford University Press, 1951), p. 30.
2. John Holusha, "Chrysler Enters No Contest Plea over Odometers," *New York Times*, December 15, 1987.
3. See, for example, Michael Oreskes, "Corruption Is Called a Way of Life in New York Construction Industry," *New York Times*, April 25, 1982; Selwyn Raab, "In City Construction Industry, Corruption Appears Built In," *New York Times*, September 13, 1987.

Chapter 10. Honest Business: Neighborhoods and Saints

1. Donald R. Cressey, "Restraint of Trade, Recidivism, and Delinquent Neighborhoods," in James F. Short, Jr. (ed.), *Delinquency, Crime, and Society* (Chicago: University of Chicago Press, 1976), discussed in Marshall B. Clinard and Peter C. Yeager, *Corporate Crime* (New York: Free Press, 1980), pp. 115–16.
2. Arthur P. Glickman, *Mr. Badwrench: How You Can Survive the $20 Billion-a-Year Auto Repair Ripoff* (New York: Wideview Books, 1981), pp. 84–85.
3. Told to the author in Baraga, Michigan.

Chapter 11. Morality and the Marketplace

1. Michael Novak to Robert Lekachman, in "Is There Virtue in Profit?" *Harper's Magazine*, December 1986, p. 44.
2. Quoted in Steven Lukes, *Marxism and Morality* (New York: Oxford University Press, 1987), p. 25.
3. See, for example, Walter D. Connor, *Deviance in Soviet Society* (New York: Columbia University Press, 1972).
4. See, for example, Mary Connelly, "Isn't Anybody Working in the Parks?" *New York Post*, July 9, 1974; Michael Goodwin, "Parks Plagued by a Shortage of Good Help," *New York Times*, October 14, 1980.
5. Michael Novak, Ibid., pp. 39–40.
6. Albert Einstein, "Why Socialism?" in *Out of My Later Years* (New York: Philosophical Society, 1950), p. 128.
7. *Co-op News* (published by the Consumers Cooperative of Berkeley, California), March 5, 1984, p. 1. Recall that in Chapter 4, one pharmacist was also eager to sell his customers generic drugs—but he charged name-brand prices for them. See pp. 77–78.
8. The most detailed account of the Berkeley Co-op can be found in Robert Neptune, *California's Uncommon Markets: The Story of the Consumers Cooperatives, 1935–1976* (Richmond, Calif.: Associated Cooperatives, 1977), 2nd ed.
9. J. B. Wilkinson and J. Barry Mason, "The Grocery Shopper and Food Specials: A Case of Subjective Deception?" *Journal of Consumer Affairs*, Vol. 8, No. 1 (Summer 1974) , pp. 30–36.
10. Karl Marx, *Capital*, Vol. 3 (Moscow: Foreign Language Publishing House, 1967; orig. 1894), p. 440. See also Lenin's 1923 essay, "On Cooperation," in Robert C. Tucker (ed.), *The Lenin Anthology* (New York: W. W. Norton, 1975), pp. 707–13.
11. See Paul M. Hirsch and J. Andrews, "The Language of Corporate Takeover," in Louis R. Pondy and Thomas C. Dandridge (eds.), *Organizational Symbolism* (Greenwich, Conn.: JAI Press, 1983).
12. Adam Smith, *Wealth of Nations* (New York: Modern Library, 1937; orig. 1776), p. 14.
13. Arthur P. Glickman, *Mr. Badwrench: How You Can You Survive the $20 Billion-a-Year Auto Repair Ripoff* (New York: Wideview Books, 1981), pp. 59–60.
14. See, for example, Raymond A. Bauer, "Communication as a Transaction: A Comment on [Talcott Parsons's] 'On the Concept of Influence,'" *Public Opinion Quarterly* 27 (Spring 1963), p. 83; see

also Bauer and Stephen A. Greyser, *Advertising in America: The Consumer View* (Boston: Division of Research, Harvard Graduate School of Business Administration, 1968).

15. Remar Sutton, *The Insider's Guide to Buying Your Next Car: Don't Get Taken Every Time* (New York: Penguin Books, 1983), p. 23.

16. Ferdinand Tönnies, *Community and Society* (New York: Harper & Row, 1963), orig. published in 1887; Georg Simmel, "The Metropolis and Mental Life," in Kurt H. Wolff (ed.), *The Sociology of Georg Simmel* (Glencoe, Ill.: The Free Press, 1950), orig. published in 1903; Robert E. Park, "The City: Suggestions for Investigation of Human Behavior in the Urban Environment," in Richard Sennett (ed.), *Classic Essays on the Culture of Cities* (New York: Appleton-Century-Crofts, 1969), orig. published in 1916; Louis Wirth, "Urbanism As a Way of Life," *American Journal of Sociology* 44 (July 1938). The essays by Simmel and Wirth, as well as by Park, are reprinted in Sennett.

17. It was not merely sociologists who were saying these things about the city; since the beginning of American history our poets, novelists, philosophers, statesmen, and intellectuals have generally said similar things. See Morton and Lucia White, *The Intellectual Versus the City: From Thomas Jefferson to Frank Lloyd Wright* (Cambridge, Mass.: Harvard University Press, 1962).

18. Manuel Castells, "Is There an Urban Sociology?" in C. G. Pickvance (ed.), *Urban Sociology: Critical Essays* (London: Tavistock, 1976), p. 38; see also Castells, *The Urban Question: A Marxist Approach* (Cambridge, Mass.: MIT Press, 1977).

19. Friedrich Engels, *The Condition of the Working Class in England* (Oxford: Basil Blackwell, 1958; orig. 1845), p. 31.

20. Martin King Whyte and William L. Parish, *Urban Life in China* (Chicago: University of Chicago Press, 1984), esp. Chapter 11; Ruth Sidel, *Families of Fengsheng: Urban Life in China* (New York: Penguin Books, 1974).

21. Whyte and Parish, Ibid., p. 288.

22. Ibid., p. 25.

23. In fact, a recent Harris survey found that during a three-year period in the mid-1980s, when the proportion of American families owning VCRs increased from 17 percent to 55 percent, and the number of viodeotapes bought or rented increased fourfold, overall attendance at plays, classical music concerts, and other performing arts events declined. According to the survey, from 1984 to 1987 theater attendance fell 25 percent, concert attendance declined 26

percent, and opera attendance dropped 38 percent. Only movie and museum attendance increased (9 percent and 24 percent, respectively.) See Louis Harris and Associates, *Americans and the Arts: V* (New York: National Research Center of the Arts/Louis Harris and Associates, 1988), p. 5.

24. Albert Hirschman noted in an important book that citizens have two general means of coping with unsatisfactory social and economic conditions—exit and voice. In a privately owned store, for example, an unsatisfied customer mainly has the power of exit—he can leave and shop elsewhere. In a consumer cooperative, he has a far more powerful and ultimately more satisfying tool: the power of voice—participation and influence. See Albert O. Hirschman, *Exit, Voice, and Loyalty* (Cambridge, Mass.: Harvard University Press, 1971).

25. Robert K. Merton, *Mass Persuasion: The Social Psychology of a War Bond Drive* (New York: Harper & Bros., 1946), p. 142.

26. Ibid., p. 143.

27. Ibid., p. 142.

28. On urban isolation and loneliness, see, for example, Philip Slater, *The Pursuit of Loneliness* (Boston: Beacon Press, 1970); David Popenoe, *Private Pleasures, Public Plight* (New Brunswick, N.J.: Transaction Books, 1985). On thriving *Gemeinschaft*, see, for example, Herbert Gans, *The Urban Villagers* (New York: Free Press, 1962), and *The Levittowners* (New York: Vintage Books, 1967); Claude Fischer, *The Urban Experience* (New York: Harcourt Brace Jovanovich, 1976), and *To Dwell Among Friends* (Chicago: University of Chicago Press, 1982).

29. Herbert McClosky and John Zaller, *The American Ethos: Public Attitudes Toward Capitalism and Democracy* (Cambridge, Mass.: Harvard University Press, 1984), p. 133.

30. See Seymour Martin Lipset and William Schneider, *The Confidence Gap: Business, Labor and Government in the Public Mind* (New York: Free Press, 1983), Chapter 6.

31. Data obtained from the Roper Center for Public Opinion Research, Storrs, Conn. Roper Surveys taken in the 1970s found similar attitudes toward American business. See Lipset and Schneider, Ibid., pp. 167, 171.

32. Lipset and Schneider, Ibid., p. 170.

33. Ibid.

34. Ibid.

35. Ibid.

36. Harris poll, May 4, 1978.

37. Lipset and Schneider explore recent public attitudes toward the consumer movement and toward government protection of consumer interests, *op. cit.,* pp. 244–55.

38. Ibid., pp. 170–71.

39. Ibid., p. 171.

40. Some of the antibusiness sentiment found in these surveys may be exaggerated slightly. In survey research, respondents tend to agree with statements read to them by interviewers—the so-called acquiescence bias. As most of the items in the surveys quoted here were stated in an antibusiness way, public suspicion of business may be a bit inflated. The general conclusions are undoubtedly valid, however.

41. See Lipset and Schneider, *op. cit.,* for an exhaustive analysis of these surveys of public confidence.

42. Ibid., p. 375; McClosky and Zaller, *op. cit.,* p. 136.

43. Lipset and Schneider, pp. 375ff.

44. Joshua Cohen and Joel Rogers, *On Democracy* (New York: Penguin Books, 1983), p. 40.

45. Adam Clymer, "Low Marks for Executive Honesty," *New York Times,* June 9, 1985.

46. *Business Week,* July 20, 1987, p. 71.

47. Marshall B. Clinard and Peter C. Yeager, *Corporate Crime* (New York: Free Press, 1980), p. 113.

48. Mark Green and John F. Berry, "White-Collar Crime Is Big Business," *The Nation,* June 8, 1985. See also Irwin Ross, "How Lawless Are Big Companies?" *Fortune* 103 (December 1, 1980), pp. 57–64.

49. Clinard and Yeager, *op. cit.,* p. 8.

50. Karl Mannheim, *Man and Society in an Age of Reconstruction* (New York: Harcourt, Brace, 1940), p. 19, quoted in Merton, *op. cit.,* p. 143.

51. Jethro Lieberman, *The Litigious Society* (New York: Basic Books, 1981), p. 186.

52. Ibid., p. 8.

53. Compare, for example, *Time,* March 24, 1986, and *Consumer Reports,* August 1986.

54. This depends on what measure of litigiousness is used. Lieberman's source claims that Britain and the United States are in a close tie for first place, with Britain occasionally ahead. See Lieberman, pp. 5–6.

55. Lieberman, *op cit.,* p. 3.

56. Steve Lohr, "Tokyo Air Crash: Why Japanese Do Not Sue," *New York Times,* March 10, 1982.

57. This term is taken from Samm Sinclair Baker, *The Permissible Lie: The Inside Truth About Advertising* (Boston: Beacon Press, 1971).

58. David Wise, *The Politics of Lying* (New York: Vintage Books, 1973), pp. 497–98. See also Max Ways, "Finding the American Direction," *Fortune,* October 1970, p. 73. Ways reports that in a Washington, D.C., ghetto the Knight survey found that *half* the respondents claimed they didn't believe the moon landing had occurred.

59. See, for example, *New York Times,* September 16, 1983; October 31, 1986; July 11, 1987.

60. On the deceptive use of language in advertising, see Michael L. Geis, *The Language of Television Advertising* (New York: Academic Press, 1982); and Torben Vestergaard and Kim Schroder, *The Language of Advertising* (Oxford: Basil Blackwell, 1985).

61. Twain's anecdote related by Baker, *op. cit.,* p. 190.

62. ABC News/Harris survey, March 16, 1979.

63. Data obtained from the Roper Center for Public Opinion Research, Storrs, Conn.

64. Edward Bellamy, *Looking Backward: 2000–1887* (New York: New American Library, 1960; orig. 1888), pp. 206–7.

65. See J. K. Johansson, "The Theory and Practice of Swedish Consumer Policy," in David A. Aaker and George S. Day (eds.), *Consumerism* (New York: Free Press, 1982), 4th ed., pp. 62–75.

66. Of course, almost everyone agrees that in some areas experts are, in fact, better qualified to judge what is best for the public interest than the public itself. Ordinary citizens, for example, cannot be expected to determine for themselves which new medicines are safe and effective; government specialists must test and screen them, and in that sense they obviously know what's good for the rest of us better than we do.

67. Robert B. Reich, "Toward a New Consumer Protection," *University of Pennsylvania Law Review* 128 (November 1979), p. 3.

68. New York City Department of Consumer Affairs, *Consumer Affairs Information Guide,* p. 2.

69. On the customary triumph of business over consumers, see Charles E. Lindblom, *Politics and Markets* (New York: Basic Books, 1977); Anthony Downs, *An Economic Theory of Democracy* (New York: Harper & Row, 1957), pp. 238–56; Mark V. Nadel, *The Politics of Consumer Protection* (Indianapolis: Bobbs-Merrill, 1971); Michael

Pertschuk, *Revolt Against Regulation: The Rise and Pause of the Consumer Movement* (Berkeley: University of California Press, 1982).

70. Quoted in Richard Hofstadter, *The Age of Reform* (New York: Vintage Books, 1960), p. 171.

71. In a well-known passage from *The Eighteenth Brumaire of Louis Bonaparte,* Marx offers a precise definition of class and explains why the French peasantry, though they may have had common interests, nonetheless did not constitute a class. "The small peasants form a vast mass, the members of which live in similar conditions, but without entering into manifold relations with one another. Their mode of production isolates them from one another, instead of bringing them into mutual intercourse. . . . In so far as millions of families live under economic conditions of existence that divide their mode of life, their interests and their culture from those of the other classes, and put them in hostile contrast to the latter, they form a class. In so far as there is merely a local interconnection among these small peasants, and the identity of their interests begets no unity, no national union and no political organization, they do not form a class." See Karl Marx, *The Eighteenth Brumaire of Louis Bonaparte* (New York: International Publishers, n.d.; orig. 1852) , p. 109.

72. Nadel, *op. cit.,* Chapter 7.

73. Downs, *op. cit.,* p. 254.

74. Nadel, *op. cit.,* Chapter 1 and pp. 121–30.

75. Pertschuk, *op. cit.,* p. 10.

76. Murray Edelman, *The Symbolic Uses of Politics* (Urbana: University of Illinois Press, 1974), Chapter 2, "Symbols and Political Quiescence."

77. The ratchet metaphor is suggested by Michael Pertschuk, *op. cit.,* p. 120.

78. What would such a system look like? For plausible models of a decentralized market socialism based on social pluralism and political democracy, see Irving Howe, *Socialism and America* (New York: Harcourt Brace Jovanovich, 1985); Alec Nove, *The Economics of Feasible Socialism* (Winchester, Mass.: Allen & Unwin, 1983); Radoslav Selucky, *Marxism, Socialism and Freedom* (London: Macmillan, 1979).

Index